KILLING TIME, LOSING GROUND

Experiences of Unemployment

PATRICK BURMAN
Brescia College,
University of Western Ontario

With a Foreword by
JAMES RINEHART
University of Western Ontario

THOMPSON EDUCATIONAL PUBLISHING, INC.
TORONTO

Additional copies of this publication may be obtained from:
   Thompson Educational Publishing, Inc.
   11 Briarcroft Road, Toronto
   Ontario, Canada M6S 1H3
   Telephone (416) 766-2763 Fax (416) 766-0398
Please write for a full catalogue of publications.

Canadian Cataloguing in Publication Data

Burman, Patrick W., 1947–
   Killing time, losing ground

Includes bibliographical references.
ISBN 1–55077–021–7

1. Unemployed - Ontario - London. 2. Unemployment -
Ontario - London. 3. Unemployed - Ontario - London -
Social conditions. I. Title.

HD5730.L6B87 1990   331.13′79713′26   C90–094614–8

64982

ISBN 1–55077–021–7
Printed in Canada by John Deyell Company.
2 3 4 5   94 93 92 91 90

KILLING TIME, LOSING GROUND
Experiences of Unemployment

Dedication
To Terri, Jennifer, and Rachel
who shared the burden

Table of Contents

Acknowledgements

I want first to thank the unemployed men and women who agreed to be interviewed. Their honesty and insight form the heart of the book.

I was fortunate to have the help of such capable interviewers as Linda McLure, Audrey Rosa, and Mark Priest. The many interviews they carried out were handled with attentiveness and compassion.

Many other valuable people have contributed to this book, though its mistakes are my own. James Rinehart has been inspiring and supportive from the early stages, and I am deeply in his debt. In England, where I was on sabbatical, I owe thanks to Robert Blackburn, who went over many chapters with a friendly and critical eye, and who greatly contributed to the conception of the social class scale described in Appendix A. I benefitted from the support and critical comments of Anthony Giddens at Cambridge, as well as David Held, John Thompson, Willie Brown, and Colin Fraser. Paul Willis provided much insight during a day in Wolverhampton. I thank Andrew Weigert for his careful comments on the manuscript while in England. I am also indebted to Fabio Dasilva for his contribution.

In Canada, I must thank a number of people who read parts of the manuscript: Kathy Kopinak, Carol Agócs, Judy Richer, Dennis Hudecki, Harvey Krahn, Graham Lowe, and Arlene McLaren. Thanks go to the Unemployment Working Centre and the people I worked with in those years, and to the supportive faculty and administration at Brescia College. My college has supported my research in ways too numerous to mention, and I am very grateful.

I also want to thank Keith Thompson, Byron Wall, and Martha Wall for their painstaking effort and support in their role as publisher.

Foreword

When the data for this study were being collected in the early 1980s, one and one-half million Canadians were unemployed. Then, as now, information on these individuals consisted largely of statistics on the extent of joblessness and its distribution by age, sex, education, occupation, and region. But counting the unemployed is not the same as understanding them. What is it like to be without a job? How does it feel to be unemployed? How do people react to joblessness? This book represents a much needed and refreshing departure from the usual quantitative treatments of the disadvantaged because it depicts unemployment from the perspectives of the unemployed, thus providing insights and understanding that elude statistical accounts of the phenomenon. People tell us in their own words and through the author's social-psychologically grounded interpretations of interviews with them *what it means to be out of work*.

In this book, we follow the jobless from remote state bureaucracies and corporate personnel offices, through local "help" organizations and the household, to the very core of their selves. In government and business offices the unemployed experience a profound sense of powerlessness and of being little more than objects. Like characters in a Franz Kafka novel, the jobless often apprehend themselves in these settings as being at the mercy of powerful, manipulative, and unfathomable persons and forces. As individuals search for work, they come to realize how indistinguishable they are from their fellow unemployed, impressing upon them a consciousness of being abstract commodities no one wants to purchase. Institutions like Canada Manpower, which ostensibly were established to provide a necessary service, are seen by their clients as sources of frustration and degradation. In bureaucratic encounters, the jobless are stripped of individuality, their uniqueness ignored. External attributes such as age, physical appearance, and credentials are scrutinized, reified and crammed into particular niches in the occupational world. As the period of joblessness drags on, there is among these informants an agonizing sense of being trapped in a maze in which the exit seems more and more remote.

For most persons unemployment entails loss of income, low income, or both. This can have a profound effect in a society in which money and the trappings of consumption suffuse social relations. Through these interviews we come to understand how low income constrains the social activities of the unemployed and restricts physical movement in the community. The absence of money generates regular household crises over food, clothing, rent, utilities, and transportation. It means not being able to reciprocate a dinner invitation, not seeing one's way clear to join a friend for lunch or a movie, and not being able to afford the price of a favorite recreation. As the weeks and months of unemployment pass, one's social orbit shrinks, placing a heavy emotional load on family relationships.

In some instances the family provides relief and solace for the bruised egos of the unemployed. In other cases, being without paid work strains family and marital relations, occasionally to the breaking point. For unemployed wives the sexual division of labour in the household often returns with a vengeance and is accompanied by "a loss of [the] sense of being an independent person."

The contraction of social relationships leaves the self exposed and vulnerable, and all too often the unemployed find themselves alone with their thoughts. Protracted periods of introspection and self-doubt are common. There is, Burman concludes, "an omnivorous preoccupation with the self" that brings painful memories, self-doubts, and feelings of futility. As one informant lamented, "The only thing I have on my mind these days is me." These centripetal processes are aptly characterized by Patrick Burman as "losing ground."

Burman's chapter on how the unemployed experience time is beautifully crafted. Typically, the jobless blur what are ordinarily discrete time units, resulting in bleak and seemingly endless stretches of shapeless time. For them, there is a virtual absence of patterned sequences of routine activity and rejuvenating respite. Days fade together. Weekend and holidays are indistinguishable from weekdays. The complaint, "One day is the same as the next," reverberates throughout these interviews. This amorphous existence contrasts sharply with the structured rhythms of employed family members, friends, and the community, and accentuates the consciousness of being isolated. Aimlessness is a natural state among the unemployed. Time without employment is regarded not as leisure but as an unwanted intrusion of idleness. As the title of this book indicates, the unemployed are locked in a desperate struggle to "kill time."

It is ironic that a study of *unemployment* reveals so much about *employment* in our society. As we are drawn into the inner worlds of the unemployed, we begin to comprehend why people "consent" to exploitative and alienated labour and why individuals become attached to and express "satisfaction" with jobs that lack intrinsic gratifications. Financial independence, self-respect, and the opportunity to socialize are job-linked elements that are extrinsic to the content of work, but stabilize and give meaning to our lives. Employment insulates us from the abyss of joblessness: a job, any job, is preferable to no job at all.

Many informants, even those who performed volunteer work, felt discouraged because they were not doing anything "useful." Even when they discovered activities that captured their interest, nagging feelings of self-recrimination were common. As the author observes on the subject of hobbies, "more often than not, there was guilt or defensiveness in engaging in pursuits so unconnected to the ethos and instrumentalism of employed society."

There are some striking parallels between the attitudes and experiences of persons in and out of the labour force. Employed people seek fulfillment and pleasure outside of work, but leisure often fails to provide meaningful pursuits and gratifications. Consequently we are drawn back to work in order to "kill time." Like the unemployed, many workers complain of being treated like numbers on a balance sheet and being insecure and underpaid. Many workers occupy subordinate positions, perform routine tasks, and, like the unemployed, are also expected to follow orders but not to initiate action. Both the jobless and the employed dream about having a fulfilling job, a job they can be proud of, a job that helps the community and contributes to personal well-being.

There is nothing in this book that will arm or comfort those who maintain that financial assistance to the unemployed destroys their motivation to work. Nor is there anything here to sustain stereotypes of "welfare bums" living it up on government handouts. What becomes clear from these interviews is that pronouncements of the decline and imminent demise of the work ethic are without substance. Only a few persons in the sample preferred unemployment to work, and, in these cases, the alternative was mindless work. The great majority of these informants tried to conceal their identities, blamed themselves for not working, and desperately searched for work. One woman put it succinctly: "I need a job. I want to work. I want to be able to pay the bills. I want to be solvent. I want to live."

Given their desperate circumstances, one might expect the jobless to mobilize politically to improve their situation. However, only a minority of the sample was able to reject self-blame and embrace structural explanations of their condition. Most of the informants perceived no meaningful and effective political vehicle to alter their circumstances. Their feelings of political impotence had several sources. One was atomization: unemployment constrains physical mobility and severs connections to social networks. This leaves the jobless isolated, a condition conducive to self-absorption rather than collective action. A second basis of political apathy, stressed by the author throughout the book, is the tendency of unemployment progressively to reduce individuals to passive objects. Over and over again, the informants described themselves as *"being nothing," "being on the receiving end of everything," "being participants in a script written by others."* They repeatedly found themselves in situations where they were ordered about and dominated by others. Instead of initiating activity, the unemployed have things happen to them. As dependency and passivity envelop the jobless, their potential to engage in political action is eroded.

Collective action also is impeded by the powerful sway of meritocratic ideology: the set of ideas that holds that the massive inequalities of wealth, income, and power in our society reflect the different levels of intelligence and effort (merit) of individuals. Being rich and powerful or poor and without work have everything to do with the individual and nothing to do with class structure and political-economic forces. The onus for being without work, then, falls on the jobless individual rather than on the economy and the state. Given the pervasive influence of such ideas, it is not surprising that Burman's informants often held themselves responsible for their condition or blamed potential allies in the work force. There is nothing inevitable about this political quiescence, as evidenced by the activities among the unemployed in other eras and in other parts of the world, but the combination of isolation, passivity, and meritocratic ideology constitutes a formidable barrier to the political mobilization of the unemployed.

Unemployment is not simply a personal trouble; it also is a *social* problem. In examining the personal situations of his unemployed informants Patrick Burman says he came to realize that he was simultaneously examining the capitalist system in Canada, a system that not only tolerates but generates unemployment. I like to ask my students to estimate the unemployment rate in this country, assuming all Canadians were equally ambitious and equally well-educated. The obvious answer—a high level of unemployment—unsettles adherents of meritocratic ideas. At Canada Manpower in London, Ontario, in 1984 there were 85 registered jobless persons for each registered vacancy. It has been estimated that in the early 1980s, when Canada was experiencing the highest rates of joblessness since the Great Depression, roughly 50,000 to 75,000 job vacancies were being sought by one and one-half million people—a ratio of one job opening for every 20 or 30 job seekers. After all is said and done, the problem of unemployment is one of fewer jobs than the number of people seeking them.

Since this research was conducted in a single city—London, Ontario— it is reasonable to ask if its results could be reproduced across Canada. I suspect the circumstances, attitudes, and experiences of this London sample would not differ markedly from those of jobless persons in many urban communities. The only difference might be that unemployment touched fewer lives in London than in traditionally depressed areas where a large proportion of individuals are and have been without jobs. London is a relatively affluent city. There are no heavy geographical concentrations of the jobless; in London, they inhabit virtually every area of the community. This dispersion renders the unemployed in London a largely invisible minority and diminishes their capacity for organization. In contrast, unemployed persons living in communities characterized by long-standing and widespread economic devastation and underdevelopment are more likely to have established modes of mutual aid and support that make unemployment a less isolating and less degrading personal experience.

Burman's research developed out of his involvement with the unemployed in London, Ontario. It was only as his commitment deepened that he became convinced that these essentially voiceless people should be given the opportunity to tell others what it's like to be without work. Patrick Burman has poured his heart and soul, not to mention an enormous amount of time and effort, into this book. He passed untold hours talking to the unemployed in London, arranging the interviews, drawing out of these very personal statements themes, subthemes, and aberrant cases, and interpreting and presenting the data.

To characterize Patrick Burman's research orientation as engaged rather than detached is not to suggest that the results of this study are distorted by ideological biases. On the contrary, the author's personal and political beliefs provided the necessary empathetic foundation for a faithful description and analysis of the public and private lives of the unemployed. The outcome is a work that represents the very best of the *engaged* genre of sociological research.

James Rinehart
London, Ontario
June, 1988

Introduction

I became concerned with the unemployment crisis of the early 1980s in my own city of London, Ontario. In the winter of 1982–83, I joined others in helping to establish the Unemployment Working Centre (described in this book). My first involvement then, was as a volunteer coping with a human and community problem. Gradually, being around the unemployed stimulated my sociological curiosity. Feeling that the unemployed were widely misunderstood, I embarked on an interview study to learn about their perspectives and problems and make them known to a wider audience.

The Research Study

I decided to use the open-ended but focussed interview as a research tool, preferring to give an in-depth treatment of a small sample rather than aim for a broad representative survey. I was convinced that *qualitative* analysis was called for. First, it best expressed both my own understanding of the people involved and their own humanity; but also because I knew that our institutions made them *feel* like statistics. I had no desire to quantify them any further.

The Sample

Knowing the difficulty of obtaining a random sample—there being no comprehensive list of unemployed, no geographical area where they all live, etc.—I at first simply interviewed people whom I knew were unemployed and asked them to refer me to others in a similar situation. I eventually widened the scope of recruiting, through ads in the freely-distributed paper called *The Pennysaver*. My assistants and I also put up notices in youth recreation areas and other gathering places, and stopped people on the steps of the Employment Centre and in the Unemployment Working Centre.

After pretesting the instrument we conducted interviews with seventy-five unemployed people in London between 1983–1985.

The interviews were taped, their length ranging from forty-five minutes to two and a half hours. The sample members (to be referred to as "informants") were asked about the impact of unemployment on their personal lives, on relationships with families and friends, on the structuring of their daily routines, and on their experiences with employers on the job search and government officials in the agencies. They were asked what they thought of their society, their future, and what could be done to address the problem of unemployment.

The characteristics of the men and women in the sample are thoroughly explored in the book. Their characteristics are presented in more structured form in the Appendices: in summary tables, in a matrix of variables, and in brief verbal portraits. To protect the privacy of the informants, their names as well as specific references to places, etc., have been fictionalized throughout this book. When compared with data on the officially unemployed in Ontario in 1984, the characteristics of my "convenience" sample were roughly the same vis-a-vis age distribution, length of unemployment, percentage of job losers, and proportion of high school-educated. There was a slight over-representation of women, single persons, university-educated, and those from the tertiary sector of services and clerical work. While this may not be that distortive of the population of unemployed in London, Ontario, these sampling biases should be noted.

A word should be said about how the informants came to be unemployed. I define "unemployment" as Statistics Canada does: being able and wanting to work, looking for work, but being unable to find it. There are various "flows" into this state of unemployment (which I have termed "unemployment statuses") (Lemaître, 1985). There are young *entrants*, trying to shift from a school- and family-based life to the labour market. There are *re-entrants*, looking for work after a long stretch of (say) child-rearing. There are *job-leavers*, who had left their previous employment for education, or due to illness, change of residence, personal responsibilities, or job dissatisfaction. Finally, there are *job-losers*, which are the bulk of the unemployed of recent years as well as the sample (55%). Their jobs were lost in layoffs, business closings, dismissals, and project completions. For this last, important type, the job termination and its timing were externally imposed upon the individual, who had to adjust to a considerable dislocation.

The City of London, Ontario

We should now introduce the city in which the informants lived. London is a prosperous city of 285,000 in Southwestern Ontario, roughly midway between Toronto and Windsor. While it has a few large auto plants and some other manufacturing within its limits, London is chiefly a white-collar town with a large university, a substantial insurance industry, technological firms, many service establishments, and a vast retail trade sector. As a city, it is conspicuously affluent—in the grandeur of its homes and the number of its millionaires, in the many gourmet shops and restaurants, and in the large number of shopping venues (in terms of retail space per capita, Londoners are more highly serviced than almost any other city in Canada).

Even most Londoners will tell you that it is a conservative town. It is a city that conceals its unemployed and poor. When the recession reached its depths in 1982, an estimated 25,000 people were out of work—but even then were not very visible,. Those laid off from factories and firms formed queues at the Canada Employment Centre and Welfare, joined other applicants at restaurants and stores, or ate sandwiches at the Sisters of St. Joseph soup kitchen—then they melted away into their homes and housing projects. Their social, economic, and psychological problems were well outside the consciousness of the average Londoner. This unthinking affluence will be seen as a formative influence on the informants.

The Organization of the Book

The organization of the book takes us from the general to the particular. The first chapter provides a theoretical and historical background to the study. Believing the plight of the unemployed to be largely economic and political in origin rather than psychological, I then begin with the job market and work down through the chapters to the more micro-social areas of family, daily life, and self.

I first look at the ways in which the job market regionalizes the spacing of unemployed persons as they approach employers (Chapter 2). The unsuccessful job search has selective impacts on different phases of the life cycle; and I look at the experiences of younger and older applicants (Chapter 3). The other major sector with which the unemployed come in contact is the government bureaucracies. I deal first with Manpower and Unemployment Insurance (Chapter 4), and then those bureaucracies which administer social assistance and family benefits (Chapter 5).

The focus then shifts down to the intermediate formations between public and private life: unions, unemployment organizations, and social networks (Chapter 6). Following that are two chapters on daily life. The first explores those practices imposed by poverty and lack of mobility (Chapter 7); the next discusses those constructed practices with which the unemployed fill their unstructured day (Chapter 8).

The informants' family relationships come under scrutiny, as the formation perhaps most heavily burdened by unemployment (Chapter 9). Unemployment gives one an often hyper-conscious awareness of *self*, whose struggles and perceptions are the topic for the last substantive chapter (10). We finish with a concluding summary, and an examination of some initiatives for change suggested by the informants and the theoretical lessons of the book.

CHAPTER 1

Setting the Stage

While becoming familiar with the unemployed as persons, I was also noting the ways in which they were discussed, researched, and treated by *employed* society. The sheer scope of the problem—large numbers of people across a huge country, millions of dollars spent on unemployment insurance benefits and social assistance, the logistics of government programs—seemed to foster an aerial view of the unemployment issue. Now, this view was often appropriate and sometimes necessary. Politicians had to deal with broad responsibilities affecting aggregates of people. Economists had to chart, quantitatively, flows in and out of the labour force. Sociologists, quite fittingly, had to conduct some large-scale sample surveys to identify the social characteristics of the large number of jobless.

Yet, while the above approaches had value, *something was missing* in social scientific and policy debate. The unemployed, generalized about from a comfortable emotional distance, seemed to be reduced to a complex of functions and attributes within a socio-economic system. For many economists, the jobless were grouped according to their type of unemployment (cyclical, seasonal, structural, etc.), from which groupings the remedies flowed accordingly (e.g. stimulating aggregate demand, training programs, taxation adjustments, and the like). To the politician, the jobless seemed reduced to the position of recipients of benefits or retraining courses; in political discourse, they became elements in a numbers game which used unemployment rates to bolster or attack government policy and programs.

These objectifying and abstracting treatments dovetailed with, even fed into, the ways in which the unemployed were handled by social and economic institutions. On the job market, the unemployed person was not seen as a concrete human agent who was the unique centre of his or her experience, but as a kind of collage of qualifications and aptitudes, assessed for its costs and benefits to the company. In the social service bureaucracies of the state, the jobless were "clients," whose eligibility as recipients of benefits and retraining had to be carefully weighed, and whose occupational classification had to be precisely set down.

The result of this two-fold reduction of the unemployed to "objects" of analysis and institutional practice was the screening out and marginalizing of the *lived experience* of the unemployed. We could not see or feel their living situation in our conventional thinking and experience of society—and were quite content to live with these blinders. The result was that even people who cared about the unemployed unwittingly contributed to a *decentering* of the unemployed from their active individual or collective lives. From failing to see them as subjects involved in their lives, it was not a great leap for employed society to exclude their participation altogether from the projected *strategies* designed to cope with or counter unemployment.

No serious critical sociology can acquiesce in this class-based inattentiveness of power, in which the lived experience of groups of people passes from view. The social analyst must come closer, using the tool of empathy. As John Berger writes, "[T]o understand a given choice another makes, one must face in imagination the lack of choices which may confront and deny him." (Berger & Mohr, 1979). When we come closer to the experiences of the unemployed—stepping out of the protected vantage points of profession or institution—we enter a material and phenomenal world at once familiar and jarringly different.

It is a life-world that is fraught with contingency and strain—located at the point where societal forces bear down with maximum weight. As one desperate unemployed father in the sample expressed it, *"The pressure is real! The pressure is here and now!"* Alongside the stress, the experience of unemployment can be so abstracting, so disconnecting, that the jobless person loses grip on social reality. An unemployed journalist said:

> I feel like I no longer have a life…I'm a participant in a script that someone else has taken over.

Expressions of dehumanization while looking for work or queueing for benefits recurred like a motif throughout the interviews: *"I'm nothing, I'm just a number, I'm a statistic, I'm just one of a million."* The sense of being an object, displaced from normal human reciprocity was perfectly caught by a woman informant, *"I'm on the receiving end of everything."*

Against this decentering drift imposed by unemployment, we see—again, when *close* to the unemployed and not just generalizing over their heads—evidence of efforts to *recenter* their lives. Many of the unemployed resisted objectification and abstraction, keeping alive their concrete social relations. Though consigned to the receiving end of society, they found ways to give (e.g. to family, friends, or others in volunteer work). They engaged in activities in the "hidden economy," or grew their own food, to get by. Some took pride in being self-disciplined and ingenious when shopping for food or clothes. There were informants who organized with other unemployed people, for mutual aid or political leverage. Though some were demoralized and inward-looking, others continued to analyze, speculate, make plans, criticize, learn. Far more than mere sources of raw data or grist for the sociological mill, they were often knowledgeable and expressive on many aspects of their situation, both objective and personal.

The Objective: Discovering the Unemployed in Their Human and Structural Contexts

This book places itself squarely in that dialectical project of recentering. It aims to make a contribution towards revealing the unemployed at the heart of their experience and restoring their faded images on the societal canvas. This is a collective project already well begun by the unemployed themselves and many of their supporters, social researchers among them. While offered in solidarity with the unemployed, the book will strive to be true to the facts of their living situation. The approach taken here is a species of critical sociology: unavoidably so when the pursuit of truth must lift so many veils which shroud the reality of the unemployed. Sociological analysis tries here to bring into "figure" those marginalized lives which are, impersonally and every day, being consigned to "ground" in our capitalist society.

The first task of the book is an interpretive one, presenting and synthesizing the unemployed's *descriptions and interpretations* of their own social practices. Far more than simply the offering of impressionist quotations and accounts, this is the attempted rendering of a life-form as it is lived. As instances of interpreting selves in action, the social practices of the unemployed must be set down accurately and with empathy, true to their moving interaction of objective and subjective features. In this interpretive task, we draw on interactionist and phenomenological concepts which provide a vocabulary of processes of the self.

While the "anchor" will be the unemployed's self-described experiences, the second step is *analysis*. Guided in part by the unemployed's formulations and other sources, the sociologist has the analytical and theoretical task of trying to relate action to that more inclusive constellation of facts in which it is set. In this book, therefore, the unemployed's social practices are seen to occur within various enveloping social contexts: family, friends, networks, labour markets, welfare bureaucracies, and history.

After all, the unemployed's condition and practices are not problems of individuals *sui generis*, but largely derive from the concerted practices of others: those of employers, politicians, bureaucrats, investors, consumers. In examining unemployment, we are also examining capitalism, both directly and "symptomatically," namely through the superfluous and marginal lives it generates. In examining unemployment, we are also examining the concrete working out of the welfare state.

Conceptual and Theoretical Framework

As a sociologist, I had been urged by Mills and others to pursue the *connections* between "private troubles" and "public issues" (Mills, 1959); I had come to believe that in *this* lay the great promise of our discipline. So I looked to the social science literature on unemployment for linkages between these two levels: the ego-involved, emotionally turbulent *action* and the broader *structures* in which it was set. Much of the literature, however, seemed to gravitate either to the pole of action *or* of structure, while neglecting or simply positing the other term. On the *structural* pole, much of the work of labour economists looked, somewhat mechanistically, at flows of labour in and out of the work force (e.g. Lemaître, 1985), motivated implicitly by self-interest. Marxist accounts of the unemployed as a reserve army of labour were helpful, but sometimes reduced subjective motives and aspirations to being mute "soldiers" following the "orders" of capital. The literature on *action* (e.g. Levine, 1979; Fineman, 1987), on the other pole, certainly shed valuable light on the effects of unemployment on people's psychic and social functioning. It did not, however, analyze the way that functioning interacted with the structural and institutional features of the political economy. I felt that *this* interaction should be addressed.

Structuration Theory

The theoretical framework I began to adopt drew from the "structuration theory" of Anthony Giddens (1984). His approach refused to be drawn to either a macro- or micro-social vantage point, and indeed he thought that their polarity was misconceived. Giddens held human agents to be knowing, interpreting beings who act, but in so doing produce unintended consequences which, through repetition over time, condition human action. It is through this conditioned action that structural properties become actualized in social systems and human action but they must be "kept alive" through social practices. Giddens called this dialectical relation between structure and action the "duality of structure," defined thus:

> Structure is the medium and outcome of the conduct it recursively organizes; the structural properties of social systems do not exist outside of action but are chronically implicated in its production and reproduction (1984: 374).

Thus labour market structures are both the *medium* in which the practices of the unemployed and employed are shaped, and the (partly unintended) *outcome* of those human, minded practices.

The focus of social analysis and research should not be a mutually exclusive one on structures or on human action, but rather on "social practices ordered across space and time" (Giddens, 1984: 374). Because it is within such practices that structural processes from "above" *converge with* interpersonal and self processes gathered from "below." So labour market and other structures are internalized by human agents who, being so formulated, act back on and shape those environing processes.

The Syntax of Social Practices

My key unit of analysis then would be social practices, within which action and structure are mutually formed through time. I now needed a way of conceiving practices, which are meaningful but are partly brought about by non-meaning factors. The factors which help shape social practices are extremely varied: e.g. the environment, population flows, the layout of city streets and buildings, the structure of opportunities in labour markets, cultural scripts, the needs of the self, and so on. Combinations of these inputs either prescribe or mutely condition social practices. The social analyst's job is to identify the most influential factors at work.

But what is shaped is not inert. Humans' *enacted* social practices, in which are inscribed so many influences, have a life of their own. These practices are carried on by mindful human beings moving ahead in the current of time, evolving understandings and relationships which are new in human history. Of course one of the products of their practices is precisely those unintended consequences that structure future action. But the flow of human action—lived as it is by knowledgeable human agents aging and leaning into time—will never be a mere passive product of causal forces, or a perfect repetition of what came before.

In this light social practices can be seen to resemble *sentences*. Our linguistic behaviour is surely constrained by our vocabulary, syntax, and the prescribed usages of our culture—but none of us believes that our future utterances are rigorously predetermined. In the enacting of language in conversation or literature entirely new formulations appear at every turn. Now the combinatory possibilities of social practices are probably much less extensive than those of language, but if we do not push the analogy too far, it may do useful work. Believing this to be so, I have made the analogy an important part of the conceptual and theoretical framework of this study.

The social practice string, or "sentence," has three constituents which are linked like parts of a sentence:

SELF (& OTHERS)....DOING A SOCIAL PRACTICE.....IN THE INTEREST OF
(subject)   (verb)   (adverbial phrase)

The *subject* of the social practices to be described in this book is the un-employed person, or self. He or she can be the real subject of the practice, and/or can be a joint subject with other people, or can be simply the "grammatical subject." As in grammar, the latter situation occurs when the verb is in the passive voice, making the subject a mere grammatical not logical subject ("the leaf was blown in the wind"). There are three types of relationship between the self and others within the practice: "personal relationships," where the attributes of persons are centrally involved; "role relationships," which are guided by expectations that attach to roles; and "non-relationships," in which the individual is forgotten, or made into an object (e.g. number, file). These three types suggest a (dynamic) continuum of decreasing human involvement—i.e. from the "personal" pole to that of the "non-relationship." We also look at the symmetry or asymmetry of "power relations" between self and others.

The *verb*, or practice itself, is seen as having a "voice" which is active or passive. The verb-practice also has a "tense" which can be present, past, or future-oriented. The tense or time-orientation of the practice is important in the light of people's need to integrate their present with past experiences and future projects.

The *adverbial phrase*, "in the interest of," refers to the combinatory potential of the practice—i.e. the amount of reciprocal development which the practice stimulates and contributes to in its social environment. When a practice is very stimulating in this regard, it is "synergistic." On the other end of the continuum, when a practice serves only self-interest and little else, it is said to be "atomizing." Synergy represents combined action that adds to the creativity and social vitality of all involved, hence is the highest form of reciprocity. Atomization is action that severs ties; instead of multiplying benefits it is the turning of one person's gain into a loss (or non-event) for others.

An example might be instructive. *Child care* can be the sole practice of the mother, whose bond with the child may be synergistic to a point. But if this practice is solely her responsibility, she may become socially atomized and economically dependent on her husband. If, however, she is joined in her child care by her husband or other members of the community, the combined agency of the practice increases its synergy in a positive direction. She is freed for participation in the community, the child learns from both parents, the couple shares more, and they are less bound by unspoken sexist expectations. The practice has shifted *syntactically* (empirically speaking), in that its linkages with others are more flexible and voluntary. The mother's role is no longer solitary but is a part of a conscious community in action—as such her practice is now grasped as a positive contribution rather than just a part of the domestic environment, and she can now share its fruits and challenges with other participants. The empirical *syntax* then refers to the shifts in relationship of the constituents of a practice as the individual copes with various constraints over time.

The description and analysis of the unemployed's social practices will in effect be a careful reading of precisely this shifting syntax. Who is the subject of these practices, logical and grammatical? What are the relations between the unemployed person and others? Are power relations asymmetrical and, if so, what shifts have occurred? What changes occur in the voice and tense of the practice-verb? What degree of synergy is the practice invested with? With whose interests besides that of the self is it allied?

Formulators of Social Practice Texts

Beyond the local reading of the social practices, we must examine the empirical "scripts" with which they are coping. The enacted social practices described herein interact with various prescribed or conditioned pressures of their environment and history. Among these pressures are: job market conditions, government directives, the work ethic, the enhanced role of money and consuming in social life, the increasing need for two salaries to maintain a standard of living, and the requirements of personal identity. Keeping with the linguistic analogy, these pressures are, in their different ways, the *"authors"* of practices, whose empirical syntax form virtual scripts for our lives. Recall the unemployed journalist's words: *"I feel like I no longer have a life…I'm a participant in a script that someone else has taken over."*

One of the important formulators of prescribed social practices—in addition to the many others we will explore in the book—is the *self*. This is the ultimate protagonist of the book, being the point at which the economy causes the greatest suffering and strain. I conceive the self as having a *project* of realizing "personal identity" in the circumstances of his or her life. This prescribes the exercise of personal agency and the weaving of past experience into present action. The notion of "project" also implies that the normal human being plans for the future, organizing present activity in the future perfect tense. The self, however, comprises more than a personal identity with its various mandates: it has a "*social* identity" composed of the regard of others for the roles and attainments it can claim. The bearing of unemployment on the requirements of both personal and social identities will be an important focus of analysis.

Since this is chiefly an empirical work, the conceptual scaffolding sketched above will not always be made explicit and systematic, but will be woven into the text. But using such a conceptual framework will allow us to see different domains as having different empirical *idioms* (or characteristic usages). It also enables us to see historical forces as formulators of social practices to which selves and groups must adapt. It is with a brief historical background to the high unemployment of the early 1980s that we conclude this opening chapter.

Recent Historical Background

Canada's unemployment rate, compared to the other Organisation for Economic Co-operation and Development (OECD) countries, has been among the highest since the late 1960s. Its rapidly growing labour force strained against serious weaknesses in the whole economic structure. Its manufacturing has been dominated by branch plants, which tend not to foster Canadian research and development or to use local components, but in effect to "export" jobs to U.S. parent firms. Associated with this underdevelopment of manufacturing has been an over-reliance on the capital-intensive resources sector, which provided relatively few jobs in the expanding urban areas.

With the inflation of the 1970s and early 1980s, came reduced investment and rising interest rates. As orders from foreign buyers of Canadian resources declined, the primary sectors suffered. Capital, hitherto flowing in from the U.S. in the form of direct investment, was dis-invested from Canadian branch plants and redirected to more profitable areas, such as the Pacific rim and the southern United States. Layoffs occurred, plants were shut down, existing plants were under-utilized.

The foundations of the Welfare state under the Liberals—resting upon the redistributions of the fruits of foreign investment and sale of resources in the 1950s and 1960s—began to crack as government revenues declined and the deficit mounted. A *monetarist* strategy and ideology was adopted by political elites. This approach favoured controlling the monetary conditions for the suppliers of investment. If a nation controlled inflation and provided incentives to investors, then, it was believed, the economy would move forward far faster than by simply propping up the demand side.

So when the recession hit in 1981–1982, the government targeted inflation, not unemployment, the former being more injurious to capital accumulation than the latter. The unemployment rate was allowed to rise and was permitted to stay high rather than risk another bout of inflation. As Kaliski has written, "We know...that the world-wide recession was caused by a policy-induced reduction in aggregate demand" (Kaliski, 1987: 689). The economy was not permitted to absorb the surge onto the labour market of the last wave of the "baby boomers." Neither could it respond adequately to the growing need of families to have two income-earners, or to the need of single parents to support their children.

The economic crisis has had severe and continuing impacts on workers in the 1980s. The years 1981–82 marked the most serious recession in Canada since the Great Depression. Between 1981 and 1984, approximately one million workers lost full-time jobs, and were not recalled (Picot and Wannell, 1987: 90). More than one-third of the job losses involved a plant closure or relocation (the largest single cause). The 1987 study by Picot and Wannell which followed up the fortunes of these job losers found that, for the most part, they did rather poorly. In January 1986, their unemployment rate, even for those who had been employed three years or more, was about 25%—more than twice the national average. Among certain subgroups of these permanently laid-off workers, the rate was between 40% and 50%. Those that acquired new jobs took an average of six months to find them and, when they did, 45% suffered "pay cuts which left them earning an average of 28% less than they did in their old jobs" (Picot and Wannell, 1987: 124).

The most severe employment declines occurred in the *goods-producing* sector which registered, between 1981 and 1982, a startling 9% decrease in employment. Between 1981 and 1985, employment in manufacturing declined by 141,000 jobs across Canada. Severe proportional declines also occurred in primary industries (fishing, mining, forestry) and in construction. By contrast, the *service-producing* sector continued its long-term upward trend (Moloney, 1986: 92). By 1985, its share of total employment had risen to 70.4%.

The early '80s, then, accelerated the restructuring of employment, producing a net shift of workers from manufacturing and other goods-producing areas to the service sector, especially trade and consumer services (Picot and Wannell, 1987: 126). The marginal workers of that sector now found themselves in strong competition with those laid-off, as well as the better-educated new entrants to the labour markets. Employers simply upped the entry requirements to jobs by demanding education and experience. Many workers—especially youth—began to experience job-finding difficulties.

This expanding service sector has brought with it an increase in the number of part-time workers. Within this number, the fastest-growing group has been *involuntary* part-time workers (i.e. those wanting to work full-time), whose growth has more than doubled every five years since

1975 (516,000 in 1985). By contrast, the drops recorded in full-time and voluntary part-time were so severe that it was not until 1985 that they began to recover their recession losses. As well, there was a trend within the service sector towards more flexible business hours in finance, trade, and personal services; this "accelerated the use of generally less-unionized and cheaper part-time labour" (Akyeampong, 1986: 148).

In this changing economic and job market environment the unemployed informants sought their place. It is with their pressing search for employment that we begin the analysis.

CHAPTER TWO

Labour Markets: The Positioning of the Unemployed

The need for employment in Canada drives thousands onto labour markets every day. The official unemployment rate fails to measure this intense activity. The official monthly unemployment average of 1.3 million in 1985 (based on twelve point-in-time estimates) gives only a static view. Taking the year as a whole, the number of people who experienced *some* unemployment in 1985 was actually *3.6 million* (Veevers, 1986: 90), most of whom spent part of that year looking for work.

As a small sample of the unemployed, the informants in the present study were probably even more active job-seekers than the average, and certainly had greater difficulty in finding work. Here are the sample figures on duration of their unemployment:

Unemployed 3 months or less:	25% (19)
4 to 6 months:	19% (14)
7 to 12 months:	27% (20)
more than 1 year:	29% (22)

Those on unemployment benefits or social assistance (true for 56% of the sample) were required to look for work five to twelve times per week.

The unemployed then, if not the virtuosi of job search, were certainly among those most exposed to its perplexing demands. For the labour markets onto which they poured were partly material, but largely unseen. Beyond their physical settings and interactions were abstract structures of inequality one could never get at. The places one went to look for work were places of power, which kept inviolate their solemn capacity to choose people for work. The present chapter deals with the spatial *positioning* of the unemployed as they ventured out to make contact with employers. The next chapter examines the bearing of the job search on the life cycle.

The Outer Zone

Modern societies are stretched over space and time, in contrast to tribal cultures which are integrated on a face-to-face basis. Large modern institutions such as firms or governments generate actions which affect people at a considerable distance from the originating context and over timescales which exceed that of a human life. The individual's positioning within modern societies is complex. It is set "within a widening range of [spatial] zones, in home, workplace, neighbourhood, city, nation-state, and a world-wide system" (Giddens, 1984: 85). To this (intentional and unintentional) arrangement of people and social formations in space, Giddens gives the name "regionalization."

From the empirical data it is possible to see that the regionalization of the informants places them in two spatial zones each containing different experiences. There was a broad "Outer Zone," i.e. the space in which the job search occurred before concrete relations with the employer were made, and the "Inner Zone," where those relations actually took place. The social practices of the Outer Zone to be described and analyzed here are:

- Dispatching Written Accounts of Oneself;
- Moving or Being Prepared to Move;
- Queueing.

The Inner Zone practices are:

- Trying to Penetrate the Receptionist's Screen;
- Being Interviewed by the Employer.

Dispatching Written Accounts of Oneself

Many informants conducted their job search chiefly through the mail. In a large country a mailing campaign was certainly a rational strategy. It could be an exploratory stage, later to be replaced by more selective methods. Whatever the case, for the informants, especially for those aspiring to white-collar or professional positions, this strategy became quite engulfing. For these groups, job-hunting meant no less than "writing oneself" in cover letters, application forms, and résumés.

The amount of research put into the "documentary presentation of self" was often enormous. Whether in response to advertized vacancies in the papers, or going through lists of companies in the yellow pages or trade magazines, some informants worked systematically and hard. CRAIG, a 35-year-old jobless engineer living with his parents, pored over the papers for ads, company names and addresses, prepared documents and résumés, mailed hundreds of letters (using a computer) for two weeks of every month, 14 hours a day. For the next two weeks he reaped a meagre harvest from his mailbox. From a good mailing, the response rate might be 25%, but only a rare interview would emerge. When unsuccessful (he had been unemployed for 18 months) he redoubled his efforts, in a belief that he was not working hard enough.

The force that drove the almost compulsive energy of these job searches was explained by DOROTHY, a 33-year-old disabled woman with training in social work. She sent letters and résumés on a rotational basis to various agencies in the city.

As long as I kept finding I could do something, I still was able to feel I was in control. The worst times are when you realize that you're done, or you feel that there isn't one more thing you can possibly do. You have made all the phone calls, you've written all the letters, you've sent all the résumés and done absolutely everything: that's when the feeling of hopelessness sets in. Helplessness, too.

So long as I can find even one more thing to do, to help get me out of this situation, I'll do it. And it gives me a little more incentive. To go on the next day and not give up.

Engaged in activity for activity's sake as much as for its results, she seemed to fear the cessation of activity. If she stopped being a writer, *she* might become "written"—lacking a subjective centre. Furthermore, what possible *form* would her daily life take without it? Without the structuring of her day which the job-hunting work gave, she might be left in a drifting self-absorption. At the very least, these successive draftings of her public role in documents kept alive the hope that one day she would be in the public script.

Some shy and distressed informants used the mail because it was the least "bruising" to the ego, keeping them from face-to-face rejections and slights. Informants told stories of how they had been "burned" by employers in the past. MATTHEW, a 39-year-old married man with four children, unemployed for three years, expressed his weariness at *"being rejected door-to-door."* He had withdrawn from the personal search, sending his résumés around as his proxies.

While an exclusive mailing approach *could* protect feelings to a degree, it was far from unemotional. CRAIG admitted to having tried personal approaches. He flew out west at his own expense on two occasions, one costing him $800, the other $1000—only to find, in one case, that the oil project had been cancelled the day before his interview and, in the other, that they were not interested in him. Lacking networks, mentors, or friends to help him get a foothold, CRAIG consumed his life-force in mailing letters to impersonal firms. That letter-writing could carry "condensations" of strong emotions of longing and aggression is attested to in CRAIG's words:

I have attacked Toronto! I wrote to 256 accounting firms in Toronto—I got one interview…. They were going to interview 50 people, to cut it down to 10, to cut it down to three, to hire one. I made the top 50. It's a joke! To try for a job that pays peanuts…. You just don't know what to do any more.

The salary offered by the Toronto firm was $13,200. Interviewees had to pay their way there.

The Résumé

The most important single document of all, especially for aspirants to white-collar or professional posts, was the *résumé*. To the employer, the résumé was the "product description" of the worker's labour power. On its basis inferences were drawn about the candidate's suitability, derived in part from the firm's previous experience of that type. For the *unemployed*, however—especially for those confined to the Outer Zone through lack of contacts or personal access—the résumé was more manifoldly significant. To the person who sent it forth into the world it was a surrogate for the self, its objectification on the labour market. While résumé-writing could be somewhat formula-ridden, most informants showed a considerable *personal* involvement in the production and circulation of these accounts, which made them important identifying activities of the self.

For those without a confident social identity—e.g. women with low self-esteem who were unused to the job market—the writing of the résumé was extremely difficult. JOANNE, a 47-year-old married woman, joined a job-finding club. There she set herself the task of making a résumé:

This has done a number on my head. It's done a real number on how I saw myself. I know my skills. I know what I'm capable of doing. But do you think I could put that down on paper?… I literally couldn't put together a résumé by myself. I couldn't sit down and say anything good about myself. Crazy!

For women repressed in the home or office environment, whose achievements had never been publicly validated, to write a résumé was to ask themselves: "What *is* my social identity?" Lacking the public vocabulary with which to describe their skills, they were cast in the role of inept translators between two virtually non-communicating domains: the public and the private.

The symbolic importance of the résumé as manifesting personal identity was shown profoundly in the case of EVA. A 23-year-old university graduate living with her parents, she was seeking work in the personnel field. Full of energy, hungry for work, EVA poured herself into her résumé-writing, even making a fetish of it. She was always writing and rewriting herself: *"What I call productive is when I get this great idea to redo my résumé again, for the millionth time…."* When she had recently made a small error on her résumé, she was upset to the point of tears.

As a personal flourish, and a kind of test of the employer, she typed on the second line of the document that, though her name was Donna Marie, she would prefer to be called "Eva." As she read through her rejection letters: *"Automatically if I see 'Dear Donna', I just want to rip it up. Because if they had read my résumé they would have known that I prefer to be called Eva."* When a firm failed to match the emotion and craft she brought to the application process, she felt insulted. Once, when applying for a job working on computer terminals in malls, she had carefully composed perfect letters and sent them to each member of the hiring committee.

> *I got back, two weeks ago, the standard rejection letter…and I was furious. Like, I spent weeks on this letter and they sent me back a form letter…. We used to call it F.O.A.D.…what the university kids call "Fuck Off And Die." That's basically what these people say. Their basic rejection forms. They say, "Thank you for your interest in …blah, blah, blah. Best of luck in your future endeavours." It's just a garbage form letter.*

She was enraged at the sheer disproportion of the exchange. She probably knew that to them her résumé was a product description, but could not accept that she was just an unwanted commodity. She was trading her *humanity* on this marketplace, albeit in symbolic form, and wanted recognition for it.

Dis-Identifying of Applicants

Many informants experienced the glutted job markets of the early 1980s as massive miscommunication. They were human beings with particular human identities, which needed to *be identified* and chosen in order to thrive. They wanted to stand out as "figure" against "ground." But the field they entered negated the image, turning unwanted applicants to "ground." The firms, inundated with applications, sought ways to *reject* their documents, winnowing through them to arrive at a manageable number. The revelations of personal detail in the résumés were so much noise in the channels. Thus the processing by the employer contributed to the *dis-identifying* of applicants.

If one listened to the people rejected—especially time after time—it was clear who suffered the most from this corporate threshing. ERICA, an unemployed housewife of 45, had been unemployed for two years, after being a consumer advisor with a business association.

> *Sending all these* [responses to] *ads in, in the paper, and you don't get a response…. Of all the applications I've made, only one company has written back, and said "Thank you." You know, one!… Employers just seem to be taking advantage of everyone. There's no consideration, there's no graciousness, you seem to be begging.*

I'm now writing in my letters, "Thank you for even taking the time for even read-
ing this letter." Because I know there's going to be 400 like them there, and maybe
this will stand out… Really, you're just a number. I'm just a number now. [sub-
dued voice]

ERICA was describing society from the perspective of one abandoned in
its outer zone. Unemployed people and their documents were entering
the labour market to be recognized as human beings capable of contributing to society. The market, impersonal, with an efficiency derived from
the *abstraction* of human encounters, often simply did not "read" them.
The effect, quite unintentional, was to repulse the individuals seeking
connection and to reduce active effort to passive waiting. Removed from
the centre of their social experience, many had to make do with mailing
more paper surrogates of themselves to distant, powerful employers.

Moving or Being Prepared to Move

Modern communications and transportation have given labour
markets great extension in space. In response, suppliers of labour power
have often been ready to move, whether through emigration, moving to
cities, or commuting (Offe, 1985: 19). The informants were no exception,
showing a similar degree of "market flexibility" in the search for work.
Several had moved to London from smaller towns. They had looked for
work in Toronto, Edmonton, Los Angeles, northern Ontario, the
Maritimes and many other places.

I was more interested, however, in the *hypothetical* reach of the informants' job search, i.e. in their readiness to move. "Being ready to move" was
not obviously a social practice, but it did entail a withholding of community participation and conviviality. Thus the comment from 30-year-
old, married BOB, who said he would move anywhere for work: *"Friends,*
as valuable as they are, are not tent pegs in your shoes." Another, KARL, who
had been a peace activist in Ottawa, kept his roots shallow in the community soil:

> *If I feel I'm going to be in one place for a long time, I will be active. Now I can't say*
> *for sure how long I will be in London so I am not very active in anything like that*
> *now. I may get started and then I may get a call from Nova Scotia…or some place*
> *else and they say "Come here."*

The informants were asked how far they were prepared to go to look
for work. Overall, 39% said they would move anywhere, usually within
Canada (the "Very Mobile"); about 17% would move on certain conditions, typically that the move would benefit a child or spouse who would
come along (the "Somewhat Mobile"); and 44% indicated that they were
very tied to the community at present (the "Immobile").

Mobility Patterns

A quantitative analysis showed what factors were related to "readiness to move in search of work."[1] If we look at the impact of sex on readiness to move while controlling for educational effects, we see that university-educated women were more prepared to be very mobile than high school-educated women (50% compared with 23% respectively), but were still less prepared to be mobile than university-educated men (83%). Looking at Immobility, university-educated women were less likely to be immobile than high school-educated women (38% and 65%) but were still more immobile than their university-educated male counterparts (0%). There were similar results in the relation of sex to "readiness to move," when the effects of parental occupation were controlled for. Once again, women of higher-status socio-economic background were more prepared than women of lower socio-economic family origin to be mobile and were less likely to be immobile. Despite the small numbers, it seemed that sex and class had impacts on readiness to be mobile that were partly independent and partly interactive.

Generally those who were single were more ready to be mobile than those with family responsibilities. Sex and class background, in part interactively, also had a bearing on the degree of spatial flexibility in the Outer Zone. *Lower- and working-class women* comprised the largest proportion of spatially inflexible suppliers of labour. Next were ranked *middle-class women*, some of whom were as ready to be mobile as certain males, but were generally more likely to be *im*mobile than were males. At the top we had the most fluid (potential) movers through the Outer Zone, the *working- and middle-class men*.

---

[1]   The variables related to the "readiness to move in search of work," especially the states of Very Mobile and Immobile, were four.

First, *family situation*: those with children at home, especially the sole support parents on Mother's Allowance, were most likely to be Immobile. Second, *marital status*: those most willing to move were single males. Single women were slightly more likely to be Very Mobile than married women, but less likely than men. Third, there was *sex*: women appeared to be more likely to be Immobile than men, and were less likely to be Very Mobile. 30% of the women in the sample were prepared to be Very Mobile as compared with 52% of the men, while 59% of the women were Immobile as compared with 23% of the men. Fourth, there was a relationship with *socio-economic status*. Those with university degrees were more likely to be Very Mobile and less likely to be Immobile than high school graduates.

A similar result was obtained when we used another indicator of socio-economic status: father's or mother's occupation. There was a rough pattern of greater readiness to be Very Mobile as one went from manual occupations (32%) to managerial ones (64%). There was a significantly greater Immobility in the manual and clerical/sales/service parental occupational levels than among the professional and managerial ones.

The qualitative data shed light on the different mobility patterns. The largest category (38%) of the Very Mobile was, predictably, single young men. They were often unskilled and untried, seeing in themselves a potential that the local job market simply could not detect. "Go anywhere" was a manifestation of the open-market diffuseness which the young and others showed in their job search. Their willingness to go *"wherever, next boat to Kenya,"* displayed an excessive market flexibility that derived from weakness not strength. Lacking credentials and job experience, they had little to protect their position in the community and were ready to be "leaves in the wind."

Even academically qualified informants were ready to go anywhere. Three of the "very mobile" who had advanced education in engineering and accountancy were embittered to find that educational credentials alone would not open the doors to employment. CRAIG, who had trained as an engineer and an accountant, had about ten years of post-secondary education behind him (*"a waste"*). Feeling that his academic years had postponed his occupational maturity, he wanted to join an *"anti-university, where you could...throw degrees away."* What made it worse was that these credentials were being deployed from an isolated base. The journalist and two engineers were all living uneasily with their parents, unintegrated in social networks: to the phrase "going anywhere" they might have added "as long as it is away from here."

Of the women, forming 45% of the Very Mobile, some were single and originally from elsewhere with little to hold them in the city. The married women showed no pattern except that, in different ways, their mobility plans pivoted around their men. One would follow her husband's travels as a training physician. A second would move far provided that both she and her husband would have jobs. A third delicately hinted that, when she improved her situation, she planned to leave her husband and take the children with her.

Financial and Social Constraints

One of the constraints on informants' job search mobility, actual and planned, was financial. Moving around was a major expense for the unemployed, who always faced the risk of the money being wasted. KENNETH, a civil engineering graduate, was called for an interview with a Calgary firm. He then lived in Peace River, about nine hours away:

> It cost me $200 for the round trip. When I got out there, it was the president and vice-president, who had 18 and 35 years experience respectively. I don't think they even read my résumé. Even though that's the only place they could have got my number. They hadn't read past my phone number.

And then when I got there, they said, "Do you have an extra copy?" and I handed them an extra copy. "Oh, your experience is field, I need someone with design experience. Sorry, bye."

EVA went for a job interview in a city a few hours away. She was invited back for a second interview—at her own expense. *"I had to drive to Markham, borrow the car, pay for gas, get something to wear. The interviews went fairly well and I thought perhaps I would get this job. And then, the rejection letter I got from them was a ditto, a photocopy. It said 'Dear Blank' and they wrote in pen, 'Miss Anderson.'"*

Prolonged unemployment eroded the financial resources to *be* mobile on the labour market. PAUL, a 20-year-old, poor, single male, felt frustrated that most of the jobs were out of walking distance; lacking transportation, he could not get to them. Another man, an unemployed labourer, almost had a job with The Weed Man, but he had to be in Komoka, a small town outside London, by seven a.m. *"If you don't have a car, you're screwed. He said, 'I could use you, but I don't want to send someone over to pick you up, I just can't do it.'"*

Generally, as we come to the Somewhat Mobile and the Immobile, we see the barriers to mobility that beset human beings, especially women, in their complex social webs. Many informants' reasons to stay had to do with the needs of others. There were men who had girlfriends who would have to be consulted and worked into any moving plans. One man would consider moving to look for work but, as a father figure to his divorced sister's son, he planned to stay put for the next five years. Another man, a Kenyan immigrant named BERNARD, tried to explain his cultural attitude towards moving. *"In our African culture, we have very close friends. I have very close friends around me here. [Speaking of a job elsewhere:] I would take it, but a part of me would be living here."*

Women especially were tied to their community by seemingly a thousand strings, and spoke with feeling of their attachments. Here are the comments of two single women:

> *I need the supports I have here, I need good friendships, I need people I know around me. I need volunteer connections.... It would be hard to leave London.... It feels so good to be independent from my parents. (DIANE)*

> *One of my fears is that all the people I know will move away from London and I won't really have the community I have now.... There are good bonding communities in London. (LAURIE)*

Even more than for the men, these community ties were enablements for the women. For these women to "head down the road" for work might be a *financial* gain, but would be a loss of resources of support and identityformation. Of course, often, more than love of community kept women immobile. Their sex role as cohesive agent within their nuclear and extended families was both enabling and constraining. The mothers among them were concerned about the effects of moving on their children, who would not transplant easily, or on their own mothers and fathers who were aging or ill. *"I'd like to stay near,"* said young KIM, whose mother had cancer. The cultural and psychic formation which kept women "near" compelled commitment and also aroused guilt if they went "far."

The market economy in a time of high unemployment seemed to penalize those who were rooted in families and communities, very often women—who could not easily widen their search when local opportunities dried up. What was penalized here was the whole centripetal development of family and community life and the people who tended it, often for little or no money. Working against this careful husbandry of local concerns, the market economy of labour exerted a centrifugal, unravelling effect on community. It conferred a comparative advantage among the unemployed on the spatially and psychically "flexible," i.e. those with shallow roots in the city. Or the system *forced* people to be flexible: some of the poor simply *had* to move to find work and could no longer afford community life.

The jobseeker had to choose between an unrooted non-relationship to distant employers in an attractive job market and real, concrete relations in the city that was home. Forced to attend to self-interest, one sat on the sidelines of the community, in which events were carried on by those who could *afford* to belong. Cut off from synergistic contacts at home, one threw a line into far-away cities hoping to start the link that would gather one into a new community.

Queueing

When unemployment deepens in a troubled economy, companies tend to retain their higher-ranked workers, who are protected by union seniority or by the extensive investment the company has made in their skills. Laid off first are the less-skilled and less-educated workers. Many of these jobless flow into low-skill job markets in the service sector, where they compete with those who have always worked in those jobs off and on, or who want to make a career in them. An example is DONALD, who had experience and training as a cook and was devoted to the restaurant world. Finding this sector impenetrable at his desired level, he was forced to reduce his selectivity and "market price," and even take pizza-driver jobs at minimum wage.

Service sector establishments such as restaurants became magnets for all manner of unemployed. To walk into this massing of applicants at a just-opened restaurant could be a formidable experience: one young man found himself amidst about 1000 people competing for 50 jobs. In these markets the unemployed person met other unemployed, but in a *queue*. The initial feeling was likely to be a shrivelling of the self. *"There are so many. What have I got to offer?"* an informant asked.

Appearing self-contained, the person in the queue was really quite busy observing and making comparisons with others. A sole support parent projected her insecurity about her worth: *"If I see a long line, I get very discouraged, because I think there's at least one there that has the education or the experience to get the work. Which I don't."* Physical attributes which could affect employability, such as age, became manifestly a deficit as one studied the appearance of the competition. EVELYN, a sole support parent in her late thirties, found herself, absurdly, competing with 60 mostly young jobseekers for an evening job in a shoe store that paid minimum wage. *"Where did all these people come from?"* she asked dazedly. In such a crowd of *"jet-set younger types,"* she felt old and hopelessly out of date. Five years ago restaurant jobs were easy to get, she recalled.

It was difficult to verify the worth of one's individuality while continually stacked in queues with competitors. The sort of ideological "positive thinking" where one was differentiated from everyone else, a winner standing out as "figure" against the "ground" of the crowd, was hard to sustain. The informants appeared to reject such individualist thinking. As 32-year-old KATHY put it: *"I knew there would be a hundred or two hundred people applying for the same job and I didn't feel I had anything better than anybody else to offer."* Her resistance to individualism came partly out of lowered self-esteem, but perhaps also out of a potentially critical feeling that: even if I *were* better than anyone else, my victory would be everyone else's loss.

The dominant impact, however, seemed to be a dis-identifying one. Pervading many informants' minds was the feeling that they were *"just a number."* One man described himself as *"one of a million people going and knocking on doors."* In a job, while spending money and controlling leisure time, even in résumé-writing, a person could differentiate self from others, and express personal identity. But in the queue, the unemployed person was stripped of what now seemed a "delusion" of uniqueness. The packing in with competitors, so worryingly different in detail but so similar in intent and capability, made one aware of self in the guise of an *abstract commodity form*. The *fact* of their expendability as labour power, suspected in their status as unemployed, was here dramatized. For these who were bodily experiencing the market glut, the words they used were *"depressing," "demoralizing," "frustrating."* It hollowed them out, abstracting them from concrete self-awareness and relations with others. The stacking of human selves like materials exacts a toll that no material has ever suffered.

Though physically co-present with other people in queues, the informants were still in the Outer Zone. Instead of concrete relations with others, one stood in isolation from fellow applicants. These others had become projective screens on which were played feelings of insecurity and invidious resentment. Ultimately the relationship was atomizing. The syntax of the social practice was passive; its tense was stuck in a present from which, it was hoped, the employer would rescue the applicant. Self and others shrank from each other and synergy was very low. The queue of jobseekers was the uncommunal mass of liberal individualism, the grey background against which the individualities of the powerful took on colour.

The Inner Zone

Trying to Penetrate the Receptionist's Screen

The shift from Outer Zone social practices to the focussed interaction with employers or their agents in the Inner Zone was considerably more complex socially. Here the applicant offered not just documents but a coordinated presentation of self in an encounter with powerful strangers. Some informants felt they needed to be coached to enter the Inner Zone. JOANNE, housewife and former secretary, was not confident enough even to call or talk to people, to get names. But, after a successful program of role-playing at a job-finding club, she learned—not without anxiety—to do a "spiel": "*Hello, my name is…I would like to talk to the office manager.*" Many of the sample members were more aggressive than that. Some would keep returning to the same offices, trying to develop personal relationships with the receptionist. One women button-holed a personnel manager when he was at a church supper. A woman who wanted waitressing work would check out a restaurant, then keep calling back to demonstrate her interest: [*"Can I phone you in two weeks?"*]

The spatial organization and norms of the typical outer office are designed to condition action. Their organization marginalizes the positioning and minimizes the personal impact of the applicants' identities. Well-behaved applicants wait on the edges of the office and fill out applications. The receptionist at her desk, the first and possibly only person the applicant communicates with, forms a defensive line in the outer office, being the farthest point the jobless person is likely to go in the employer's direction. Part of her role is to contain and cool out the applicant, and keep him/her from penetrating the inner office. Her role is not an easy one, for she takes the brunt of the human energy that flows into the office.

On occasion the applicant brought into the office a compelling need to reveal the self. LAURIE, 24, single, captured the informants' view of this confrontation:

I don't feel right just leaving an application and walking out; I want to talk to some-one, at least introduce myself, ask how long the application is going to be on file and remembered, so that I can reapply even if there are no jobs at that one period. If I see it, if I hear it…if it's a concrete experience—if I'm going in and seeing someone, talking to someone, you know, I feel I'm there! They'll know me and remember me…. It just keeps the adrenalin going to see people…to be presentable, to be polite, to communicate what ideas I have. [Emphasis added]

This articulate statement hinted at the tension between the dynamic human being and the resistant analytical space of the organization. Her efforts to concretely identify herself had to contend with the spatial and normative power of the office which sought to "abstract" her from her human need.

The receptionist's front-line role became a magnet for harsh feelings from certain often-rejected informants. As one older female informant put it: "*I don't have to tell a receptionist my business…. I just want to get on the in-side track. I want to work.*" "*What do they know?*" asked another, who often pushed past the receptionist to see the man in the inside office, only to be told that he was too busy. The gate-keeping function, to the frustration of informants, would also be exercised on the phone, discouraging a job-seeker from even coming into the office. Some informants judged the stalling tactics that were the receptionist's stock-in-trade in strict moral terms. BRIAN, the oldest sample member at 60, could not even get in to talk to employers. He called the receptionists "*liars.*" "*That person's a buffer, they can be as kind as they want to be, but eventually they get just as hard as anybody else. One day would do it. 'I'm sorry, he's out of town. I'm sorry, he's tied up at a meeting'…and they've learned to lie and they can keep on lying like that for the rest of their lives, and if they'll tell those lies, they'll tell any lies. I've had every excuse in the book given to me.*"

In contrast, the receptionist's guarding of the gates of the inner office stimulated in others a sense of compassion. One man found the receptionist at first "cool"; but on the second visit, she warmed up to him. ERICA had an acute reflection on this role: "*I know it's important to impress those people. And I really strive to do that. I mean they're doing a job, and just because they're handing out applications, doesn't mean you should treat them like furniture. A lot of people do. But it's not their fault. I think it's us, the applicants. I think we tend to treat them as non-people. And I find that if you put out a little with them, you get a little back.*" Later, ERICA commented that unfriendly receptionists were "*probably reflecting us.*"

This last was an extraordinary insight into the more negative encounters. The receptionist and the applicant met in a context of structured miscommunication. The unprocessed, unsheltered applicant brought a human identity into a processing organization which simply could not assimilate it (or employ it). The applicant sought a relationship that was warm and the gate-keeper sought to cool it. Unable to help, the receptionist developed a protective veneer against the personal hurt to which her front-line position exposed her. ERICA pointed a way, if not to synergistic community, at least to a recognition of common humanity beneath the shell of these stifling roles.

Being Interviewed by the Employer

To encounter the employer was to deal with someone who was *serious*, being the controller of scarce, valued resources. An informant whose father was a businessman described the type as making a big show of being businesslike, *"not allowing feelings to show."* To encounter the employer was to deal with someone who did not *"know what the poor are going through nor do they care,"* as a single parent commented. The employer was the representative of a superior class. When asked if business could do something about unemployment, one woman answered: *"The average businessman is above that, is sort of in a class above the type of people who are on unemployment."*

The informants felt that the hard economic times tended to play into the hands of business, increasing their power. Certainly they did not want reduced productivity, said a 28-year-old technologist named CHRIS, but they definitely benefitted from the high unemployment. The most *"unhappy"* situation for business would be if they needed people and workers were scarce. But now: *"it's a good thing for industry.... They can pick the best people, or the best-looking people.... I think their choice of people is better than ever right now."*

Many informants put it more strongly than that, talking of *"business riding it high"* and *"they're loving it now."* Businesses were cited as lowering salary levels or withdrawing benefits earned by workers in a previous contract. ERICA was even more specific, drawing on her work experience with a business association. *"Any applications that wanted more than $10,000* [in salary] *they just threw them in the garbage."* Others pointed to working friends in the clerical field who were being absolutely overburdened with work, their employers refusing to take on additional staff. As 26-year-old FRANCES put it concisely:

> *I think large businesses profit by unemployment. They can keep their wages lower. And their workers are happier to be employed at a lower rate and in conditions worse than usual...than to be unemployed.*

As diminished figures trying to relate to a powerful class over which they had little leverage, some informants found themselves victimized and cast aside by employers. While good encounters with fair and helpful employers were reported, in many other encounters the usual ethical standards of concrete social relations—fairness, truth, and sincerity—seemed to be suspended. An informant was promised an interview for a restaurant job in a week, waited for ten days, and then found that the job was filled. Two persons were duped into working for employers for up to six months for nothing. One was an immigrant, BERNARD, 27, who did not know he could sue a tree farm that had refused to pay him for a work spell. Another—MARTHA, a sole support parent of 44—trained in a travel agent course and, as part of her practical experience, worked for an employer. He persuaded her to stay on for six months, promising that she would be paid—but she never was. Both people were personally *shattered* by the exploitation; they felt demeaned, depressed, and intensely disillusioned.

There were informants who, after years of working for a company, were laid off without proper notice, without a kind word. This happened to MARIANNE, a divorced woman of 60, who wondered: "*What is wrong with these people that they can act this way?*" Or, worse, they may go on to ask as she did: "*What is wrong with me…that people should treat me as though I was dirt?*" Whether it was callousness on the part of some employers, or routine instances of the inattentiveness of power, the response of the unemployed person was often internalized.

Jungle Ethics

Being used by employers, or ignored, or lied to, could encourage a similar "jungle ethics" on the part of the job seeker. The knowledge that employers and other applicants "cut corners" carried the lesson that, in this game of self-interest, lying was okay. One fellow recalled an acquaintance being interviewed for a private librarian's job who was asked, "Do you know something about art history?" The person brazenly said "Yes" and got the job. When the informant asked his friend later if he knew the Group of Seven painters, he knew nothing about them. In another instance, ERICA was urged by her husband to lie about her skills "*just to get in the door.*" Maybe she will have to do it, she said, but it was against her nature to be a "*trickster.*"

Performing for Employers

Many of the job seekers had grasped that employers expected them to sell themselves, to *perform*. In upbeat family restaurants, for instance, the young staff were expected to be full of energy and verve—applicants were selected for these qualities. But a few of the younger informants resisted being used in this way, as did PETER, 21:

> *I'm usually not much of a talker. So they ask me a question and I answer it. But I don't give them all the accessories.* [And you think they want that?] *Oh yes.* [Why don't you give it to them?] *Because I don't think there is a need. An example was when my brother started at Chi Chi's. They had people up there, and they were giving cheers, like "RAH RAH Chi Chi's" and stuff like that. People were based on how they performed there.*

> [Speaking of the employers] *They all want to make money. They want to make as much money as they can. So they expect people to perform in a way that will make them money…. They want to know what they can get out of you for themselves. I'll work hard for them, but I won't cheer or be loyal to the company.*

PETER counterpoised to this phoniness a model of honest communication: "If people said what they meant and meant what they said—if a person said 'I can do that,' then the other person would know he could do it."

Other informants, however, would have judged PETER's expectation as naive, sensing that the victories on the labour marketplace go not to the honest, but to those who make their mark. LAURIE's analysis of how the self had to "work the system" to get ahead was both astute and cynical:

> *It's like a big game…and you need to go through the act as gracefully as you can without being a hypocrite about it. Not being a goody-two-shoes, not being so naive about it that you can't play it to win. That's very prominent here—you do have to be something of a games-player. It's not just if a person likes you or knows you.*

> *Too often, in a capitalist society or country, you don't know 99.999% of the people you're talking to or walking in on. You don't know them, you've got to make that good first impression. And I find that pressure to make that first great impression somewhat annoying, 'cause it's like putting all your eggs in one basket. You've got to be tops all the time. You learn to face yourself, to be good on the days you've got to be good on.*

The Poor Gamesmanship of the Unemployed

The game, so ably described by LAURIE, was the "presentation of self" before powerful strangers, but an ambiguity remained. *Which self* should be displayed, in this formal, unequal audition called the job interview? This from HEATHER, a 27-year-old housewife and mother:

> *I guess when you go in for a job, the way people look you over, that was the thing that bothered me the most. Interviews make me nervous…. My true self doesn't come across when I go into someone else's office. I can talk more freely on my own.*

The sense of being scrutinized, of being on stage, was magnified when one did not know what was wanted. There were even painful attempts by informants to *modulate* personal qualities to fit into the employer's processing mode. STEVE, 21, reflected on a seven-minute job interview for a silk screen position:

> *I'm really worried about putting out my personality full force. I'm very wary about being introverted, I don't have a happy medium. I don't have enough experience. I felt in that interview that I was too introverted. They didn't get a chance to know me in the format they presented, so I didn't feel positive about the experience. I didn't see how they could make a decision that was positive.*

What made the unemployed poor gamesmen, in LAURIE's sense, was that they held so few cards in their hand. Sooner or later, the unemployed wore down on their job search, while the employer (who was not trading the self on the market) did not. People talked of the *"loser look"* one acquired. A small number of desperate informants reported that they have begged for work. BOB, laid-off as a computer operator, living in poverty with his family, would tell employers: *"Look, this is my résumé; it does not look favourable for my hiring. But I am a student trying to get through school and I have to eat. I will wash your dishes."* MATTHEW, 39, who had been unemployed for three years, made the sad statement: *"I don't think there's anything wrong with grovelling anymore."* After one employer had asked, "Is there anything else you'd like to say?" he could not keep it in. He told her, *"I need a job. If you want, I'll push a broom for you."* This humbling before the employer exploded the fiction of the rational exchange between buyers and sellers of labour power on the marketplace. Being an act out of the prescribed role, a ripping-off of masks, begging was not much appreciated by employers. When MATTHEW begged for work, the female employer *"sort of backed right off, and you could sort of see this glass come down."*

The unemployed were poor gamesmen partly because their interaction with the employer was a *poor game*, with a different set of rules for the employer's side than theirs. Informants pointed out how asymmetrical the communication with the employer was, even on the level of information exchange. Employers ran ads and asked applicants to write in care of the newspaper, preventing the applicant from knowing who the employer was. They asked, illegally, the ages of applicants either directly or through such questions as year of graduation. They pried into childcare arrangements, gaps in work history, and family ties. When ANDREA, a single parent and feminist, bridled at these violations of privacy *during* the interview, the employer reprimanded her. She and others told of privately resolving to behave better, to "bite their tongue." The employer could survive the standoff, not the unemployed; sooner or later people would come into his or her control.

Applicants received no comparable flow of information about the companies. Their only constraining tactic in this information game was the control they exercised over their *own* information (though some were convinced while waiting for a response that the employer was checking up on their past). So KARL, for instance, concealed the names of companies he had worked for, not wanting to be tracked down and penalized for past labour activism. People omitted educational qualifications, fearing that they would be considered overqualified.

Conclusion

Looking at the prescribed job search practices laid out for the unemployed in the Outer Zone, the coldness and lack of humanity which the employer projects is striking. The place to which the applicant brings or mails his documentary offering blandly conceals the exercise of power within. The employer is aloof from the applicant's approach, and his judgements are those of an inscrutable deity. His power is everywhere, shaping the society in unseen ways, yet it is nowhere and cannot be brought to account for its decisions. This is a power which masses and stacks and arranges applicants for bureaucratic assessment.

In the Inner Zone, the informants were again conscious of being in the presence of a powerful Other, who wanted to dominate the flow of communication and information. Though not knowing what was wanted, the applicant felt pressured to either shape the presentation passively to the employer's wants, or opt out. It was an atomizing relation in that it stripped the applicant down to the employer's measure. It was the employer who decided whether the applicant would be admitted into full membership in the society. A positive choice conferred a membership that was given and could be taken away. A negative choice could cut yet another thread binding the person to solidarity with others.

We are struck by how impersonally *formulated* the informants' enacted practices were—their "authors" being macrosocial forces, faceless institutions, structures of opportunity. Very few relationships had a personal content. Even the role relationships seemed to lose their shape under the pressure of numbers and the institutional coping and containing mechanisms, and would dissolve into non-relationships.

The self was mere grammatical subject, having little part in the authorship of its enacted practices in these domains. But when seeking for the real subject of the practices, the unemployed self met no communicating interactant, simply people in a system or processing field. Rather than contribute to personal and social identity, the unsuccessful job search left people feeling *dis*-identified, abstracted—like particles in a field.

It may be Habermas (1970: 93) who provided the most accurate framework for considering the distorted communication between unemployed and employers. The employer's criteria constituted "instrumental action," oriented to success/failure in the processing of applicants. The unemployed, while certainly acting to succeed, also acted within the framework of *"communicative action."* They tried to achieve understanding of their possibilities and place in the social world. They were stunned by the frequent failure of employers to respond, to give reasons for rejection, to give encouragement. As discourse, it was systematically distorted not only in the manner it was conducted, but because the rejected achieved no illumination from their experience—only personal pain from an impersonal refusal or neglect.

CHAPTER THREE

Labour Market Experience of the Younger and Older Unemployed

I mean, my God, we're talkin' Rejection City here.
    EVA, 23

Having explored the general idiom of job market practices, what *particular* inflections exist for certain segments? The factor of age has proved important. Many younger and older workers found they were even more discriminated against than others on job markets. Many were left in the cold by employers, or pushed involuntarily into part-time work or undesirable jobs. This chapter presents the accounts of these informants regarding their job search experiences. After a short conceptual and empirical background we examine four social practices:

- Suffering Youth Discrimination;
- Prolonging Youth Dependence on the Family;
- Suffering Old Age Discrimination;
- Hastening Old Age Dependence.

The accounts chart a similar movement at both ends of the adult working span, entailing (unsuccessful) approaches to the job market and a subsequent retreat into enclaves.

In recent studies of aging an important emphasis has emerged which focuses on "life-course transitions." It draws on Hughes's distinction between *objective career* (entailing well-defined social statuses and experiences) and *subjective career*, which is:

> the moving perspective in which the person sees his life as a whole and interprets the meaning of his various attributes, actions, and the things which happen to him (Hughes, 1971, quoted in Marshall and Rosenthal, 1986: 151).

Objective careers—taking into consideration, for example, the age at first marriage, spacing of children, and "empty nest" period—are important but limited. Built upon them are those *subjective* careers in which we assess (among other things) whether our life events are "on time" or "off time" in the light of accepted "social timetables." To be "off time"—to expect but not experience a transition, or to have it happen too soon usually creates problems of adjustment for the individual, either because it affects his sense of self-worth, or because it causes disruptions of social relationships (Neugarten and Hagestad, 1976: 51).

I will be analyzing the accounts of the informants to find how the unemployment of the younger and older informants is assimilated within their subjective careers. Does their joblessness put them "off-time," postponing or hastening crucial life-course transitions? If so, how are life plans re-scheduled, or projected anew into the future?

Empirical Background

Economic downturns have a disproportionately heavy impact on young people. "In addition to unemployment, they are the last hired and first laid off, and they are given the least rewarding jobs, financially and meaningfully" (Levine, 1979: 6). Of the unemployment of recent years young Canadians suffered more than their share. The probability of 15- to 24-year-old men or women experiencing some unemployment during 1985 was 41.9%, almost twice that of 25- to 44-year-old's and nearly three times higher than men 45 and over (Veevers, 1986: 92). Although the young make up around 20 percent of the labour force, "they account for a staggering 40 percent of the unemployed and about a third of those out of work for more than 12 months" (Lowe, 1986: 3). Especially vulnerable are those young people who leave high school without finishing, though more educated youth are not unaffected (Deaton, 1983: 17; Shaw, 1985: 149).

Although the youth labour market is very active—with large and frequent movements between the various states of employment, unemployment, and being out of the labour force—the seriousness of their unemployment should not be minimized. Hasan and de Broucker's (1985: chapter 7) detailed analysis points up some significant findings:

- While brief spells of unemployment among the young are numerous, they comprise only a small fraction of youth unemployment—*long spells*, suggestive of job-finding difficulties, take up a disproportionately large part;
- Young unemployed persons would seem to experience disproportionately more "discouragement" than other age segments, i.e. are more likely to stop looking for work because they think there are no jobs (extending the real duration of their spells) (1985: 70).

Much of the volatility in the flows of youth in and out of the labour force can be traced to those aged 15 to 19. For young adults (20–24), more apt to be seeking a permanent work attachment, their unemployment is entrenched and "full-grown." The average length of their unemployment spells and their concentration in long-term unemployment matches the figures for older groups; their flows into joblessness actually exceed their seniors. Furthermore, young people are much more likely to be *under-employed*: they eclipse every other age group in measures of involuntary part-time employment in the 1980s (Jackson, 1987: 109). In short, when economic times are difficult, this group (especially women) face relatively bleaker employment prospects than other groups (Hasan and de Broucker, 1985: 72).

The problems of *older* workers are somewhat different. Older workers generally experience lower unemployment rates than their younger counterparts. For 1985, the probabilities of men 15–24 experiencing some unemployment were 41.9%; for men 25–44, 21.6%; and for men 45 and over, 14.5% (Veevers, 1986: 92). The reasons for this have more to do with "employment stability rather than success in finding a job once unemployed" (Shaw, 1985: 152). Older workers are less likely to work in those cycle-sensitive industries which are hardest hit by recession, such as the manual work sectors of manufacturing, durable goods, and construction. Senior workers are often protected from layoffs by collective bargaining agreements (Shaw, 1985: 152–153).

Still, the unemployment rate for those 55 and over rose from 4% in 1981 to more than 8% in 1985, and that was probably understated, given the number of older jobless who become discouraged and drop out of the labour force. As well, for those older workers who *do* become unemployed, their unemployed spell will last much longer than younger persons. They will have much more difficulty finding a job. The reasons for this are various: outdated skills, the reluctance of employers to invest in contributory pensions schemes and training for older workers, and the view that they are less pliable than younger workers. Older unemployed persons eventually react to this greater impermeability of the labour market by withdrawing from the labour force in greater numbers than other age groups. As mentioned above, once they are inactive, they are more likely than other age groups to be "discouraged," i.e. to want work but not seek it, believing it to be unavailable to them (Shaw, 1985: 153).

Both younger and older workers, then, are alike in having experienced discrimination on job markets in the 1980s. Keeping in mind this discrimination and its bearing on transitions in the life cycle, we begin with the younger informants.

The Experience of the Young Unemployed

Suffering Youth Discrimination

The entry-level qualification requirements of the youth labour market were judged by some informants to be smokescreens. They would scoff at the restaurant that would require the applicant to be 19 years old to wash dishes, or to have grade 12 to do some other menial task. Many of the young people could not meet the educational qualifications demanded. Of the 29 sample members, aged 15 to 24, about two-thirds had not finished high school—typically they had been in Grades 9, 10, or 11.

When asked why they had abandoned schooling, their reasons were varied. A few had quit school because their financial situations were desperate. Some had found their classes boring or too stressful. ALLEN, 22, a former construction worker, admitted that leaving school at 15 was unwise—but, at the time, school was driving him *"stir crazy"* and construction jobs were his for the choosing. In another case, LORNE, a 19-year-old, living alone, had been rejected by his high-achieving family—partly because of poor school work. His father a doctor, his mother a computer science professor, the young man preferred welfare to the pressures of a school environment which humiliated him. Other informants, resenting the authority of teachers, reached out for the prospect of adult independence represented by the job.

Most young informants, however, cited "youthful appearance" and "lack of experience" as the two principal barriers they encountered on the job market. We will deal with each in turn.

Youthful Appearance

The first hurdle was the first look at them by receptionists and employers. Receptionists and employers seemed to size up the young in a single, rejecting instant—as if no other criterion mattered. NORMA, a 24-year-old single woman who had been dismissed from the London Transit Commission, described how difficult it was to seek work in an occupational market where the average busdriver was male and in the mid-forties. Young and female, she first felt the rejection as a look. Asked how it felt on the job search NORMA replied:

> I hate it!... Because you keep getting rejected. People look at me and think I'm not serious, because I don't look like a busdriver. I'm 24, but I look about 19.
> [emphasis added]

In what seemed to the young almost a discriminatory reflex, those who did not "look the part" were discarded. The "part," a kind of collage of marketable traits, was the moveable benchmark of that market's structure of opportunities. It expressed what was acceptable and what was not. Attributes that *differed* from this normative profile became stigmatizing, i.e. problems for social identity. As such they were potential raw material for a negative self-evaluation within *personal* identity.

Young informants expressed frustration and a bemused contempt for the superficiality of employers, who would negate relationships in an instant, rarely allowing even *role* relationships to form (let alone "personal"). *"Employers aren't dying to hire you, when they look at you,"* laughed HERB, a 21-year-old "New Waver." *"You're wearing funny clothes, your hair's a different colour than what it should be,…you have an earring or two. Looking like that, you're going to get a job working in a kitchen, someplace where people aren't going to see you."* HERB recounted the reaction whenever he applied for a "public" job such as retail salesman or waiter:

> *Once in a while I have had experiences where they have said "Ha ha ha. Are you joking?" And I just thought, "Well, it's your loss." Because I feel I deal very well with people…[What about secretaries?] They always sort of look you over and go, "Oh, yeah." Some of them look as if they're trying not to break out into laughter.*

The employers' perception was skin-deep, even myopic. Judging *"people on just the way they look"* (HERB added) prevented a deeper vision: *"looking at how potentially you could do so much for them."* The young found the marketplace blind to the hidden dimension, the untapped potential of youth.

The appearance of the young as judged by adults is a social confrontation. As a discriminant, appearance norms cut two ways. For one thing they reinforce *class divisions*. It is as though one has to pass through class-operated turnstiles whose admission ticket is a middle-class appearance. LAURIE, who has known poverty, described it well:

> *I've been stopped, evaluated and dismissed by the receptionist who's…there to spot people who are respectable or not at the door. Her job is to filter people out from others.*

> *I feel intimidated by that sometimes…. That person's secure, that person's behind a desk. It's the old authority bit. She can just hold up her hand and that's it. If I have a hair out of place or a button undone, that's it, I'm not going to get a job.*

Another woman was told that she was dressed too casually when she showed up at a sports store for an interview. Wearing the best clothes her income could afford, she wondered why one needed to be formally dressed in a sports shop in the first place. The stress on fancier dress, whatever its motivation, has the effect of raising barriers to low income applicants—who will simply withdraw from these markets.

The confrontation is also a *generational* one: the employer, a tangible symbol of the older generation, applies his superior resources to pressure the young to conform. To force compliance on appearance is to challenge unconventional youth's expressed social identity. For this sort of youth, distinctive appearance serves as a rallying point for the like-minded, and symbolically identifies the person with the peer group or generation. To give up that expressive symbolism for what the young call *"shitwork"*—washing dishes, cleaning tables—was judged by some as not worth it: *"I won't change the way I look for the sake of working,"* as one informant flatly put it.

Even when employed the young feel the pressure to conform. VINCENT, a 23-year-old single male, lived in poverty in a small room of an old warehouse. He described his trouble working as a part-time dishwasher at a university residence. He once had a Mohawk haircut, the only trace of which was a sort of tail at the back. His supervisor, antagonistic towards his appearance, would mock and badger him about why he did not finish high school. *"I told her to kind of 'Butt out, I'm trying to do my job.' And then I got reprisals from that.... She began to pick up on little things, like 'You missed that spot,' and egging me on. I just sort of blew up at her. I didn't show up for work for eight days,"*—in effect, quitting. VINCENT heard later that the supervisor was talked to about the affair, since she was the first one who had experienced trouble with him.

In the context of the stigmatizing social practices in which the market has cast them, the struggle of unconventional youth to retain their appearance must be seen as a *resistant* social practice. Rather than agree with the market's implicit message:

- Your appearance marks you as an undesirable loser;
- If you improve it you will increase your marketability;
- You will then be able to earn and purchase material for your social identity;

the informants have chosen—with peer group support—to use precisely that appearance as a collective and personal symbol of a dissent (or at least distance) from the conformist labour market. Those stigmatized traits were pulled away from their downward negative spiral and became, instead, expressive resources for building community and self-esteem.

Lack of Experience

Young informants found that, after appearance, loomed the mountainous obstacle of "lack of experience." As one young man put it, *"Once I tell them my experience, right there, their interest is gone."* As BOB wearily recited:

> They want experienced kitchen help, they want experienced waiters, they want experienced cashiers, they want experienced construction workers.

Even youth jobs that said "No Experience Required" would turn out to demand it. The young were turned away from the coveted adult world of work because they were seen as untried and inexperienced. "But how are we to gain experience if you will not employ us?" the informants asked.

This dilemma applied not just to the young and unskilled. Even in labour markets with a high formal educational requirement, a market glut in a period of high unemployment will "raise the ante," i.e. will increase the stringency of entry requirements by adding experience. DOROTHY described her efforts to get into the social work field. This profession had suffered in the early 1980s from a thinning out of grants to agencies and from a cutback in government positions. Many unemployed graduates with Bachelor of Social Work degrees, tired of knocking on employers' doors, went on to acquire their Master of Social Work. They then discovered that the desirable jobs demand M.S.W.'s *with experience*. But, asked DOROTHY, how could we be getting experience if we were working on our Master's after the B.S.W.?

These authoritative evaluations of informants' life histories by powerful officials and employers were a major concern of informants. When people like DOROTHY or CRAIG (he of the "the anti-university," in the previous chapter) were told that professional work experience was central and that, by implication, academic preparation was peripheral, they were likely to devalue or despise their schooling. Consider the case of DONALD, a jobless cook. In the 1970s, he took a five-month Manpower training program in cooking at a community college in Waterloo, a city about an hour's drive from London. Logging approximately 14,000 miles on his car from the daily commuting, DONALD got a rigorous training in a kitchen by a first-rate chef. The student chefs, treated entirely as professionals, expected to be prompt and exact in meeting deadlines, were given such challenging tasks as catering events at the local university and cooking for restaurants in real operational settings. After the arduous course, DONALD received a certificate as Second Cook.

When he then went to Manpower and told them he had six months of short-order cook work and five months of on-the-job training in the Manpower course, the Manpower official counted only the short-order work as experience. To DONALD, it was as if the five months of training—far more instructive than the short-order work—had never happened. Here was power, authoritatively redefining the life-course; it superimposed on personal histories a cruder binary version, which judged past episodes as Experience or non-Experience. Experience was life history made into a commodity, a currency on the labour market; all else was shunted off to the periphery of the life span. As a result, the personal sense of one's past becomes more fragile and subjective, drowned out (as it were) by the official version. Disconnected from publicly validated future roles, one's past becomes a bridge to nowhere.

The requirement of *experience* for even undemanding jobs, or jobs which people could learn by doing, is in part an arbitrary "valve" for the efficient streaming of applicants. From the experiential view of the young, however, it looks like an oppressive instrument of power. Young people reported their hearts sinking when they were asked their experience. VINCENT put it incisively:

> *The first thing...put it down on a piece of paper..."What experience do you have?" Bango, like that. You think, there's got to be more than experience. One word doesn't explain it, and that misrepresents quite a bit.*

VINCENT was right, in use-value terms. Young informants pointed proudly to the work they had done. There was the volunteer work of 16-year-old KIM, involving a host of tasks dealing with public and written records at a community library (not counted). There was the time young LORNE spent building the cottage with his father, from beginning to end (not counted). There was DONALD's work in a general restaurant where he occasionally cooked fish, which he thought qualified him for Manpower's recommendation for a job at a fish restaurant (not counted).

Young informants resented the patronizing stereotypes held by employers that would not recognize their commitment to the work world. They felt employers thought they were not serious, or that they would move away from the job at the first opportunity, going back to school or onto something else. The informants' response (especially of those in their twenties) was firm: we *are* serious, we want a foothold, we want to contribute. EVA, when asked what was the lowest wage she would work for, responded emphatically:

> *Christ, I would work for two dollars an hour. It's the experience I need! OK, I mean minimum wage. If there was a job that came up that couldn't pay—there was just work that needed to be done—I would do it for free, just for the experience. Oh yeah, the experience is worth eight dollars an hour, I swear!*

Hungry for experience, EVA wanted to move her life into step with a society in motion, into historical time, and out of the ego- and family-time at home.

One *consequence* of labour-market rejections of young people is a defensive and complementary social practice. One is forced to extend one's dependency on others well into adulthood.

Prolonging Youth Dependence on the Family

An important life-course transition in late adolescence and young adulthood is the shift from a chiefly familial and local attachment to autonomous involvement in the institutions of the public sphere. In this "normal" model is contained an expected social timetable against which most people evaluate their subjective careers.

The most vital social formations for the 26 single informants between 15 and 24 years old were, in order of importance, the family of orientation and the peer group. Judging from their accounts, emotional and financial support tended to come from:

- The Family Only;
- The Peer Group Only;
- Neither Group ("Isolates");
- Both Family and Peer Group.

We will deal briefly with each category.

Those supported by the *family only* were not doing that well and were often poorly integrated with peers. The teenagers in particular were pressured while at home to go back to school or at least look for work. There were a few "home bodies," mostly female, who stayed home perhaps because mother was sick but actually preferred the life of the family. More often, however, there seemed no credible role for teenagers at home. A small number were loners who found it painful to test themselves outside. GLENN, an 18-year-old who quit a restaurant job because they would not pay him more than $4.00 an hour, lived at home with his parents. His few employed friends did not understand him. The home had become, by default, his social world. Thoroughly discouraged in his job search, he blamed himself for his unemployment, and felt guilty for living off his parents. Introspective by nature, his joblessness had driven him deeper into the self. Confused, desperate, he had decided to return to school.

Of course unemployment provided good reasons to avoid peers and stay at home, even to non-loners. Being with friends, who were either in school or employed, meant answering difficult questions about idleness or social assistance. One could not pay one's way or entertain reciprocally. A few found it impossible to borrow from friends, even to accept a lift somewhere: *"too proud"* as a young man put it. The home, although a place of safety, seemed to deepen the marginalization of some youths. When no longer linked with relationships and activity in the wide world, the home encouraged an inward-turning and could become, psychologically, harder to leave.

Of the half-dozen youthful informants with little or no family support, three were integrated with peers and three were isolated. HAROLD, 18 and gay, was thrown out of his home by his father, though he still received a little financial help from his mother and friends. Having recently "come out of the closet," he was enjoying acceptance in the gay subculture. He wanted work in the restaurant sector, which is (selectively) hospitable to gays, partly because his friends were there. It was their empathy which sustained him in this deprived time. Constant visiting, talk about job prospects and unemployment, the odd beer at the club now and then, occupied the better part of HAROLD's free time.

The "isolates" had a much heavier burden. There were two teenagers who had completely broken from their families. Eighteen-year-old MARJORIE, no longer in contact with her family (some were out of town), lived in poverty on social assistance with her fiancée and another person. Having left school in the middle of Grade 11, she was unable to break into waitressing or even babysitting and then found it was too late to transfer to another school. When she was interviewed in June she was floundering: up until three a.m. watching television, sleeping most of the day, moody, and down on herself. A second case was LORNE's, who had been rejected by his family. Living alone on social assistance, this young informant seemed hopeless and cut off from life—having no connections, few friends, little work experience, or education. To resolve adult identity for people in LORNE's position is extremely hard, being deprived of the successes or relationships needed for the task (Levine, 1979).

When the support of *both* family *and* peers was available, the interaction could be competitive *or* synergistic. An instance of the first was provided by MICHELLE and JUDY, two sisters. The youngest informants at 15 and 16, they lived with their mother, who was on welfare. With a negative attitude towards school, their attendance was irregular. The only available work in the neighbourhood for them was babysitting—a diminishing prospect as the local children were growing older. Bored in their poor and limited home, the sisters frequently quarrelled, especially if one or the other got work. When JUDY acquired money, she was out of the house with it like a shot—as though fearful it would disappear: "*go to movies, shopping, downtown, friend's house. All over the place.*" The girls' adolescent lives oscillated between mother and peer group, the motion depending largely upon earnings. A job provided money which sped the movement outward to the peer group and intensified its activity. Lacking both success in school and job prospects, the sisters could at least bid for social success with their peers. When there was *no* job—meaning they had to borrow or go to parties empty-handed—they made a reluctant return to home and mother.

More typically, however, there was a *synergistic* interaction between family and peers. The family offered financial support, advice, and a home; at its best, it hewed to an unconditional belief in the worth of the family member regardless of the insults of the outside world. When the accumulated pressures of family life proved too much, the peer group was on hand as a safety valve. Peers gave emotional (occasionally financial) support. Most importantly, the peer group was a mediating link to the outside world, giving access to perspectives, people, news, and contacts. At *its* best, it made one feel a part of a generation, part of the larger forces of one's time. LAURIE articulated this solidarity, which tempered the naked individualism of the labour market:

> [My friends] *are facing the same change that I'm facing. I think the economy is changing, and we're young enough to change with it. But for the next five years I think we'll all be adjusting and trying to survive—month to month and year to year. And we'll be getting our long-term career goals clearer-focussed and getting the preparations together.*
>
> *So we'll all be struggling and…there's nobody I know looks down on me for doing what I'm doing and thinks I'm a lazy bum. None of us are…really stuck in that way of acting…. We're all pretty active. We see each other fairly often….* I'm not alone in this. [Emphasis in original]

LAURIE, significantly, lived with and had a very close relationship with her mother. She was therefore supported by the two key social formations of youth. Let us look further at this important enclave into which unemployment protractedly places the young: the parental home.

Living With and Off Parents

Of the 18 younger adults, aged 20 to 24, most were supported by their parents, with a small number of the others dependent on spouses or boyfriends, or a "social wage" like Mother's Allowance. A few planned to return to university and were content to live out in the suburbs with their parents in the meantime. They contributed to the household by housework and gave some money for room and board.

A less conventional case was HERB's, a young gay man of 21. While oriented towards his peers and a job congenial to his lifestyle, Herb lived contentedly with his parents. Living at home helped to organize his life. *"I've got two dollars in the bank, but I've got Mom and Dad. And I don't have to ask them for money. They just sort of say, 'Here.'"* His mother was trying to impress on him that he must choose between school and work. While he did admit she was getting through to him—he was looking for more secure work—interactionally he tended to brush her off, saying "Awww, Mom." In another case, STEVE would allow himself to be inspected by his mother each morning on what he was wearing before job-hunting. He felt it was a bit of theatre for his mother's sake, as he himself was somewhat cynical about the job market.

Some of the people in their twenties quite consciously humbled themselves before their parents in order to survive. This was roughly PAUL's case, another gay male, unemployed for eight months. While not living with his parents, he depended on his mother financially. He and his partner were so poor that they were forced to steal food. He justified his dependence on her by pointing out that it fulfilled her parental role. While this may be a rationalization, PAUL's situation left him few options. He had to find some way of living with a humiliating extension of his childhood. Living in the lee of a resistant labour market which offered him only the role of loser, at least "mother" and "son" were familiar roles which he could draw on. The government's safety net was pitiful: his U.I. benefits, based on a low-paid restaurant job and soon to run out, paid $100 every two weeks.

Living with parents can help the young sort out their confusion for a while, as with 24-year-old ROSS. A graduate of the Co-op program in mechanical engineering at the University of Waterloo, ROSS found himself out of work when the firm he was training with went bankrupt. He then became involved in volunteer artistic work during International Youth Year, out of which grew an intense interest in music and recording. While he doubted that he could make a living at music, he was thrilled by the experience of exercising his powers at something he loved. Another of his goals was to start his own business, an enterprise which he feared steady job-hunting would detract from. Admitting his confusion, ROSS's job search for positions in mechanical engineering waxed and waned. Living with supportive parents prolonged—in a comforting but perhaps not advantageous way—his state of irresolution.

Playing up the filial role, generally, had its cost: it exposed the young person to the overprotective, interfering, and nagging behaviour which anxious parents display to their children. That behaviour in turn stimulated the manipulative reaction of the young person—in a familiar but somewhat immature spiral. Deprived by the labour market of the opportunity to test their mettle as adults, they were often without the status of adults at home. This prolonged dependence on parents, a known result of hard times generally, extended even to informants *over* 24 years old. Of that number, six were living with their parents, and a much larger number were partly dependent on parents for resources or services. Peer groups and networks thinned out for the older informants, leaving them with few stepping-stones to the people and opportunities of the larger society. Relationships would contract to the family and kin network.

This prolonged dependence on parents, while understandable and partly synergistic for the family, extended the social role and self-conception of "youth" well beyond its conventional span. It put them "off-time," postponing the life-course transition to autonomous adulthood. The first cause, it must be stressed, was the exclusion of these youth from a role in the labour market and society-at-large. None of the "safe harbours"— peers, family, Mother's Allowance, social assistance—seemed enough to support the transition. The thrust of many of these unemployed young people was unmistakably towards the work world. At a deeper level, it was a thrusting *outward*: beyond egocentricity, beyond the attachment to home, beyond the subordination to teachers. While not everyone wanted full-time employment—many indicating they would like to help others in volunteer work—as long as the link between employment and a satisfactory income and status existed, they wanted employment.

The Experience of the Older Unemployed

Suffering Old-Age Discrimination

If the labour market *over*values experience in the young applicant, when it turns to the older person, suddenly experience is not enough. About 15 informants aged 35 and older linked their jobfinding difficulties to age discrimination; their accounts point up the different kinds of discrimination as well as their responses.

Blatant, Objective Discrimination

A good deal of the discrimination was quite open and objective. EMMA, a 52-year-old single parent with a teenage daughter, had worked at a variety of jobs: tobacco farm worker, factory worker, laundromat attendant, housekeeper/nanny. Social assistance and alimony provided barely enough support, and she had been seeking satisfactory employment for four years. One job-hunting day, she brought an application in to Jean Junction. The employer told her point-blank: *"You might as well rip that up…. We hire young women, not women your age, because we're selling to youth and not to older women."* EMMA was stunned by his words:

> *I felt really disappointed. I went out of there crying. I think you get a slap in the face, just because you're trying. Then people tell you you're not trying, that there's jobs out there. And I said "Where?"…*
>
> *It's frustrating being discriminated against. I was young once, and I tell them, you're going to be old one day too, young man. We all get there.*

A few other informants were told by the employer in no uncertain terms that younger workers were preferred.

Since this form of discrimination violated the Human Rights Code the screening was often subtle and indirect. Thirty-nine-year-old MATTHEW was sent by Manpower to apply at a hardware store as a clerk. *"And the minute he [the employer] saw me and shook my hand…he just kind of backed off and looked at me and said, 'He said you were a student.' And I said 'Yes.' So I filled out the application form and, he turned his back on me and said, 'I know I'm not supposed to say this, but how old are you?' And I said 'Thirty-nine.' 'Oh, well, we pay minimum wage.' 'Fine, I'll take it.' Then he said, 'We work funny hours.' All of a sudden these little things started coming out. It became obvious to me that he didn't want me."*

The Discrimination in Youthful Displays

Another, more perceptual, type of discrimination was based on the sheer public and symbolic visibility of the young in offices and public places. The employer did not have to indicate anything: his office was studied by the candidate as a kind of exemplary tableau of job-marketable attributes in order to get a sense of his or her own chances. *"There are so many young women from 16 to 24,"* observed an older woman, who might have noticed them more due to their symbolic status as rival or usurper. Another woman suggested the typical inference: *"When you go into an office, and you see a melée of...none of them are over 25, wellll* [chortles]...*you know."*

Of course this form of discrimination was more than perceptual—as women who were involved in staff change-overs attested. ERICA, 45, described her last few months as a staff person in a business association. *"We had hired two new staff people, both young, gorgeous ladies....* [After an office manager left] *they put a girl in her job, who hadn't been there as long as me, but she was a beauty, she was a model."* Why would they want young beautiful girls? ERICA answered:

> Because you're out amongst businessmen, you're doing seminars, you're doing meetings—and this is the thrust he seemed to be taking.... I really feel that there was too much of an emphasis on superficiality, on youth and beauty, rather than on hard work and conscientiousness.

The unwitting effect of these discriminatory hiring practices is to *divide* two generations of women workers against each other. The older informants were somewhat disparaging towards their younger counterparts and dismissive of their skills—reactively fostering their own stereotypes. Less confidently, older informants (especially secretaries and office workers) would talk of being passed over for younger women.

> I'm now 52—and I find that the younger women are more available.... I imagine a lot of employers would like younger women.

> My age, you know, I'm 51. They're going to pick a girl of 17.

> If you're 19 and don't know enough to come in out of the rain....

> Maybe I don't throw anyone into sexual desire but...it's the job!

It is as though these women were shorn of their skills and experience and cast in the passive role of "wallflowers" at a dance, waiting to be chosen by the desirable male.

An instance of intergenerational rivalry was recounted to an informant by a friend of hers in the Over-55 Club. This woman was interviewed for a job by a much younger woman in a personnel department. The interviewer told the friend outright: "With your experience, I would not hire you. Because…I would be looking for a job down the road." On the other side of the confrontation, certain middle-aged informants indicated their nervousness when the interviewer was young. The rivalry never seems to end: even if the older woman, with her decades of experience, can overcome the boss's youth-preference and land the job, she still must deal with the younger employees' sense of threat. The labour market— win or lose—fosters the belief that youth and maturity are enemies.

Are there any informants who resisted this atomizing, competitive ethos of the market? GAIL, 50—an intense, chain-smoking woman—had quit her job as secretary because of a tyrannical boss. She was called into a placement agency one day, to have an interview with an employer. Suspicious, GAIL wanted to know: "Why here? Why not at his office?" They explained that he had acquired a "girl" from the placement agency a few months ago with whom he was not happy. He was interviewing for a mature person at the agency location so that the girl would not suspect. GAIL, angered by this deviousness, said she would accept the interview but would tell the boss what she thought.

> That to me is bloody cruel. They cannot expect a 19-year-old to have the experience that another one has. Yet they want the younger ones.

She was not recommended for the interview.

More than just the office, *society in general* was seen as a display-case from which all traces of older people were vanishing. BRIAN, 60, once a well-paid interior decorator, had had a firm that went bankrupt. In the last few years, he had only been able to find work in a gas station and had been often rejected on the job search. His words were bitter:

> You don't see the old people any more. They don't want old people around…. Walk down the street and see how many old people you really see…. They put them in places like this [a senior's apartment] and hope they'll die! Or else they put them in Extendicare. If they're well enough not to be there, well, then they get their hair dyed, they get their faces lifted, they do anything and everything to stay young. Nobody wants to have anyone very old around them.

When asked what contributed to the emphasis on youth, he pointed to the television set: "*That thing there governs what kind of lifestyle we have.*" Television—like the rooms of office workers, like the streets in Brian's part of the city—offered its own selective display: highlighting the faces, figures, and activities of the young, while keeping those of older and marginal types in shadow.

Many of those with the characteristics considered "unmarketable"— the non-conforming young, older people (especially females), blacks, the physically disabled, the overweight—had an acute awareness of the symbolic character of social types. PAULA, a black single parent of 22, reported feeling caught in a cultural blind spot that made her unemployable. Being an attractive black woman, she thought, automatically pegged her to others as a prostitute or an entertainer, certainly not as intelligent and industrious. The marginalized tested reality with a different figure/ground configuration than the mainstream. What were usual attributes to the majority were, to the marginalized, *normative* and exclusionist. As for their *own* characteristics they seemed erased from the consciousness of society. As a black informant stated forcefully: *"There is no black man working in any major office in London."*

Self-discrimination

According to Statistics Canada's annual survey of discouraged workers, older workers were much more likely to be "discouraged"—to give up looking for work—than younger groups. In 1985, out of the would-be workers under 45, only one in 20 had given up looking for work. For the over-45s, one in *seven* had given up. This points up the importance in that group of the subjective assessment of labour markets and of one's own chances within them.

To define the mechanisms whereby market discrimination leads to discouraged withdrawal from the market we must explore a third form of discrimination: *self*-discrimination. This is the social-psychological "completion" of job market rejection. As in the youths' situation, unmarketable attributes become negative elements of social identity and then are turned into interior themes in a self-rejecting *personal* identity. This negative self-concept is then projected onto employers who are gradually avoided, as part of a slow disengagement from social practice.

Most of the informants who complained of age discrimination, indeed most of the over-35s, had been unemployed for over six months. They knew the experience of repeated rejections from employers first-hand. Having been ignored or refused jobs for which they felt qualified and, crucially, *having not been told the reasons why* they were rejected, many of the older informants were free to speculate. The very vagueness (or absence) of the employer's response formed a kind of Rorschach projective test which demanded an interpretation. Being denied a reason in objective reality, from what sources did they draw their interpretations?

Often they were drawn from personal reflection as in ERICA's case. When asked to what she attributed her unemployment, she pondered. She had a very solid business background as secretary and consumer advisor, so she was (surely) not being rejected on qualifications and competence. *"The small reason is weight, I've got a bit of weight on me."* But having only been interviewed three times in 19 months, she doubted that her appearance was decisive. Having seen younger and less qualified acquaintances get jobs within that time, she concluded: *"I think it's age. I can't for the life of me think of any other reason, it's age."*

Within this information vacuum, furnished with mute rejections, thoughts tend to drift down to the self. Decades of individuating experiences that have added dimension to the self-concept no longer seem to be operative, in what is now a rejecting social field. Elderly features are stigmatized and become problems, even enemies, of the self. *"I've got too much grey hair,"* said BRIAN. *"I was never old till I was told by so many people I was old.... I don't think anyone wants you around. They see sixty before they see the person."* SILVIA, a 57-year-old widow, was asked how it felt looking for work:

> *Degrading. Although you don't have to state your age, they can tell by looking at you.*
>
> *...[Or] with a résumé, they can tell right away what age you are, and they have you. "Hey lady, if you finished high school in 1945 ..." Right away they have you.*

"They have you,"—the dirty secret of aging has been uncovered again on the job market.

Older women were particularly vocal on this penetration of job market rejection into the self. Older informants showed an astonishing capacity for personalizing social problems, even when they knew structural explanations. Consider GAIL's important formulation, when asked what keeps her motivated in her search for work:

> *Because you can't die!.... Maybe it's not blaming everyone in the world for what you're in. And realizing that the main problem is me. And therefore I have to overcome this in some way.*

Perhaps she resisted the structural explanations because she wanted to believe she was still the credible subject of her life, who could still, individually, solve her own problem. Given the changing structure of opportunities for women GAIL's age (55) at a time of high unemployment, her unemployment could be intellectually explained. But, *existentially*, most of the informants felt personally involved, personally rejected, and hoped that they personally could find a place for themselves.

Note their words—analytically questionable, but humanly comprehensible—swirling down to the point of gravity, the self:

> *If I'm out of a job today, it's because I'm too old.... Nobody said, "Hey listen lady, don't you realize that you will never get anything steady, or a decent job, because of your age." So, if it's anyone's fault, yeah, it's mine. [bitter laugh] Been around too long.*
>
> [SILVIA, 57]

There's something I do wrong [in interviews]. *I have a fantastic letter of recommendation...a very good résumé.... There really must be something in my personality that turns people off.*

[AGNES, 54]

I really am questioning my self-worth. I really feel, Hey, I've got nothing left to offer.... You know, I just don't have it, nobody wants me.

[ERICA, 45]

What is wrong with me that I can't hold a job?.... That people should treat me as if I were dirt?

[MARIANNE, 60]

After the rejection is taken into the self it colours the informants' perceptions of other people, particularly employers. Though partly derived from a realistic assessment of marketability, the vision of the self is distorted by its felt uselessness and superfluousness. The feeling is quickly generalized to many other unproven settings and can distort the feedback from others. BRIAN at 60 felt that he had to find a career or trade—he was taking a course in upholstering—because at his age no one would hire him.

Nobody is going to employ me at this stage of my life. And I could prove that, I'm sure, tomorrow morning if I went out of here with you in tow and I applied for 44 different places....

Even applying for the upholstery course was difficult: "*I never thought I'd be accepted, because I'm afraid of my age again, you see.*" Instead of lending value to his age, the stigmatizing zone of the job market makes BRIAN "afraid" of his age.

Feedback from others may be too quickly judged as critical of self. When one 57-year-old woman presented herself to receptionists, she found they were kind enough, but "*maybe because they think...you know, we have a real winner here, maybe we have to* [humour her]." Another woman found that when she would go to a doctor or lawyer, "*they look at you and wonder why you're not working.*" Likewise before employers: "*They look at you as if to say, 'What are you doing here?'*" As part-projections, these views of others have a spreading, self-fulfilling character. They may become even more deterministic and disabling than the (highly constrained) "objective" reality would make it.

Hastening Old-Age Dependence

If older unemployed persons often "solve" the problem of unemployment by withdrawing from the labour force rather than finding or continuing to seek employment, to what enclaves do they retreat? Does their joblessness put them "off time" in their subjective career, affecting an important life-course transition? If so, how is their future re-drawn? We will examine each enclave in turn.

Into the Family: Grown-up Children

The case of AGNES, 54 and divorced, is instructive. She had spent her young adult years caring for her children while her husband was in school. Then, *"as soon as things started to get easy, he walked out and left me with five children."* After much "sub-employment" she was hired, in her forties, for a modestly-paying but interesting job in the editorial department of a city newspaper. During her five years there, she judged children's art submissions; typed newspaper articles into a terminal; followed up complaints; and interviewed and researched. Then, with one week's notice, she and 25 other employees were laid off. Management pointed to the decline in advertising revenue due to the auto industry downturn in the city. As well, technological change in the office had decreased labour needs (e.g. stories now came in from the wire services pre-typed on the terminal, resulting in fewer typing jobs).

At the time of the interview AGNES had been unemployed for 27 months, despite persistent jobseeking and excellent references from the newspaper. She was beginning to despair. Her reduced circumstances had forced her to move close to London, even though a daughter of hers was in college in the former city.

> I don't have a place to live. I'm living right now on the charity of my son…. My son is giving me a roof over my head, paying for the food I eat. And he has enough problems of his own…. Life has been very bloody unfair.

Her family were trying to understand: *"They don't like the fact of me not being self-sufficient…. It undermines me as a person, my insufficiency. I don't qualify for welfare because I receive some alimony and the alimony is not enough to live on."* Family members were mobilizing to help: a brother and married daughter had each offered her living space. She knew their offers were generous but her burning desire was to live on her own and provide for herself.

Even in her well-meaning family, power relations and the control over information were slowly shifting away from her. She sensed uneasily that the family was starting to feel responsible for her. Her relationship with them was shrinking: she felt less a person than someone cast in a role— the *family problem*. They were arranging things behind her back, finding excuses to make things easier for her. While trying to contribute to the home as best she could, the syntax of action was slipping into the passive voice. She was initiating fewer projects, lingering instead on the fringe of the family.

Over and above the aging of her body, unemployment had accelerated her *social* aging. Her "off-time" life transition to a dependent "old age"— in her mid-fifties—was being slowly engineered by the conditions of the job market. The slow societal movement—a structuring which impersonally consigns social categories and people to the background—determined both her suffering and her struggle. For her human task now was not just to find work, but to find life within a forced social disengagement.

The essential role into which society casts its prematurely "terminal cases" is, from a caretaker's view, quite benign. But it offends the human spirit. In a clear and anguished summation of the social impact of unemployment, AGNES expressed the offense, "*I seem to be on the receiving end of everything.*"

Into the Family: Spouse

Of the older workers living with and being supported by spouses, only a few were content with the arrangement. BRIAN's close relationship with his working wife enabled him to take his joblessness more calmly, to enroll for an upholstery course, to cope with less money. Given economic stability and a good marriage, the burden of unemployment could be lightened, even in the deeper sense of being freed from the pressure of getting and spending. "*Our lifestyle is more rewarding than it was before. We take time to do a lot more things together than we did before. Spending time together, time rather than money.*"

For most women informants, however, dependence on the spouse was not liberating; rather it altered both relations with the husband and the syntax of daily practice itself. JOANNE, 47, had emerged from an emotionally abusive office situation, dominated by a boss's unstable daughter who slammed phones and threw things when she could not get her own way. Taking pills for stress, experiencing muscle spasms, crying before going to work—JOANNE realized that the job was ruining her and finally quit. Being at home with the children proved so enjoyable that she felt sad about having to work again.

The support offered by her husband, however, had its drawbacks. She was stuck at home and in charge of all the housework. She and her husband could not even afford holidays. He had beaten her in the past (though this was no longer a problem), and his attitude about her quitting work was ambivalent. Her insecurity was expressed in a kind of vision:

> [I have this dreadful] *anxiety about the future.... I seem powerless to stop it. I will take it right to the point where I have to sell the house, my husband and I will be divorced because he will hate me so much. [Laughs] Really! I will spin this great daydream.*

She was starting to take the job search more seriously.

None of the informants expressed the indignity of dependence more poignantly than those older married women who, once employed, were forced back into the home full time. ERICA, after her layoff, spent her time at home doing housework and ruminating sadly her on her life-course. Her husband was supportive to a point but was also in authority. He strictly controlled the budget. He urged strategies on her that went against her grain: wanting her to lose weight and look more glamorous; suggesting that she lie about skills, such as running a computer, just to get in the door; goading her to be more assertive. She was expected to do all the housework (*"I'm the lackey."*). She even brought her husband and daughter their tea, feeling that because she was being supported, she owed them this. Like AGNES, ERICA was close to despair. Calling herself a *"has-been,"* her life over, she cast herself in the role of an irrelevant old person. We see how societal discrimination descends into social identity, then personal identity—particularly when the self's social environment cannot repel or counter the negative elements.

On the Social Wage

Many of the older informants were eligible for "social wages": unemployment insurance benefits, social assistance, Mother's Allowance, alimony. While providing support in the rough seas of the labour market, few social wages yielded an adequate income. They also drew from the informants a complex mix of attitudes—from shame to dependence to longing.

Among the groups most vulnerable to poverty in the eighties are older unattached individuals. MARIANNE, who was a secretary for 23 years, was laid off three weeks prior to the interview. Though on U.I. benefits, her situation was precarious. She raged at being deprived of her right to make a living as an autonomous adult.

> My daughter and her husband and my mother and dad and my gentleman friend, they all say, "If you need help, we'll help you"...but I don't want this. I've been independent for so many years. And neither do I want a handout from the government! I don't want to go on welfare. I went down to Canada Manpower and I said "Find me a job".... I was so mad at them.

She was far from sympathetic to the social wage. Even when raising the children alone, she never had a *"handout,"* apart from U.I. benefits— and criticized the system for paying young women to sit around and have babies.

But later, her distaste for social wages had to be abandoned. If the *"depressing job hunt"* bore no fruit, she would put in for early retirement and try to find a senior citizen's apartment with rent-geared-to-income.

"Everybody gets a handout, why can't I? You know? I hate to look at it that way, but times have changed..." Being forced to exit from the autonomous worker role had hastened her social aging, and she prepared herself mentally to "head for cover." That the worker was still alive in MARIANNE was evident when she told the interviewer: *"I will work. I would even like to help you with this interview. Type it or whatever."*

Some older informants yearned for the protection of social wages, particularly those just outside the margins of age eligibility. Just as some of those slightly over 25 envied the under-25s for the social programs targeted to youth, some middle-aged informants felt they were too old to work but too young to receive the social wages of the "officially" old. The middle-aged did not seem to occupy as clear or secure a definitional niche as the "senior citizens." In the words of EMMA:

> *Nobody really understands your problem. I think when you're middle-aged, there really isn't anything for you. Like, for senior citizens they have discounts, and even for the youth...but for middle-aged persons, there isn't anything: not a discount, nothing at all. They're a forgotten breed.*

The word used by a few informants of this age is "limbo," which describes the no man's land between the private and the (legitimate) public wage. This hole in the social safety net means that an unattached woman in her fifties who is struggling to find work with no success feels like an oddball. If she is not a mother with dependent children, or disabled, there is really no (undemeaning) safe harbour—except a husband (which some have considered and rejected). Functionally or socially "old" in being denied work and the means of independence, she is not yet eligible for senior housing (age requirement of 60) and the other senior benefits in the community.

This tending or straining towards zones of safety away from the rejecting jungle of the job market could be accompanied by a kind of anticipatory socialization for being old. GAIL persuaded a friend to let her join the Over-55 Club, to help her find work (her comment about getting in the club was revealing: *"It must be 'Be Kind to Senior Citizens Week'"*). She would go to events at a special price with a senior citizen friend of hers. At 50, however, she was too far from cover and faced the job market exposed. *"I always had a father who took care of me or a husband who had a good job. Now, I have me."*

On the job search for five months, GAIL was trying to contain a growing sense of panic. When asked what she would tell her M.P., she answered passionately:

> *I need a job. I want to work. I want to be able to pay my bills. I want to be solvent. I want to live!*

The desire to surface into the world of socially alive men and women seemed to struggle in GAIL with a pull downward and inward into egocentricity—even going beyond the reputed disengagement of the old. She, AGNES, ERICA, and others like them hinted despairingly at fading away, departing, or even committing suicide. Yet they would snap out of it and talk of the bright world they still hoped to join. This inner struggle of light and dark was caught in GAIL's words:

Sometimes you want to crawl into your little world, close the door and...be afraid. Or go out and meet people, go out and talk, hear somebody else's point of view.

Conclusion

Both younger and older informants faced a discrimination in the form of a negative reaction to appearance. Beyond that, they faced a gauntlet of employers' requirements and stereotypes about their capability—erected not by careful assessment but by the need to sift through the oversupply of applicants flooding onto markets. The job market, though billed as an efficient coordinator of employers' needs and jobseekers' skills, was *experienced* by its "rejects" as an arbitrary defining medium which discriminated unfairly against them.

These refusals, however impersonal, had the effect of degrading the social identities of young and older people. They interpreted their rejection as a public dismissal of the value of youthfulness or maturity. The distinguishing marks of these phases of the life cycle could become stigmas, marks of a rejected social identity that began to infect personal identity. For the young who conformed, these stigmas and the passive practices left to them as jobseekers were the vehicle whereby judgements on the marketplace worked down into the self-concept. For the unconventional young, a space for the self and community was defended against the atomizing trend of the market, but the pressures of unemployment were still felt.

For the older informants, being rejected or ignored by the job market seemed to hasten their social disconnection from productive, independent life. Deprived of a vital social identity, their aged features could become enemies of the self. Their personal identities would be possessed by a feeling of obsolescence and decay.

The selves, from which the means of expressing adult autonomy were withheld, looked to their support networks to preserve their dignity and social existence. But these enclaves to which both younger and older unemployed would retreat could never provide the valued social identity of self-supporting work and independence. Though the families and social wages did provide relief from being an object of market forces, the inability to reciprocate the support others were giving, and the cramped livelihood that one had, made the enclaves imperfect places for the restoration of dignity.

These largely passive practices left to the unemployed led to two distortions in life-course transitions within the subjective careers of informants. For the young, the prolonged dependence delayed the autonomy needed to form adult identity. For the older informants, adult autonomy was withdrawn before its usual time, and social conditions led to a premature disengagement from social existence.

High unemployment would seem, in general terms, to have the unintended consequence of regionalizing and depriving two major phases of the life cycle: late adolescence and young adulthood, on the one hand, and middle age and later life, on the other. Class society distributes productive opportunities, income, and status to the prime-age and educated mainstream—while consigning, indeed banishing, certain younger and older members of society to dependent, inactive enclaves at its periphery.

CHAPTER FOUR

The Impersonal State: Manpower and Unemployment Insurance

To be put out of work in Canada typically involves a major shift in one's linkage to the public realm: from a relation to an employer to a new involvement with the offices and disciplinary structures of the state. The unfamiliar terrain onto which the unemployed step is that of the government agencies which process and extend benefits to them. In these settings the informants were handled in ways that ranged from the most blandly impersonal to the most up-close and intimate.

The accounts and analysis have been divided into two chapters. This chapter explores the experiences of the unemployed with the large universal programs known as Unemployment Insurance and Manpower (to receive U.I. benefits, one must register with Manpower). The next chapter takes us into the more particularizing social programs, where the local state monitors the client, even intruding on private life: social assistance ("welfare") and family benefits. We begin with an historical introduction to this important state sector, focussing especially on its bearing on the unemployed.

The Background of the State

Economic circumstances of market behaviour in goods or labour do not shape us in a direct, deterministic fashion. While economic factors do affect changes in employment or unemployment levels, these levels cannot simply be read off from economic statistics but rather are partly entailed by the *response* made to these economic circumstances. Increasingly in modern times, the responding party is the state (which of course has its own impact on economic environments). The policy of that state and its institutions and practices are the result of the play of contending interest groups, classes, and deep-seated social processes.

The Voluntary Response of the State

To gain a sense of the partly voluntary nature of this response, we only have to read the history of the Great Depression in this country. Just as the Conservatives had resisted old age pensions in the 1920s, their prime minister of the early 1930s, R. B. Bennett, refused to have the federal state take a leading responsibility in suppoiting the unemployed. The essential responsibility lay with the self-reliant individual and his or her family, next with the municipality. As year after jobless year went by, however, Bennett's position proved politically untenable. Spurred on by continuing social misery, hunger, and protest, faced with the inability of municipalities and provinces to fund massive relief costs from their limited tax base, the federal government at first made *ad hoc* responses, content by and large to underwrite the efforts of regional and local governments. There were labour camps for single men, sporadic funding of work projects, and loans to provinces to set up assistance boards and help with municipal relief. In response to the inadequacy of these measures, pressure for social welfare reform—especially of a social insurance variety—began to build: from the unemployed themselves, from the Cooperative Commonwealth Confederation (C.C.F.), from the Workers' Unity League, from unions, churches, and provincial parties. Even employers' groups and the right-wing Social Credit party in Alberta supported reform, calling for the redistribution of social "dividends" to help purchasing power and demanding that the burden of welfare be lifted from municipal property taxes (Heidenheim, 1984: 98).

The Rowell-Sirois Commission report of 1940 articulated a new Keynesian motif for the role of the federal government upon which the then Liberal prime minister, Mackenzie King, calculatedly began to play. The report asserted that national unity was threatened by relegating welfare funding to the provinces. In the case of the less wealthy and less populated western provinces, dependent as they were on vulnerable primary industries, their requirement to pay the main cost of social welfare was unfair, divisive, and financially ruinous. In the Keynesian spirit the report indicated that unemployment transcended provincial borders and was essentially national in scope. An unavoidable byproduct of the economy, unemployment required large fluctuating financial commitments. Only the federal government, with its control over the money supply and its wide-ranging tax base, could be expected to deal effectively with the problem. It should be prepared to engage in deficit spending in hard economic times and to gather surpluses and pay back debts in prosperous times. It should gather personal and corporate income tax revenues to itself in order to mount effective social programs and reduce regional disparities (Struthers, 1983: 204–205).

The Unemployment Insurance Act

Mackenzie King and the Liberals realized that, especially as the government began to assume new powers during the mobilization for the Allied war effort, the government must take on a larger role. It was intolerable that people who were being asked to make great national sacrifices should pay such unequal amounts for local relief, or suffer so unequally from economic distress. Moreover, after the veterans returned from war, they would not tolerate unemployment (Struthers, 1983: 206).

Fearful of the explosive reaction of the returning soldiers towards post-war unemployment, wanting to keep the country from turning "left" towards the more expansive welfare policies promoted by the C.C.F., Mackenzie King and the Liberals ushered the Unemployment Insurance Act into law in 1941. The pace of legislation picked up after the war and, in the next three decades, the edifice of the Canadian social security system was slowly erected—on a foundation, it must be added, of economic growth and stability. It included family allowances (1944), Old Age Security (1951), disabled persons assistance and mother's allowances (1954), Canada pensions (1963), public assistance under the Canada Assistance Act (1966), an upgraded Unemployment Insurance plan (1971), medicare, grants for housing, workmen's compensation. Of these "cords" of the government "safety net" the programs most widely approved and expensive were universal and non-discretionary. In 1983–84, the largest federal direct transfer programs were the "demogrant" programs, Old Age Security and Family Allowances, which paid out $7.8 billion and $2.3 billion respectively. Federal transfers to the provinces for welfare, social services, and health insurance have also become enormous: $6.7 billion in 1982 (National Council of Welfare, 1985: 76).

The Erosion of Government Spending

What these large numbers should not obscure is a new trend that has been observable since 1975: the relative *erosion* of governmental spending in Canada, brought about by a weakening of economic conditions and changing government policy. The Canadian economy, among others, was subjected to a series of shocks, first stimulated by massive increases in oil prices in 1973 and 1979. One result was rapid inflation: between 1974 and 1984 Canadian prices doubled. Along with rising prices came a considerable slackening of growth, partly exacerbated by the weakened state of Canadian industry and its balance of international payments. There was an increase in the federal deficit which reached a record figure of $4.8 billion in 1975. There were rising levels of unemployment, partly brought on by computerization and the international movements of competitive industrial capital away from high wage areas (Dumont, 1987: 2). As profitability sagged and inflation undermined investment, a conservative response formed among many Western capitalists and state officials, Canadians included. Social spending and the "inflated" workforces of public service workers became prime targets of this ideological attack. The state's public spending was attacked as simply adding to its crippling deficit while diverting funds from the profit-making sections of the economy. The view was that "Canadians had come to 'expect too much from government' and the social security provided to Canadians was 'undermining market discipline'" (Social Planning Council of Metropolitan Toronto, 1985: 52).

The erosion or undermining of social spending in Canada has been more subtle and less ideologically strident than in Britain or the United States (except for British Columbia), but it has been very real. Reduced levels of social spending have been spread ever more thinly across a expanding caseload. The late 70s and early 80s saw the proportion of state expenditures devoted to social security decline, even in the face of growing demands for social services due to the fast-rising numbers of unemployed. During the eight years of economic decline between 1975 and 1983, Ontario's total real increase in social spending was 17.3%. This was matched against an increase in social assistance beneficiaries of 71.2%, chiefly due to higher unemployment.

One result of this significant excess of demand for social assistance over the provincial provision for it was that "general welfare rates in Ontario were eroded by more than a third between 1975 and 1982 in terms of real purchasing power" (Moscovitch, 1986: 81). From 1975 to 1983, the cost of living increase of 100% contrasted with an increase in monthly benefits for General Welfare of only 41.4% and in Family Benefits of 52.8% (Social Planning Council of Metropolitan Toronto and Ontario Social Development Council, 1983: 94). Governments have pushed for more selectivity and means-testing in an attempt to save money on the more expensive universal social programs. One example among others was the reduction in Unemployment Insurance in the form of tightened eligibility requirements. The entrance requirement for U.I. has been increased from 8 to 10–14 weeks; the qualifying period for new entrants and re-entrants has been increased to 20 weeks, for repeaters 16–20 weeks; there was an increased disqualification period of six weeks for "voluntary quits" or those who are fired; benefits were diminished to a maximum of 60% of past earnings, while the number of weeks they could be collected was reduced (Canadian Council on Social Development, 1985: 1; Moscovitch, 1986: 85).

To summarize: we have seen how state social security developed historically into a *large-scale bureaucratic* phenomenon, organized by federal, provincial, and municipal governments. Additionally, in the past decade, social security has been stretched more thinly, responding to economic crisis and its victims not (in Keynesian fashion) by expanding its programs but by cutting them back relative to need, making them more selective. So in addition to a bureaucratic state, we have an *eroding* state. The two other features of state social security I wish briefly to examine are its role in the capital accumulation process and its need to make itself legitimate.

Social Security and Capital Accumulation

The Canadian state has always been an ally of capitalists, building infrastructure, giving tax advantages to capital accumulators, and deploying legislative and coercive means to protect the owners of property and their prerogatives. The social security system aids the owners and investors of capital in a number of ways, of which I will mention four. First, payments of benefits, family allowances, pensions, and social insurance to millions of people allow them to continue to consume in the marketplace, thus keeping effective demand from being depressed as it was in the 1930s. Second, the existence of a governmental safety net to "catch" workers after they are laid off allows marginal businesses to cut or expand their workforces whenever it is in their competitive interest to do so (Heidenheim, 1984: 104; Butler, 1980). This is related to a third, more general factor: the way social security blunts extreme social discontent, making political combinations of discarded workers during a recession far less likely. Fourth, governments are committed to pegging social benefit levels below the lowest industrial wage (termed the "principal of less eligibility"). This is thought to avoid undercutting small businesses who would presumably lose workers to higher "social" wage enclaves.

The State as Self-legitimizing

The state is far from synonymous with capital, however. Dependent on electoral support, it must continually show the people that its governance is *legitimate*, i.e. rules in the national, not the capitalist class, interest. As an example already cited, the welfare provisions inaugurated by the Liberals after the war took place in an atmosphere of concern about the returning veterans facing possibly high unemployment. But beyond this, there has grown up in political and social policy circles a conviction that the state must provide opportunities and safeguards so that those less advantaged on the labour market can have good schooling, medical care, job retraining, and so on. The very considerable social support for such universal measures as family allowances, pensions, old age security, and medicare has not only been shown in polls but by the wide-ranging opposition to recent government efforts to eliminate or reduce the indexing of Old Age Security and the Canada pension. Efforts by doctors' groups to erode Medicare have also been resisted.

On such measures as unemployment insurance and social assistance, however, the government knows that the public support is ambivalent, often quite negative. People appreciate unemployment insurance but want the minority who receive it not to abuse it. Towards *social* assistance, which is based on need not merit—hence is in opposition to the work ethic—the public is far more negative. A Canadian survey in 1977 of urban residents in Alberta found that over half the respondents thought that "Most welfare recipients do not tell their social workers the truth about their financial matters" (53%) and that employable recipients "do not try to find jobs to support themselves" (55%). Also "78% of respondents believed that 30% or more of the people receiving public assistance 'do not deserve it and are abusing the system'" (Alberta Health and Social Development, 1973, quoted in Heidenheim, 1984: 131). Canadian Gallup poll results show that the most frequently chosen response to what areas of government spending should be cut back to control inflation was "welfare," chosen by 35%.

In another poll (1977), the most frequent response (made by 20% of respondents) to the question of how to handle the unemployment problem was to tighten or get rid of unemployment insurance and welfare payments, and pressure people into taking any job available (Heidenheim, 1984: 133). Governments, then, must take into account (and their personnel very probably reflect) the negative stereotyping and desire to control recipients of public benefits—those citizens appearing to get something for nothing.

Two major elements of the state's conduct of its social security responsibilities which we have discussed are relevant to this chapter:

- The state is now large-scale and bureaucratic, carving up its social security components among federal, provincial, and municipal jurisdictions—hence is less susceptible to individual and local influence;
- The state is eroding and weakening its support by allowing social wages to decline in real terms, by reducing staff-client ratios in social programs, and by trying to increase the selectivity of coverage of social benefits.

These large-scale tendencies of the modern state formulate themselves in institutional practices to which the unemployed must adapt or modify with social practices of their own.

It is to these latter practices that we now turn.

Practices

This chapter looks first at the experiences of "Being Processed" by the state, as thousands registered and applied for unemployment benefits. We follow with the next step the registrants were expected to take: "Looking for Work with Manpower."

Being Processed at the Canada Employment Centre

Of the tens of thousands of unemployed Londoners who entered the Canada Employment Centre (C.E.C.) from 1983 to 1985, most had probably been put out of work due to layoffs, business closings, or dismissals. This category, the "disemployed," formed 57% of the total Canadian unemployed in 1984 (Lemaître, 1985: 153).

They came initially to do the two things required to be recognized and supported in the government's social security system: to register for work and, in some cases, to make their claim for unemployment insurance (U.I.) benefits. Many were returning for queries, interviews, or the mandatory job search. All were being processed by a vast bureaucracy. Drawing on the informants' interviews, what was the experience like?

Relation to Other Unemployed People

The informants had fairly different experiences of three groups of people in the C.E.C.: fellow unemployed; front-line staff; and officials and counsellors. Let us take first the relation to *other unemployed* people—the "looking-for-work-force," as EVA called them. The informant typically encountered fellow unemployed persons as atoms in a milling, shifting crowd: *"You're one of 5000,"* commented a young man. One joined people standing in queues, shuffled through them on the way to a counsellor or desk, or stood beside them staring at the job boards. *"I feel rather herded,"* an informant remarked. People were often placed in a serial formation which discouraged eye contact or communication. In their inert positioning and bored postures, they seemed to invite contempt. Middle-class EVA commented on the big circle of people waiting for their number to come up in order to speak to a counsellor about a job: *"Some of these people are real losers. They have to go to the Employment Centre to show they've been looking for work. There are all these losers and they've all got their numbers for jobs they're not going to get."*

The bureaucratic setting seemed to discourage collaborative ties with other jobless persons—and not only because the arrangement of space, furniture, and bodies made them difficult. Even within great milling crowds of people, the *interest* of the unemployed person was focussed intensely on self. The process of identifying one's self and personal facts on form after form hewed one to the individualistic line. The others around one were cast in the role of competitors. Given that in London in January 1984, there were 85 registered jobless persons for each registered job vacancy (Ontario N. D. P. Caucus, 1984: 95), it was an understandable perception. The competition at Manpower could be found standing around the seven boards containing the job listings. One informant talked of *"getting the jump on other jobseekers who will be going after these jobs."* As BOB resolved, *"I'm going to zip down there tomorrow and see if there are any jobs I can fight for."* What inhibited him was his family responsibilities: *"You can't stand in front of the boards eight hours a day and wait for the card to come and snatch it. You just can't live that way, not when you have a kid."*

Relationships with Front-line Staff

Relationships with the *front-line staff* in the C.E.C. were similar to those with receptionists in private firms, but seemed more polarized. One young man found the front-line people at Manpower to be *"just like robots. They have this set basic thing they have to say to you, right? They're not really encouraging you to go out and look. They have different people there every few days."* Another man said that U.I.C. people treat you *"something like a bank teller would treat money, as if you were nothing really. Just very impersonal.... I'm surprised they could get away with things like that."*

That this treatment could be so upsetting to informants probably indicated higher expectations. Informants expected government staff to be *servants* of the public, helping with leads and opportunities instead of shielding the person in the inner office. The emotion directed towards the front-line staff could be intense: informants resented their ample salaries and job security, found them smug, uncaring, and even, in one man's word, *"cannibalistic."* However they behaved, they were the natural targets of emotion for the thousands of frustrated jobless people. Some informants understood the difficulty of being pleasant under such conditions. The impersonality the staff adopted was a way of coping with the high level of unhappiness among certain clients—a device which ironically may have fed the discontent.

Sometimes the clash between a needful clientele and an eroding, understaffed service like Manpower revealed painful truths about the government's powerlessness or unwillingness to help. ERICA spoke on the phone to a Manpower receptionist. *"I said, 'I really want to talk to somebody. I've been off work for 19 months and I've had one call.' She said, 'You can't talk to a counsellor.' I said, 'Why?' 'Because,' she said, 'there aren't any. There are 25,000 people looking for work. If they each had a counsellor, they would be bothered no end.'"* ERICA then asked what she should do. The woman suggested looking at the paper, checking the boards, etc. *"What she was saying to me was 'Good luck, dear, but do it your own way.' And that really blew me away."* Bureaucratic erosion degraded relationships: human persons entered role relationships which dissolved into non-relationships. The strangeness of it as human experience was well caught by the Kenyan immigrant, BERNARD. He spoke eloquently in the tones of cultural shock:

You're a number, a social insurance number to them, the moment you are unemployed. They pass out your cheque, cheque, cheque. They ask you questions they know the answer to.... We are not known as humans. They should make us feel people again. Motivate us. Then find our real interests, our creativity. Because you can't know about me if I sit here outside the office looking at the board. Try to find more about us.

Relationships with Officials and Counsellors

The third group with which informants sometimes dealt—after the other unemployed and the front-line staff—were *officials and counsellors*. The relationships here were potentially more consequential than other ties. When these officials counselled with empathy—understanding the informants' experience of discrimination, for instance, or respecting a woman's decision to change careers—they were warmly appreciated. But the fact was that positive evaluations about counsellors were held by only about a dozen of the informants.

For one thing, it was difficult to form even minimal relationships with Manpower counsellors. The officials and front-line staff changed so often that, even over a brief period, there was no guarantee one would deal with the same person. Changing counsellors made "role" and especially "personal" relationships hard to form, and may have increased the likelihood of mistakes. After dealing with *"several different people* [at U.I.], *my claim keeps getting messed up,"* commented an informant. Relationships *between* staff at the C.E.C. seemed inconsistent and fragmentary as well. The U.I.C. and employment sections, for instance, were thought by some not to know what the other was doing. A woman remarked: *"the person sitting at that desk doesn't know what the person sitting at this desk is doing. The person sitting at that board doesn't know what the person upstairs is doing."*

The Domain of Administrative Power

There is a deeper level to the relation with officialdom. For many, to enter relations with counsellors and officials was to enter an intractable domain of administrative and disciplinary *power*. The power exercised by officialdom constituted a "field" of distributed bodies and spaces, administrative posts, rules (legal and informal), procedures, and classifications which compose the bureaucracy (Foucault, 1979). By constituting itself as a labyrinth of esoteric knowledge and rules, the C.E.C. bureaucracy immediately changed the syntax of action of those who entered from an active to a passive "voice." The unemployed person had to constantly seek information and orientation from officials: "What forms do I need?" "What floor do I go to?" "How long is my waiting period?" "Have I worked the minimum number of insurable weeks in my qualifying period?" But officials were far from simply guides roughly equal in status to the confused traveller, pointing out places on the map. After all, officials controlled resources necessary for living, and their rules and procedures had the authoritative backing of law and of administrative directives. Making mistakes on a form or allowing oneself to be steered into a particular classification had serious consequences for the claimant.

Filling out forms epitomized the passive practice of "being processed." An action keyed to individual self-interest, filling out forms forced the informant to process himself or herself not as a unique person but as an analytical benefit category, with distinctive consequences for level of support. Not surprisingly, many informants complained of the difficulty of filling out the forms to qualify for U.I., a task made more burdensome by the lack of informing help and by the unpleasant consequences of errors. MYRA, a college-educated nutritionist with a husband who was an intern, found it an *"awful experience.... Nobody helped me with them. My husband and I are reasonably intelligent, and we worked them through, and there's no way we got them right. How could someone who didn't have the education we had get through these forms?"* Though a necessary processing step for the bureaucracy, the constant filling out of forms abstracted the individual from real-world contexts, and left an atomized portrait for the bureaucracy to process.

The officials' power consists of not just superior information (about the Unemployment Insurance Act, for instance) over the lone claimant but of *information control*, i.e. being selective about what a claimant would be told. Informants were not told things they later learned were important, e.g. that one could earn up to 25% of former earnings without reduction of benefits. EVELYNwas being pressured to take a minimum wage job (with the implied threat that she would be denied welfare) and was not told that one could not be refused welfare for at least two weeks. Enraged that so many people are isolated and uninformed, she commented cynically on the state's attitude, *"You have to keep them a little ignorant."* Certainly there was greater ease of processing if the client was not too well informed about the details of his or her rights (Kelvin and Jarrett, 1985: 87).

Classification of the Claimants

The initial processing of the person as a client at the C.E.C. was a ritual encompassing two stages. First was the filling out of forms, as the person submitted to the minute recording and coding of his or her life facts. Second was the formation and enforcement of the classification itself. The person had been analytically reconstructed into a manageable, stereotyped benefit category, distinct in regulations and privileges from other categories. This is at the heart of the government's exercise of power. As one author put it:

> The creation and management of these divisions among the working class have become the fine art of government (Dickinson, 1986: 138).

Here was created a new basis of division or internal stratification of the working class. An example is the administrative distinction between those who voluntarily quit their previous jobs or were dismissed *versus* those who were laid off—the first two groups having to wait longer for benefits and having less chance to get welfare. Here was revived the old division between deserving and undeserving poor. The endless differentiating rules thus created new bases for invidious comparison—often based on real injustices—among the unemployed. Young unskilled informants were split between the qualified and unqualified, some of the latter finding it difficult to work the minimum number of weeks in a year to claim U.I. One young man had only 11 weeks and now was rooting about for a low-paid job that would let him make the "floor" of 16 weeks—otherwise the 11 weeks were a *"waste."* Here, out of a lack of work, life conformed to the bureaucratic rule instead of the reverse. ANDREA was injured at a factory and has been off work too long to be eligible: *"I paid nine years into the son of a bitch and I can't draw a dime."* Those already marginal in the labour force were penalized by U.I. regulations, which further marginalized them.

The unfairness (from the agent's standpoint) of U.I. went farther than that. By pegging U.I. benefits to salaries (up to a ceiling or maximum figure), those workers who are ill-paid from private wages are ill-paid in U.I.'s social wages. To those who worked in a service station or grocery store and were making benefits of $400 a month, it was galling to see people drawing benefits of $900 a month. As COLLEEN, 28, commented:

> *Where's the fairness? I worked for over 10 years and have paid into it. Maybe my jobs weren't all well-paying but I've always worked. Finally there's a time when I'm not working. I feel like I'm punished—for not having had really high-paying jobs. I'm just as able to work as the next person. I'm looking just as hard as the next person. Yet I don't get money to live on.*

Stereotypes of Claimants

Before dealing with the processing complications and conflicts between officials and U.I. claimants, we should emphasize that hardpressed bureaucrats use not only classifications but also *stereotypes* to manage their contacts with clients. From the vantage point of the busy official, there is the "single parent," the "chronically unemployed," etc. Kelvin and Jarrett suggested a more general typology of the role occupants which officials face. There is the "model claimant," who is easy to process—being courteous, co-operative, having the right documents, familiar with procedure without having detailed knowledge. There is also the "awkward claimant," who, while perhaps not having essential documents, is "full of having been told of his entitlements; and [is] perhaps especially awkward in wanting to be treated as a unique individual with unique personal problems, rather than in his role within an inevitable bureaucratic system" (1985: 87).

Many informants would probably be perceived as model claimants: sixteen reported "no problems" with U.I. Some complained about the six to eight week delay, but, for many, the cheques were fast and regular. This efficient, but bare-bones service of providing people with cheques—instead of counselling or rapport—was judged with some cynicism by a few informants. Young "model" claimant HERB felt that the government was using cheques and grants for young people to keep them quiet. The government was saying, *"Hey, the world's great and we're doing fine. Here's some money. Be happy. And don't criticize us."*

Whether one views the model claimant as commendable or conformist, he or she certainly fits passively into the assigned role. But many informants did not. When they sensed that their interests or rights were being violated, they would fight. WARREN, a long-term unemployed man of 42, put it this way: *"You put into it* [i.e. Unemployment Insurance], *you've got to fight like a son of a gun to get it. And if you don't, they couldn't care less."* What awakened individuals from the passive to the active voice was their shocked discovery that *Government did not care* if the individual had to wait eight weeks, or did not receive benefits at all. The individual, now institutionally "awkward," had become briefly a "fighter," in what he or she now saw as a conflict zone. So CONNIE, 49 and single, who was earning a little money as a free-lance advertiser, had to struggle with a counsellor who wanted to define her as self-employed. BOB, who sought help from the Unemployment Insurance Commission for his wife's maternity leave, put it this way: *"We had to take a gun to their head to give us the money. They didn't believe she was at home with the baby."*

Before examining species of awkwardness, a word should be said about their foundation. Due to the complexity of U.I. rules, the differing situations of the unemployed who flowed into the Canada Employment Centre, and the changing of counsellors and staff, processing errors and mix-ups by officials or claimants were *bound* to occur. The vast computerized system of accounting for U.I. claims was not very flexible in adjusting for processing errors; it caused punishing delays for people in need. But a crucial ingredient in turning a mix-up into what informants called a "hassle" was the unspoken assumption by some officials that it was in the nature of claimants to try and get whatever they could; they were rarely given the benefit of the doubt.

MATTHEW, a low-income married man with children, put the wrong date on his card. He showed it to the girl in the office and she approved it and sent it on its way. The cheque did not come in the expected two weeks, just a notification of his error. Another two weeks passed. Instead of getting the cheque, he received a form to correct the old form.

I went down there and said, "You know, I've got a family of six to feed. Could you not expedite things?" I was harassed and very tense, and she said, "We have so many applications here, we can't single you out individually" [emphasis added]. *We literally went hungry here a few nights because we had run out of food.*

Desperate, they asked a welfare man to come by; when he found out MATTHEW was on U.I. benefits, he refused them emergency relief. One of the difficulties in fighting for benefits, in MATTHEW's view, was that *"they really make you seem like you're begging. Their whole attitude is, 'You don't deserve this but, out of the goodness of our heart, we're going to give it to you.'"*

The most awkward claimant of all among the informants was WAYNE, whose story was most instructive. In his thirties, the father of two sons, his marriage was somewhat stormy. His youth was spent as a foster child in Toronto, going from one family to the next. He was dismissed from a tire shop in his small town an hour away from London, ostensibly for being late for work but really because of a conflict with the boss. Having tried all the other shops and factories in the vicinity, his wife also out of work, he had come to London to search and take a course at the vocational college. He lived in a room in a rough part of town, with no one to speak to but his wife on the phone each night. Because he was dismissed from his job, Unemployment Insurance slapped him with an eight-week penalty period. When he tried to explain the reason he was fired, they told him he could appeal it, but it would take an additional eight weeks. He could not afford to wait.

Everything went smoothly until his move to London. His third U.I. benefit cheque was delayed. The weeks went by, but no money. They explained to him that, because he was going to school, they had to enter different information into the computer. He then found that they had gotten his address in London wrong. They told him, mistakenly, that he had to go back to register with Manpower in his small town—he took a special ride in just to sign his name on a form. They had obviously lost track of the cheques and in the meantime he was entering the fifth week with no benefit cheques.

After being stalled once too often, with the rent coming due and with less than a dollar in the bank, WAYNE's patience snapped. One Friday afternoon, he walked up to the floor where the officials were and demanded his money. His hands shaking, he threatened to throw them out of the window if they did not help him. No matter how the money was gotten—they could pass the hat in the office—he insisted on being paid. Finally, after much consultation, emergency cheques were issued to him, though he had to go to several banks before he could find one to cash them that afternoon. The fine points of his feelings were hard for him to articulate. He felt almost uncontrollably enraged and deeply victimized at having to ask for his money this way. His case, while not typical, suggests the drama and even cruelty perpetrated upon some individuals by the bureaucracy's business-as-usual behaviour.

A general concluding point about the very "awkward" should be made here. The half dozen or so informants who had severe conflicts with the Unemployment Insurance Commission or with Canada Manpower—to the point where two informants were denied help from Manpower and recommended for psychiatric care—tended to be socially isolated. Lacking contacts which could alleviate their intense focus on Manpower, having no measure of support within the bureaucracy, or no outside organizational ally that could speak for them, they seemed to exercise little effective power. As we will see in Chapter Six, *with* advocates who could help present their case in a professional way, their position made a more impressive challenge.

The Program vs. the Experience of Being Processed

There was a marked discrepancy between the helpful *program* known as unemployment insurance and the *experience* of being processed for it at the Canada Employment Centre. On the one hand U.I. did offer financial support in a difficult time; most people qualified for and received their benefits promptly. One activist held up unemployment insurance as a definite gain for the working class, whatever its flaws. U.I.'s coverage of the unemployed was very high: 87% in Canada in 1982—the highest of all industrial nations (Therborn, 1986: 80). On paper, it seemed to be a healthy universalist insurance policy to cover labour market risks.

But the experienced reality, as we have seen, was otherwise. Being processed for U.I. was found by many informants to be demeaning and stressful. The wait for benefits could be six to eight weeks—placing a strain on finances, even forcing informants to borrow from friends. The counselling service was erratic and understaffed. A few informants reported that the possibility of cutting off benefits had been used as a threat. People reported that *"it makes you feel like a beggar."* Officials had been known to scold people for quitting even bad and dangerous jobs. The most ringing statement may have been that of GAIL, who invited Prime Minister Brian Mulroney to *go down to the Employment Centre, no salary. You apply, you wait your six to eight weeks, you go through this rigmarole, you feel demeaned, humiliated...but that's what you're going to depend on, a certain amount every two weeks. And* [mock-scolding] *don't make any mistakes about declaring anything extra, because you're in trouble. They do not and could not understand, but people are going through it.*

Looking for Work with Manpower

Manpower's mandate was to keep the registered, state-supported unemployed toned up, properly assessed, trained or retrained, and generally presentable for emerging job opportunities. Its computers, elaborate tests, and the apparently vast governmental resources behind it inspired hope in many unemployed people that it would help them find work.

Yet the Manpower they entered and were processed in had three major constraints on its activities that would defeat hope. First, especially in 1983–84, there simply were not enough job vacancies to meet the demand in the area. Second, because many employers were dismissive of Manpower and were using their own channels for recruiting the employees they needed, Manpower's listings covered only a small fraction of the job vacancies that did exist. A final constraint was the understaffing of the service, as well as the failure of funds, courses, and services to keep up with demand. The laying off of 35 Manpower staff in London during the hard times of late winter, 1983, was not unnoticed by the informants. The meeting of this irresistible force of the newly unemployed with the immoveable weaknesses of a curtailed Manpower service, drew fire from many informants (not always fairly). Even among those who had long withdrawn from Manpower or were *"buried in the files,"* few were indifferent.

Positive Views of Manpower

Before examining the accounts of the majority of informants—who were negative towards Manpower—it might be instructive to look at the dozen or so who were *positive*. (In fairness to Manpower, we would have to add to their number those who had benefitted from the service and found work, and thus would not show up in my sampling.) What do the "positives" find good about Manpower? Generally it was the quality of human contact between the counsellor and the unemployed person. In the positive encounter, the person was looked in the eye, listened to, allowed to recount the unique facts of his or her life. People were thus permitted, even if briefly, to act as a human subject. JOANNE, who had just left a very harsh job, said of her counsellor:

He was very encouraging. He had a lot of empathy. He just made me feel he cared about people, for starters. He made me feel better about myself....

"When you're ready to go to work," he said, "I want to talk to you. Because the way you're feeling right now, you're just going to take any old job that comes along. And you've got a lot of skills. You've worked for a lot of years. I don't want you just taking any old job." He made me feel good about myself.

Another counsellor understood why a woman informant could not undergo a job search while supporting a small son, and did not insist that she go through the usual job search routine to qualify for benefits.

A general point here is that good counselling of people in troubled circumstances, while certainly a "role" relationship, must import into it elements of a "personal" relationship. In the following continuum:

PERSONAL RELATIONSHIPS	ROLE RELATIONSHIPS	NON-RELATIONSHIPS
(A)	(B)	(C)

the counselling encounter should be a creative mixture of (A) and (B). This was not simply to make people feel better; rather it was needed to empower them as human agents. Good counselling was *synergistic* in its effects in that it allowed the individual to confidently expose his or her many sides to a complex contact with the outside world. The opposite, i.e. poor counselling where the individual was merely passive, was the carrying out a role relationship (B) which slid into the void of non-relationship (C). Instead of being treated as a person—complex, particular, capable of opening up into an interaction with the world—he or she was simply seen as an instance of a general type. The effect was precisely an atomizing one, a reduction of prismatic individuality to a neat bureaucratic classification.

Negative Views of Manpower

Most reported encounters in Manpower were of this latter, atomizing type. The initial interview with a counsellor was judged to be far too short, even perfunctory. *"They don't put enough into the interview,"* said one woman. Much of the contact time was devoted to assessment, through vocational aptitude tests and computer choices. One informant, KARL, 38, described how *he* came out:

There is some sort of thing where you punch in your interests and your skills and your education and it comes up with a job or an area that you are suited for.... Well, I went to this and punched in all this stuff and it turned out that I wasn't suited for anything [laughs].

While some *counsellors* had supplied good advice in the choice of a new career, the *computer* earned little praise. The end of this assessment was the assignment of a single job classification to each client—presumably to facilitate the matching of clients' categories with incoming job listings. Now this reductive and somewhat arbitrary single classification would be tolerable if, as was intended, it had led on to opportunities in the real world. But, usually, it was the end of the contact with Manpower. COL-LEEN: *"They classify you as one thing and send you off with your little card and tell you to check in once a month. Big deal. What's this classification for if you don't let me know when positions come up, or if I can't find anything?"*

The most widespread criticism of Manpower was that, after the initial processing, one was utterly forgotten. In a kind of vast institutional amnesia, the relationship became a non-relationship. According to DICK, 22: *"You speak to a counsellor, right? And he says, 'What kind of work are you looking for?' You tell him and that's it. And you don't hear from them again. So what's the use of filing in?"* People have waited as long as two years, with no contact from Manpower. Even more than with employers, people felt that, in Manpower's eyes, they had no identity, no name. There was a wounded feeling of being cut adrift, of being atomized. *"You're just a number." "It's very depersonalized." "Just another statistic." "Simply another file." "They don't care about you." "They couldn't care less." "I don't feel any of them give a shit." "They'll never call you." "You'll never hear from them again."* This was one microsocial response or "after-shock" of the eroding state—a feeling that the public sector no longer knew your name.

Always there was waiting, which had the effect of weakening the desire to act and turning the voice of action passive. There was a two-year waiting list for computer courses and long waits for several other courses. KATHY waited several weeks for an interview; she was then placed on a waiting list for a course for one year. *"When you want to do something, when you finally decide to do something, you want to do it. You don't want to sit around and wait for a year."* To this untrained woman the official said: "You have to decide what you want to do for the rest of your life," and would let her on only one waiting list. BRIAN, never having heard from a counsellor, finally decided to call for an appointment. He was told he would have to wait for six weeks. *"But I want to see you today or tomorrow, not in six weeks."*

In an eroding social security system, kept by monetarist logic in parallel with a difficult economy, the structure of opportunities was almost as tight as in the job market—in this case the opportunities for good counselling, good training, and useful courses. As on the job market, the individual's impulses to act, his or her personal desire to use the present as a means to a meaningful future, were disengaged. People's desire to act *now*, to see an employer right away, not when the counsellor recommended, were healthy impulses of people trying to experience agency. The state, however, reformulated "looking for work" into a practice that not only was passive but whose *tense* was shaped by slower bureaucratic time frames, not personal ones. The tense of this reconstructed syntax was, for the client, a yawning, anticipatory present which made the future indeterminate and fateful. *"What do you do while waiting a year for a course?"* asked an informant. *"Do you try to find a good job, only to leave it for the course?"* Or, *"should you just take poor jobs and wait for the course?"* Once again the state, unwittingly this time, contributed to the marginalizing of the unemployed.

To the question "Is Manpower a good place to look for work?" the answer of the informants was an overwhelming NO. The listings on the boards were few in those years, and tended to be short-term, poorly-paid, with few benefits, often favouring those on U.I. (The latter were jobs where companies "topped up" U.I. benefits, as part of the C.E.C.'s limited work-sharing scheme.) Many jobs on the boards were waitressing, dishwashing, baby-sitting—"with experience." Qualifications were rarely spelled out, so that after taking the trouble to reach the right people, one discovered the job was unsuitable. Some listings were months out of date.

In response to this last problem, one official told an informant heatedly that *employers* were often the careless ones, not Manpower. Employers would ask for one type of worker and, when they showed up, would say they wanted someone else. They often would not tell Manpower for weeks after the post was filled, leaving the out-of-date card on the board. It might be fairer to say that it was not always Manpower that was so ineffective, but *its liaison with employers.* Yet, as the front-line representative of a state, it was Manpower that drew the negative emotions of the jobless. The employers neatly sidestepped any such responsibility and were spared much of the venom.

A conversation with a Manpower counsellor suggested to me that its staff was somewhat demoralized. He told me that Manpower was an "awful place to work." Very often counsellors would tell clients that there was nothing else they could do. AGNES was told at Manpower, *"Don't come here to get a job. We can't get you a job. You look in the paper—you probably won't get yourself a job from the paper either. You have to know somebody to get a job."* What made its often ineffectual workings so offensive to informants was the fact that these unproductive, often unhelpful Manpower employees were paid comfortable salaries out of public expense. The level of invective towards the staff was quite high, comparable to the words chosen for politicians. Here is a sampling: *"twits," "terrible,"* a *"dumping ground for civil servants who want to spend their lives filing paper clips," "rude," "inconsiderate," "pen-pushers," "counsellors who aren't counselling."* They sit there *"filing their nails, answering the phone."* They are paid $18,000 to just sit there, remarked a man on benefits of $106 a week. *"I'd like some of that $18,000 too."* Informants reported violent impulses when they stood in front of an indifferent staff person, who might not have known something that *they* knew, whose job they could very well do: *"that's when you want to plow them in the mouth,"* said BRIAN.

There were complaints about rude remarks to a client (*"You're getting up there in age and should have a job"* said a counsellor to a 28-year-old single parent). Some of the questions were needlessly intrusive. A counsellor said to MARIANNE, *"Oh, I see you're divorced. What happened to your husband?"* Then later, *"What about your family? Can't they help you?"* She was deeply upset. Instead of piling up more instances of ill treatment, we should ask: was there any *pattern of discrimination* among those treated well or ill? Looking at the severe complainers, there tended to be a high proportion of medium- and long-term unemployed among them. This fit in with the report in Kelvin and Jarrett's (1985) literature review. It would seem that the recently unemployed tended to be more often recommended for jobs by officials than those unemployed for longer times. They make the speculative but plausible point that the career of

> many a discouraged worker will probably have begun by his image within the agency as a discouraging prospect—which grows steadily as the period of his unemployment lengthens (1985: 82).

The counsellors' possibly different treatment of clients on the basis of their duration of unemployment might then replicate the discrimination they suffered in the job market. Once again, the state contributes to the marginalization of certain subgroups of the unemployed.

Conclusion

Both enacted practices (being processed and looking for work) within the Canada Employment Centre tended to be heavily "scripted" by the bureaucratic system. Both were largely passive adaptations to highly objectifying institutional practices (processing, assessing, classifying, keeping "on file"). The unemployed self was the grammatical but not the real subject, the latter being a highly directive maze of officials, forms, rules, procedures, as well as controls of spacing and timing. That system—particularly when understaffed—constrained action in regimented ways that prevented community among the unemployed. Relations with government officials tended to be role relationships which "faded away" into non-relationships. At Manpower, this was due to the inability of staff to cope with demand, especially given its poor support by higher reaches of government and local employers, and the minimal job-finding role settled for by the organization itself.

The power relations were subtle but nonetheless hierarchical, embedded in administrative procedures and classificatory practices. When the bureaucracy was challenged, the informants found that the supervisors closed ranks with counsellors against the client and that appeal procedures were sufficiently unwieldy to minimize disruptions to the system.

Nonetheless, individuals were not as compliant in allowing government agencies to formulate their practices as they were on the job market. Hassles would occur—made probable by the complex rules, processing errors, and the stereotyping and mistrust of clients by many counsellors. Individuals would begin to fight for their own interests, becoming "awkward" from a system point of view. In many of these situations, "awkward" meant an eruption of individual agency cutting against the bureaucratic grain. Here the unemployed self was reaching for the authorial pen and trying to "write" his or her own practices. These struggles, though painful, were synergistic responses to a domination which was experienced as unfair. At their best (often with the assistance of an advocate), they knowledgeably penetrated the mystique and professional pretensions of that system.

The government ground was felt to belong to the citizen in a way that job market sites did not. An expected accountability fueled anger when it failed to materialize. When occasionally the counselling was *good*, the informants appreciated the firm support and attentiveness of an agent of the public sphere— felt less atomized. As for the U.I. *benefits*, they were immensely enabling in many different ways—though they did not adorn the social identity to the extent that private wages did.

CHAPTER FIVE

The Intrusive State: Welfare and Family Benefits

For many poorer and dependent informants, the power of the state had a distinctly different "feel" to it than existed in the large impersonal programs: now the state was a judging and intruding presence. Outside the agency walls as well, the person who had become dependent on particularizing state programs found a marked shift in the social reception from others. Suddenly one had been thrust into a "bad neighbourhood" of the social system. One now had to contend with the social stigma of being one of "those people on welfare."

At the time of the interviews 15 informants were on social assistance and seven on Mother's Allowance, and several others had been involved in welfare at one time. While some received additional support from families, all were heavily dependent upon their social assistance or family benefits cheques. Of the 15, nine were males—mostly young, underemployed men who had not worked enough insurable weeks to qualify for U.I. benefits. The women were also young. Compared to the sample at large, this group contained greater proportions of unattached individuals; long-term unemployed; class III backgrounds[1] (47% compared to 28% in the sample). Most of the women on Mother's Allowance had class III backgrounds, with few having finished high school. There was a range of ages, though the majority were in their twenties. Not surprisingly, their joblessness had been prolonged; most of them had been looking for employment from six months to a year and a half.

---

[1] Social class background is a relative scale of the background of advantage and disadvantage of the informants. The components of the index are outlined in Appendix A. They are: education, father's (or mother's) occupation, ranking, and income of last important job. "Class I" would typically apply to persons with a post-secondary certificate or better, with parents from a white-collar background, and a previous job that was white-collar. "Class II" would apply to white-collar or manual workers with some post-secondary education. "Class III" would take in low-income persons with high school or less and a background of social wages or low-paying employment.

Before presenting the practices of these people within the state agencies, a brief background will place state social welfare into a broader context. Hopefully it may be rescued from its pariah status as the only dependent niche in a self-reliant society.

The Social and State Frameworks of Welfare

In Canada, as in other industrial societies, many states of dependency are now under collective responsibility. These states arise for most people "whenever they are not in a position to 'earn life' for themselves and their families; they are then dependent people" (Titmuss, 1963: 42). Included are the "natural" dependencies of childhood, old age, and child-bearing. There are the dependencies which are partly cultural, e.g. physical or psychological illness. Finally, there are the bulk of dependencies which are almost entirely determined by sociocultural factors. Some examples are: schooling which delays the entry of the young into the labour market; unemployment or underemployment; discrimination on the job market based on credentials, sex, or race; compulsory retirement (Titmuss, 1963: 43). Since our life span is longer than that of our forebears, the cessation of earning power threatens in a more prolonged way the satisfaction of human needs—and we have collectively organized to meet this challenge. The collective responsibility and provision for these burgeoning needs we can call "social welfare."

Not surprisingly, the social division of welfare has become quite complex—involving such institutional components as the state, family, occupations, and private organizations (Moscovitch, 1986: 89). *State* welfare provides, via its policies and agencies, various services and cash benefits to people. The cash benefits can be either direct, i.e. a cash transaction involving a specific benefit, or indirect, i.e. an allowance or exemption from income tax. The latter is not usually seen as a social service expenditure, but actually involves for the state considerable forgone income. For the largely upper-income people who benefit from it, it is "fiscal welfare,…a tax saving that accrues to the individual [which] is, in effect, a transfer payment" (Titmuss, 1963: 45). Corporations also benefit from state largess, whether in grants or tax breaks. *Family* welfare refers to the providing for the needs of the working mother, the young, the aged, and so on, by family members and extended kin, even the informal care available in the neighbourhood. *Occupational* welfare takes in the benefits available through employment: pensions, dental and medical insurance, housing, flexible time-tabling, cheap meals, automobiles, and other incomes-in-kind. These function, in Titmuss's phrase, as "the hidden multipliers of occupational success" (quoted in Inglis, 1982: 153). Finally, there is the *private* welfare provided by "'para-public' welfare agencies and self-help institutions, such as the range of co-operatives, non-profit corporations and benefit societies, and social services purchased privately" (Moscovitch, 1986: 89).

The *informants*, then, were really experiencing only one sub-type out of the vast panoply of social welfare. Unfortunately, their corner of this field was the most culturally visible, most socially stigmatizing, and most personally humiliating as well as being the poorest paying. The negative reaction to "welfare bums" held by the well-off *and* many of the poor obscured the other social forms of welfare which embrace virtually all of us.

In assessing these ideologically visible and needy members of society, the "normal self-reliant" majority—and reflectively the government which seeks its favour—distinguishes between the *deserving* and the *undeserving poor*. The "deserving poor" are those whose personal situation makes it impossible for them to work: e.g. the severely disabled, children, the aged, the sick and, in lesser measure, single mothers. The "*un*deserving poor" are

> those who have chosen not to work and those whose poverty results from unemployment, job discrimination or low wages. The former have been the object of punitive measures; for the latter, protective policies have been hard won. (SPC/OSDC, 1983: 71).

Because these groups are seen to deviate from the norm of self-supporting families adhering to the work ethic, the public wants them controlled, disciplined, and returned to self-reliance (i.e. dependence on a wage) as soon as possible. It does not want its tax-supported public programs to be enclaves of undeserved dependence.

Behind the state's "mandate" from the majority regarding programs for the poor—i.e. its legitimation function—we can see hints of a second major tendency or function of government social security, i.e. *capital accumulation*. By keeping its benefits lower than the minimum private wage, by degrading and patronizing its clients to make welfare unattractive to the working poor, by continually urging clients to look for work, the government keeps the workforce of the marginal business sector in its place. It thus indirectly helps keep viable those businesses whose profits depend on keeping their wage costs low. Even minimum wage laws, while unpopular with certain small businesses, probably benefit business in the long run. In their absence, private wages would sink so low that marginal workers would leave them for government's social wages.

Practices

The *institutional* practices of welfare departments which flow from this diverse mandate are at least three:

- Testing for and Monitoring Eligibility;
- Stereotyping and Patronizing Clients;
- Enforcing Work and Wage-reliance.

These formulated the social practices in which our informants were engaged, and form our topics for analysis:

- Proving and Maintaining Eligibility for Assistance;
- Coping with Paternalism;
- Testing the Marginal Work Role.

It is to the first of these practices that we now turn.

Proving and Maintaining Eligibility for Assistance

To present oneself as a claimant for social assistance is to undergo more than the usual bureaucratic processing. The claimant must submit to an examination which is an induction into a system of disciplinary power. Once accepted as eligible, the claimant must allow the officials to *continue* to monitor his or her "worthiness." According to Foucault's historical analysis, the examination introduces "a whole mechanism that linked to a certain type of formation of knowledge a certain form of the exercise of power" (1977: 187). Power relations, in other words, are expressed as knowledge relations within the examination.

One is struck by the asymmetry of these knowledge relations between welfare officials and claimant. To satisfy the many rules ensuring that assistance is given only to those who have no other recourse, a person must prove that he or she owns nothing of significant value. Possession of a car, money in the bank, expensive appliances, or property of any kind will disqualify the client. Sources of income, real or potential, are intensively queried. If the claimant is employed, or making money through baby-sitting, the official wants to know. Significant income will disqualify a person, or will be "taxed."

Information Gathering

Then there are the "gate-keeping" questions: "Is the claimant receiving alimony?" "Are there adult children or siblings who could support the claimant?" "Is there a husband, lover, or parent who is helping out financially or who could?" "Is the person you are living with on welfare or employed?" If so, he can support you. "Do you have a stable address?" If not, you cannot qualify for assistance. The information-gathering even extended to home visits. A claimant would be instructed to stay home for a particular three-day period to receive a visit. The home would then be open for examination: the state of the furnishings, the children, evidence of the presence of a man, cleanliness, and so on.

No comparable flow of information came from the caseworker to the claimant. *"They won't tell you anything if you don't ask about it. Some will tell you things, some won't,"* said one young man. Those caseworkers who served the educative function, which the profession of social work proclaimed, were few, according to the informants. MARY, 41, a woman on Mother's Allowance, put it emphatically: *"Welfare never told me they'd help me with the fridge and stove; they never told me they'd help me with glasses; they never told me they'd help me with moving; they never told me they'd help me with a lot of things."* Not only did the claimants not know the regulations of the complicated Welfare Act and the various supplementary assistance programs (and were often too intimidated to ask), the officials seemed not disposed to tell them. This virtual "information barrier" (Piven and Cloward, 1972: 152), where officials controlled the flow of information, may have functioned to minimize the "awkwardness" of the claimants.

Swelling Caseloads

This is not to impute an evil intent to welfare officials; often this under-informing was an unintended result of swelling caseloads, untrained staff, and overworked officials. It was common that, under conditions of overload, caseworker interactions with claimants tended to be brief, even abrupt, from the claimant's view (Kelvin and Jarrett, 1985: 86). In the summer of 1983, I interviewed a caseworker who had recently left the city welfare office. She described the ideal caseload as about 75 cases with two new referrals a day. That gives the worker time to talk to claimants, to follow through on their concerns, to tell them about services, to listen.

But in that hectic spring of 1983, her caseload was 200 cases a month with three or four new referrals a day. She and other staff were pressured to work overtime; staff turnover was high with new staff being *"thrown into it"* with only two weeks training and very little help from other people. This, for a job that could have as many as 35 forms for one applicant. The focus of management on *quantitative* output was apparent in its stated policy that if the average caseload ever fell below 139, layoffs among staff would begin. She was very dissatisfied with the effect this had on interactions and services with clients, as well as the harried atmosphere in her office.

Relationships between Client and Caseworker

The relationship between the client and the caseworker was judged positive if it contained a personal element. In about a half-dozen cases, informants reported that the worker showed a personal interest, was "kind," "understanding," "sympathetic." Those workers who singled them out as living individuals, not just as cases in a stereotyped pool of claimants, were appreciated. HEATHER said the counsellor made her *"feel special, not just one of those people."* Young HAROLD was gratified to find his female worker so accessible:

> *It was almost as if she had been on welfare, she knew what it was all about.... I used to go over there and just talk to her, about the problems I have been having, not just relating to welfare. She'd sit down and listen to me.*

MONICA, a single parent of 28 who had found most of her workers unsympathetic, was astonished when she found one who agreed with her that the benefits were inadequate. *"He said, 'I don't know how they could ever give this to people. I'm against it, I don't like it.' And he just went on and on and on."*

For the most part, however, the relationship was encased in *roles*. The first interview often set the strict mould in which the relationship was to proceed. One woman, JANE, just wanted her worker

> *to relax.... I am concerned with the prejudice that she's the worker, and she sits there and takes down notes, and I'm no less of a person sitting on the other side. It was very official. There was none of her personality in the whole situation.... That can't be cut up, that can't be attacked, because she's fulfilling her role as an official. If she had any negative feelings, she hid them well. If she had any positive feelings, she hid them well. I can't complain because she was very businesslike.*

JANE seemed ambivalent in her reaction. She resented the withholding of personal involvement from the role performance of the worker. She felt it necessary to assert her own humanity in the face of the note-taking and objectifying. Yet it *was* minimally correct; at least she had been spared any expression of contempt. Other informants were more clearly negative about the fact that some workers *"just do their job, are just standard, are not really personal."*

Caseworkers as Moral Deputies

Whatever the personal style, the worker's role as moral deputy of employed society who penetrated deep into your home and your private facts gave that worker an up-close, intimate power. *"They come out and look at your surroundings, and if you're not living in a hovel, they don't like it and they'll turn you down as often as possible,"* said one woman. Not surprisingly, the worker on a home visit aroused a moral defensiveness and anxiety in the claimant.

One woman, KATHY, who needed welfare for a month or two, said she was made to feel *"guilty of something...and they were going to find out what it was."* She almost felt challenged to prove that she deserved the assistance, against the assumption that she did not (i.e. unworthy until proven worthy). During the interview she actually did begin to feel guilty. She was nervous that she would do or say something wrong and would not get anything. She was afraid to ask the worker the date of her first cheque, or anything else. The worker thought her house was too much for a single person and suggested she move into a cheaper place. Striving from self-interest to be a model rather than awkward claimant, KATHY—prompted by the worker and out of her own felt deviance—was learning to fit her action to the passive syntax held out to her. These were the encounters in which knowledge and power relations were reproduced.

In the rhetoric of modern social work, welfare workers are to reach out to the disadvantaged. "The emphasis in the modern welfare state is on rights, not deterrence; on letting the needy in, not keeping them out" (Reisman, 1977: 72). In practice, however, the rules blocking eligibility seemed to lie like a minefield between the claimant and the needed help. EVELYN, a single parent with a child, who had separated from her partner out west, was in Toronto, poor, and on welfare. Anxious to take a Manpower course, she asked Welfare if they could find a subsidized day care spot for her daughter. *"You can't keep dragging a child around on the subway, I mean, it's just terrible."* While filling out the forms, she was asked if she owned any property. EVELYN and her partner had bought a little property in Quebec—it was in his name but was half hers—which was worth very little. They had no intention of doing anything with it.

The worker's response to her disclosure was disconcertingly swift:

> *She wanted me to get all the documents on whether it was income property, and I'm just looking at her, you know. I said, "The property isn't worth anything." She says, "You have to get a lawyer and you have to do this and you have to do that." And this is all to get this course through Manpower; I'm starting to get the ball rolling!*

She called Legal Aid and they were not helpful. She called Sole Support Mothers and another organization. *"There's all these places to call and everybody tells you something different. I mean, honestly they do!* [Raising her voice.] *And I was getting so confused."* When she contacted the Ombudsman's office, they wanted

> *papers and formulas and letters and I thought this is crazy. I'm asking for help and nobody has an answer and nobody knows what to do. And here you are broke and all alone with a child in Toronto, right?*

In the end, she never received the day care subsidy.

Caseworkers as Rule-Enforcers

Some welfare workers would make the system appear more minutely directive and rule-bound than it really was. While this certainly was an authoritative bureaucratic system, actually there *was* room for negotiating. Though directives came down from the provincial ministry, the local office had considerable discretionary "room" in its handling of individual cases. Informants reported occasional success in pressing for their own particular needs, against the grain of standardized practice.

So VINCENT, described one of his workers as a *"rule-book type of person"* who, at first, did not understand his need to live away from home. In VINCENT's words,

> Then I had to explain, right? So I said to him, "Listen, listen. Don't just have preconceived ideas." I had to forcibly make him listen, you know.... And then his rule-book started to melt a little bit, right? And then I could come across with some tangible things to tell him, and what's going on. And then he was pretty good about it.

In defending his experience, VINCENT was engaging in a form of resistance. In the conventional bureaucratic syntax, he would be "positivistically" reduced to a case, then codified with others of the same "type," to which certain rules and benefits would apply, and so on. VINCENT and others would have to, figuratively, grab the worker by the lapels and say, "I am the real subject of this experience, and you must listen, not just dictate." Negotiating with the worker was difficult for an individual (there were organizations that could help, as will be reviewed in the next chapter), but firmness and aggressiveness did help to unfreeze the rigid syntax of bureaucratic practice. To a positivistic model based on control, the self demanded that it be analyzed qualitatively, with human understanding.

After the claimant was found to be eligible for assistance, the status had to be continually maintained: tested for by the caseworker and defended by the client. Important now were not so much family characteristics and assets as the continued acceptability of the client's behaviour. Policies and practices, often indirect and unpublished, which monitored and controlled behaviour, called forth coping practices which we will take up now.

Coping with Paternalism

Human contact between client and caseworker is thought, in social welfare circles, to be essential. No negative income tax or benefit arriving through the mail can replace it. Not only valuable in itself, personal contact is needed to find the hard-to-reach who might need services but be unaware that they are available. Discovering old people, for instance, who need preventive action against blindness and arranging services to help them, is one way that social work can enlarge the scope of people's freedom (Reisman, 1977: 72).

But the human contacts between welfare workers and the informants were not so liberating—in fact, were in some ways the opposite, judging from the accounts. Despite some favourable reports on caseworkers, the best way of describing the officials' relationships with informants was "paternalistic." This is defined in the dictionary as the "attitude or policy of a government or authority that manages the affairs of a community [etc.]...in the manner of a father; esp. in usurping individual responsibility and the liberty of choice" (Collins English Dictionary). One informant described it as *"being under the thumb of the government."*

The authority could be wielded quite aggressively. VINCENT's first welfare worker went to the wrong apartment in his building, found no one there, and the next day upbraided VINCENT for not being in. It took the young man quite a time to convince the worker that he had made a mistake. Here was the description of their first meeting:

> *He comes down the next day...and I open the door, and he sticks his foot in, and goes, "You're Vincent?" and walks right in and bang, "Let's get down to business, blah, blah, blah...."*

> *Right! "Hi! [laughs] How are you?" He just barges right in and I'm going "Whoa."*

Later the worker criticized him for moving around too much, *"playing games."* VINCENT replied that he was trying to survive and the worker was not making it easier. The worker answered, *"Look, you're talking to your superior."* VINCENT shot back:

> *"No way! Nobody is my superior, right. Nobody is supposed to have anything over me, or try to push me around like this."* Apparently this guy was some sort of war vet.

Certain welfare workers seemed to share the negative images of clients held by the general public and were found to be condescending to informants. While there was probably an element of projection involved, many informants felt degraded in their contacts with workers.

> *My worker talks to me like I'm down there, way down there.*

> *They make you feel like you're awful, an unworthy person.*

> *I feel belittled. I didn't want anyone to know how I was getting money to live on.*

> *They just look at you, "You're collecting welfare, why don't you go out and get a job?"*

> *The welfare worker was just sort of..."Yeah, you're a free-loader."*

One informant who had worked in social services commented that it depended on the individual caseworker, but she knew many who thought the clients' only goal was to beat the system. ANDREA put the client's view rather succinctly:

> *They have a real looking-down-on-you attitude, and my back just gets right up. I don't find them very pleasant people. I keep thinking how people less assertive than me deal with that. I bet there's a lot of people that cry. Because they're so negative*

to you. There's no understanding. It's like, "You quit your job, and you did this just so you could do nothing." [emphasis in original] *I really hate that.*

Informants resented not only the lower status in which they were unjustly placed, but also the moral pedestal on which their judges stood. Informants talked of the "holier-than-thou" attitude. The welfare workers appeared to stand apart, in a haloed zone of self-reliance. But the informants knew that taxpayers paid their salaries, that their jobs depended on the very clientele they were supposed to serve. The enormous *interdependence* in capitalist society, which also took shape in the various kinds of social welfare, was so veiled ideologically by market relations based on exchange that each person had "the illusion that he or she labours for him or herself alone. It is from this spurious sense of self-reliance that our Victorian forebears attacked all forms of undeserving dependence" (Zaretsky, 1986: 94). From the same sense of self-reliance came the condescension of the caseworkers.

Thus the paternalistic treatment of the welfare poor was an atomizing practice that cut *two* ways. It made the poor seem undeserving, as though their poverty were self-determined and unlinked to anything else. And it made even the public "servants" of the poor feel spuriously enlarged in their vaunted self-determination. Once again, mutualities were severed—as "big atoms" and "little atoms" were released into their supposedly free-floating interactions.

Being Seen to be on Welfare

Mutualities were severed outside the welfare office or interview as well. Such a strong *definition* attached to the welfare stereotype—especially in a city like London, fairly bustling with exchange relations—that people reported feeling strange, as if they were putting on an ill-fitting coat.

> *When I went down there, I felt that I just stuck right out. I thought, "Oh my God, people think I'm on welfare." Typical stereotype I guess you're led to believe. You used to think, "It's those people who are on welfare," and now you discover you're one of those people.*

Note that HEATHER, the speaker, was reacting not to *being* on welfare but to being *seen* to be on welfare. Whatever welfare was paled in comparison to inhabiting its dreaded public stereotype. Friends or schoolmates who knew that you were on welfare would feel the irresistible pull of the public image: the "bum" who just sits around. GORD, 47, said of the moment when his welfare status was revealed to others, *"There's a wall there, there's a wall there,"* hinting at the break in mutuality.

The experience on its own, of course, was degrading enough—some informants expressed a moral revulsion for welfare (or for the role it offered). People referred to it as *"going nowhere," "the lowest thing you can do."* It was a kind of subsidized stagnation. GLENN was on for three months and got off:

> I feel that I'm just sitting around and waiting. Everyone is paying for me to sit around. That's the way I feel about welfare. I could be collecting that now, but that's why I don't. I just feel the government's paying me to sit on my ass, more or less.

WAYNE, whose situation was described in the previous chapter, found he could not bring himself to apply for a $20 food voucher. He simply could not beg. Several people stated that they would avoid welfare at all costs. MATTHEWsaid feelingly: *"I might be eligible for some. I feel I could do it on my own, given the chance. I don't want welfare. I don't want the city to support me. I'm willing to work. I even called the Mayor's office and asked for a job cutting the grass. But no, union, you have to go through the proper channel."*

Surveillance

Most resented was the sheer invasion by the state into private life. The state assumed the ultimate paternalistic prerogative to maintain surveillance on its "charge" and to penetrate the screen of privacy whenever appropriate. Describing Mother's Allowance, ANDREA commented: *"That was the worst year and a half of my entire life. I hated it. I hated those people having that right to knock on my door anytime they feel like it, to comment on whether my house was clean, on how I brought up my son. I resented it totally."* JANINE, 18, married with an unemployed husband, discovered that her worker had complained to her mother about the husband. The worker was worried that if she put support for JANINE on the husband's cheque, he would drink the money away. JANINE was understandably furious at the intrusion—her husband did not drink anyway.

Women on Mother's Allowance expressed resentment that, under their rules, *"if I want to live with a male, I can't do that."* Evidence of a male living-in so that he appeared to be supporting the woman were grounds enough to cut off a woman's benefits. (This was changed in a spring 1987 ruling in Ontario, which declared that a person's benefit levels were not affected by those of a partner.) Many caseworkers were on the lookout for "intense relationships" that might compromise a woman's status as a single person. A young male caseworker whom I interviewed had spent most of one night in his car watching to see if his client's male visitor would leave or stay.

The rules regarding surveillance of the habits and sexual mores of clients were part of the "deep structure" of a Family Benefits office and were not for public consumption. In spring 1985, guidelines sent from the office to caseworkers on how to conduct home visits were uncovered by the London Union of Unemployed Workers. After suggesting questions and tactics if a man happened to be present during the visit, here were some of the things to look for in the investigation:

- Men's boots, clothing, hats, tools, lunch bucket;
- C.B. equipment;
- Hunting dogs;
- Car treads in snow early in a.m.;
- Awareness of sounds to indicate presence of other person;
- Casual remarks: "My daddy is still in bed"; "My daddy is gone to work"; Reference made to "We" or "Our."

(London Union of Unemployed Workers, 1985)

This sort of intrusive "snooping" occasionally drew on the collusion of other welfare or family benefit claimants, who might "tip off" the worker that someone was hiding a man. When lone parents were concentrated in a government housing project, suspicions multiplied in a kind of contagion. MARY, after separating from an alcoholic husband, was forced onto benefits and into London Housing. She explained the atmosphere in her project:

I get the feeling that I'm under such scrutiny, like I'm trying to hide something. And I'm not hiding anything, and they should try to get some of the women who are hiding men.... It's insane. Yet they question the ones who aren't.... They treat us all suspiciously.

[Lowering her voice] Everyone's spying in everyone else's window, waiting for you to do something you're not supposed to, or have someone walk into your house you're not supposed to have. And if you have a Mother's Allowance worker in here more than five minutes, everyone thinks you're telling them about all the rest of the neighbourhood.

What added substance to MARY's portrait of her community was her account of the Children's Aid incident. The winter her car had broken down she had become overwhelmed with her household and other responsibilities. She firmly insisted that her two sons, 15 and nine, help her with the duties at home. She told them she was not a slave; that she wanted them to help with the dishes, to clean up their rooms, and do a little vacuuming. At that point, somebody in the housing complex complained to Children's Aid that her children had been assigned too many responsibilities at home. In response to the complaint, a counsellor visited her home to interview her and the children about whether their housework was excessive. The young ones denied it, and the matter ended with a caution.

This incident suggested that MARY's almost paranoid statements above probably had a basis in reality. That reality seemed to have been that some members of her community were afraid and insecure and used their imaginative powers in endless conjecture and comparison about the others in their homes. It was also true that the government made use of informers to control the behaviour of their "wards." Surely no more chilling account of government paternalism and its lack of respect for privacy could be given.

Yet Mother's Allowance, like welfare, could mean good things for the informants. These programs could stabilize a person's life. People who had known the insecurity of poverty with a child were grateful knowing that the rent and bills would be paid. But virtually everyone who was or had been on Mother's Allowance was critical, or at best ambivalent, towards it. They wanted to be free of its compelling dependency. They wanted to work but did not know where they could find a job whose pay would be good enough to abandon the subsidized housing, the free medical insurance, dental work, prescriptions (partial), lenses, and frames. They yearned to be off benefits so their children would be proud of them. Rather than asking the worker for everything, they wanted the financial security, self-esteem, and independence of earning their own living. PAULA tried to describe herself through her son's eyes: she is *"stationary,....she doesn't move, she doesn't go anywhere."* Will he lose respect, she worried, and be without a role model? Will he lead a life without motivation, *"sitting around?"*

A human life outside the weird theatre of society's stereotypes was yearned for by some of the informants on Mother's Allowance, many of whom seemed trapped in a kind of pariah status. When MARY moved into London Housing, she vowed to her children: *"I will get us out. It's not the end of the road. It's not the end of life. There's got to be something for me out there!"* When she answered job ads in the paper and did not even get a response: *"I get so angry, I could just scream!"* All she wanted was normalcy, to be out from under the gaze of government and suspicious others; to live in *"a little house, with a little yard and a few trees on it. And I could raise my kids on a street where there is no label hung on me."*

Testing the Marginal Work-Role

The welfare system evolved as an adjunct of the labour market. The historical precedent was the 1834 Poor Law Report of the British government, which became very influential in Canada and the United States. That report argued that relief to the able-bodied should be in every way less "eligible" (desirable) than the situation of the lowest-paid worker. Otherwise, poor workers would be induced to leave their employment for the more eligible status of state-supported pauper. An important goal, then, of early social policy was not to meet the needs of the poor "but to preserve the motivation of those who worked, particularly of those in the worst jobs society had to offer" (Struthers, 1983: 7). It also preserved the profits of the employers which rested on the low wages paid to the workers. The means devised to separate out the "deserving" from the "undeserving" poor was the "workhouse test." Relief that used to be provided from parish funds to paupers in their homes would now be administered in workhouses, whose conditions would be so degrading that only the genuinely destitute would submit to them—hence the "test."

Enforcing work, especially low-wage work, has been a major part of the practices and policies of the welfare state to this day (Piven and Cloward, 1972: chapters 4–5). The ways in which this pressure was applied to the informants and coped with will be examined first. After that, I will present accounts from the informants' recent work histories. Far from being two separate worlds of experience, social assistance and employment often interpenetrated, even in some cases were symbiotic.

Methods of Enforcing Work

We have already presented some of the practices of welfare officials which acted to deter people from applying for welfare. But, more specifically, how did the welfare bureaucracy induce clients to get off benefits and on to reliance on a private wage? There appeared to have been two methods: direct pressure and the manipulation of social wages.

The number of job searches required of the informants on social assistance ranged from five to 15 searches a week, for which a job search form had to be filled out. In some cases the worker did not "lean" too heavily, requiring only that the client ritualistically check the boards at Manpower and fill out some applications. Quite often, however, the worker was more insistent that the job search requirement be carried out and that the client not be too fussy about the jobs on offer. Little sympathy was offered by these caseworkers even when their clients faced age discrimination which made their job search painful and rejecting, or when low-paid jobs made no practical sense (due to transportation and child care costs, for example). Pressure of an insulting, personal kind was applied, backed up with the threat of sanctions.

People would find themselves addressed by caseworkers as though they were cardboard stereotypes and not human beings. EVELYN had separated out west from an unsuccessful musician who had fled to California leaving her with the child and the bills, and had been forced to live with her elderly father in a small town. EVELYN's very young caseworker in London had the temerity to say to her: "*An intelligent person like you should be able to get a job.*" Other informants with educational credentials—especially men—thought that their jobfinding difficulties were not taken seriously by female caseworkers, as though they were automatically *assumed* to be undeserving poor. So LORNE found that welfare was getting impatient with him. His benefit cheques were now being delayed, even though his job search sheets were in on time; they were not as nice to him now and called him often, asking, *"Are you really looking?"*

Those whose workers insisted on three job searches a day found it difficult to afford nearly $5.00 in transportation tickets that was required. Poor informants could rarely afford monthly bus passes, and the city had refused to provide discounts on passes for the unemployed. Confrontations and ill-feeling between informants and caseworkers were the result. WARREN told his worker one day to *"get the hell out of the house."*

> They were bugging me that I didn't have my job search sheet the way they wanted it, but I kept on trying to tell them that I can't afford a bus pass. I can't take $32 out of there—that's $32 for a pair of shoes for my son, or $32 worth of food for my kids. I can't do it.

The caseworker's response had been, in WARREN's words: *"If you can't afford to go out and look for work, we can't afford to feed you,"* and they cut him off. This forced him to move out temporarily and live with his parents.

The second method of enforcing work was welfare's *manipulation of social wages.* When a client had an opportunity to be supported by someone on private wages, welfare would cut off or reduce benefits. Shortly after WARREN moved in with his parents, his wife applied for welfare. Welfare workers immediately came after him to see if he could provide support. In practice, this usually worked out to be quite sexist. One woman with a child was living with an underemployed artist; she was refused welfare because she was living with him. This woman, a fine arts student during the year and unable to find work that summer, wanted an equal relationship with her man rather than being his dependent. But the welfare worker judged him to be "head of the household," and she could not convince the worker that they shared expenses. Even when both members of a couple were unable to find work, Welfare thought that one of the two should be out working and would reduce benefits. The vaunted "self-reliance" towards which Welfare supposedly pointed its clients had in this case achieved an ironic reversal, i.e. in driving the woman to depend on the male partner's wage.

Of course, keeping benefits *generally* low served the end of enforcing work. It pushed clients precipitously into the (mostly) marginal labour market and induced mothers and other disadvantaged people who worked in that market to stay put. The general social assistance rates produced a poverty income that was generally *less than half* of what was considered a minimum adequate income (SPC/OSDC, 1983: 20). Single persons in 1984 could expect welfare benefits of slightly over $300 a month, compared with a poverty line for a single person of $825 monthly. A family of four in that year could expect a benefit of about $800 a month, while the poverty line was over $1600. While the shelter allowance did make a difference, there was still very little left over after the necessities were paid for.

How low a wage would the informants take? And was there a relation between low income floors and low benefits? Of the 58 who gave clear answers, 60% would accept minimum wage or less, ($4.00 an hour in 1984) with some of the younger informants going as low as $1.50 or $2.00 an hour. Of the remainder, most would accept $5.00 or $6.00 an hour; only nine informants set their income floor at $7.00 an hour or more. Apart from indicating the informants' extraordinary wage *flexibility*—the majority settling for wages well below the poverty line—the figures suggested a general correlation between level of social wage benefits and income floors. People on social assistance would generally settle for minimum wage or less (though this had partly to do with their limited marketability as youth), while those on Mother's Allowance and Disability Allowance wanted $6.00 or $7.00 or more. To pay for the benefits associated with Mother's Allowance, along with child care, these women would need appreciably more than the minimum wage. Likewise, those on Disability, having relatively high social wages, had a higher acceptable minimum. For those on general welfare, it seems fair to conclude, their low benefit levels partly *conditioned* their readiness to take on low wage work. Low benefit levels helped prepare people to take the lowest private wages—a case of governments "tuning up" the low wage workers which the marginal employers might one day need.

In sum, the form of pressure on the claimant to take on marginal work might be personal (*"You don't really expect to get a job for $5.00 an hour, do you?,"* an official asked EVELYN)) or institutional (e.g. policies about claimants living with a partner). The welfare system's prying, stigmatizing practices held up the dependent poor as a example for the working poor to see and avoid. At the same time as it kept marginal workers at their posts, it prepared its malleable, fragmented clientele for new low-wage jobs that might materialize in the competitive marginal work world. As Piven and Cloward pointed out, the degradation of that clientele

> serves to mark the boundary between the appropriately motivated and the inappropriately motivated, between the virtuous and the defective.... Relief practices are not a mere reflection of market ideology; they are an agent in nurturing and reinforcing that ideology (1972: 149).

Doing Marginal Work

Now it should be noted that an unusually high proportion of those who came onto the welfare rolls in the 1983–85 period were relatively recent workers—they had been laid off from full-time work, had exhausted their U.I. benefits, and had been forced onto assistance. But even those people who had more regular recourse to social assistance were no strangers to employment. They often had recent work histories and many would return to wage labour—often to go back on assistance at a later time, in a cyclical pattern (Heidenheim, 1984: 122). They tended to work in marginal enterprises in primary industries and, in the cities, in the personal services and restaurant sectors (Butler, 1980, cited in Heidenheim, 1984: 122).

The informants who had experience of social assistance or family benefits were no exception. Keeping in mind the relative youthfulness of this group, here were some of their recent jobs:

- A former cook was reduced to being a driver for a pizza house, then for a Chinese restaurant;
- An ex-musician worked as a cook in a university fraternity house, with only one operating stove;
- Library clerk, fired after being wrongly blamed for an error;
- One of a number of sales managers, demoted to part-time sales (therefore "forced" to resign);
- Waiting on tables;
- Sales clerk in a boutique;
- Part-time worker in a home for mentally retarded;
- Receptionist;
- Dishwasher;
- Telephone sales;
- Laundromat attendant;
- Demolition work, labourer;
- Journalist;
- Baby-sitting;
- Labouring in a home repair firm;
- Picking tobacco;
- Engineering work, for recent graduates.

As we can see, the jobs these "welfare" informants' had were typical of the marginal work world: low-wage, poor benefits, low skill requirements, no unions or job tenure. When all the work experience of the other informants is added in, much of which was also marginal, the result is a considerable body of descriptions.

Some of the flavour of the informants' marginal work can be conveyed by three examples. KENNETH, 31, worked as an adult paper carrier in Edmonton. He was expected to deliver the papers from three a.m. to seven, using his own car (for which he received a gas allowance). On some mornings, the temperature was 45 below zero. He would be shifted to a new route just as he was learning the former route. The addresses for his 200 customers were hard to read and the customers often complained. He was rarely finished by seven a.m. and delivery was seven days a week. For this job, which he *"wouldn't recommend to his worst enemy,"* he was paid about eight cents per paper (15 cents on weekends), which amounted to $16 a day. A second example involved HEATHER, who worked as an investigator for a security firm, whose job was to arrest people for shoplifting. On that job a man pulled a knife on her and chased her through the mall. She was knocked over by shoplifters a number of times. As London is a small city, she would run into people she had charged and witnessed against in court.

In the third example, KARL had got a job in a wholesale hardware warehouse in old Montreal. The job was to pack nuts and bolts and heavier pieces in boxes. Among the workers were the very old and the under-aged, the latter being paid less than minimum wage. The building was well over a hundred and fifty years old and had been used as a barracks and stable from the 1840s. The floors were earth, and there was no heat in the winter. In the man's own words:

> The third floor where they put the heaviest goods like the rolls of barbed wire and the rolls of tar paper, the clearance between the floors and the roof was less than five feet two. There were no safety devices. To unload barbed wire: we had no hooks, hard hats, nothing. You passed a roll of barbed wire to the next guy and so on.

They had a policy of paying the English workers more than the French workers, causing some of the francophones to throw things at him. When KARL proposed that the workers organize, *"the workers were too afraid."* In another factory at which he worked, he and the other workers had to work in the basement from eight to nine a.m. The elevator, however, only started working at nine a.m. and it was the sole exit; until then they were effectively locked in. He had to badger management to activate the elevators earlier. KARL suspected that his known interest in workers' rights may have followed him and was hurting his present prospects.

As a social practice, "doing marginal work" was judged by informants to be highly unsatisfactory. The informants' relations with the *employer* seemed blighted by the low-wage, interchangeable nature of the workers' roles. As a woman bluntly put it: *"below a certain wage, the bosses treat you like dirt."* If you worked for $4.00 an hour, another man added, employers were *"looking down their nose at you. And maybe they have a right to."* Power relations in these circumstances tended to be abrasive and direct, lacking the mediation of union or professional procedure. VINCENT was backing away from marginal jobs for the time being; when asked why:

> I don't know, it could be fear. I've been kicked around a bit at jobs—no respect, eh? [laughs] *"Me boss, you slave."* OK, you get paid, but that's law.... If I was a boss, I'd have respect for the people where it was due—especially in the lower jobs like dishwasher. There must be some good bosses, but they're few and far between.

Informants resented the way they were manipulated by employers on marginal jobs, as if the employers thought, "These people are desperate and can be made to do anything." There was some revulsion shown towards the training of voice and manner on telephone sales jobs, which seemed utterly to distort the human relationship with the customer. *"It's like a recorder,"* commented JANE, 25. *"I don't like talking to human beings who are turning themselves into robots. I can't do junk like that. I despise that kind of job."*

Relations between the agent and *co-workers* on short-term jobs rarely went beyond the roles into personal relationships: they tended to stay partial and transitory. GORD, who had been underemployed for years, felt that the kind of people you met on labouring projects *"aren't the kind of people who go in for friendship. They're transient people. They're here and there, low wage. They might be out to Vancouver next week."* ERICA, speaking of temporary office work, sounded a similar theme. While she loved to work and appreciated some of the novelty of temp work, her work relationships never quite took root. Not knowing the others in the office, she felt watched, like a stranger in a small town.

> *I don't like temporary work. The learning and the being new and the newness.... Taking notes at night, learning a whole job that you're going to do for two weeks...and getting such a low wage for doing so much. Feeling isolated, feeling that they're checking me up. Going in there, and everybody has their own little group—they go out for lunch and you're left sitting there, because you don't know anybody, don't know the routine.*

The voice of action tended, on short-term jobs, to be more passive than on most full-time jobs. One was not recognized as having entitlements, "perks," seniority, sponsors—anything which might lever one into a sense of agency in the work environment. The jobs were assigned with little heed for the personal preference of the temporary worker. As for the tense of the practice, doing short-term marginal work *could* be, at its best, an "engaging of the gears" of personal life so that one seemed to be moving ahead—especially compared to the enforced idleness at home. But so low were the wages, benefits, and prestige of the work, so unlikely was any advancement from it that, for many, marginal work left them even more marginalized, working in a stagnant present with no lines to a future.

Indeed, women informants found marginal work to be even *regressive*, returning them to the jobs of their early years before they had grasped their own possibilities. With their prospects reduced as their unemployment wore on, they were pressed to take jobs that did not engage that heightened sense of self. *"Maybe you can't always carry that pride around with you,"* commented DEBBIE, 34. Still, human dignity required that a line be drawn somewhere. *"I don't want the kind of job I was doing when I was 14...you hope to move beyond that."* As JANE added:

I had my little piddly jobs. I'm not looking forward to having that kind of job put on my résumé. I've done my waitressing.... There's a point where you pay out your dignity for a job that's asking you to be overqualified for a poverty wage.

Summary and Conclusions

In "proving and maintaining eligibility," the person passively submitted to a governmental power which was far more intimate and thorough than that wielded from the Canada Employment Centre. There was an "examination" (which became ongoing) assessing eligibility for assistance. The person was firmly set in a role relationship of self-exposing claimant before judgmental authority. The syntax of the action was shaped in the interest of the "real subject"—the welfare bureaucracy—which was serving its societal mandate to screen out undeserving claimants to public benefits. Claimants could occasionally count on being taken seriously by a good caseworker, but often personal elements were screened out as the claimants found themselves encased in a highly stereotyped role relationship.

The second practice, "coping with paternalism," described the ways informants dealt with a state authority that was scrutinizing morals. The client, as in effect ward of the state, was always open for inspection; the real subject was not only the caseworker, but the whole of employed society for whose work ethic the caseworker was moral policeman. In this and the previous enacted practices there was, again, some resistance—where informants vigorously defended their own unique experience against the system's abstract classifications and rules. Overall, however, neither practice offered a credible formulating role to the self. The self's largely reactive practices were atomizing, keyed to narrow self-interest.

Doing marginal work was atomizing in a different way. It involved the worker in a less secure and self-determining association with co-workers than was available in (some) regular jobs. Temporary workers moved as travelling strangers through employee groups rather than engaged as participating members. Part-time workers in many offices and service establishments had fewer benefits or bargaining rights, less determination of their working schedules, less of a voice than full-time workers. Marginal work-forces generally had a patchwork, residual character—sewn together out of individual necessities and group discrimination—whose workers lacked collective force or craft identity. The agent who moved through such loose, dissociating social environments became something of an unbonded atom of self-interest.

The consequences of these practices for social and personal identity were severe. First we must note the important social roles that were vacated while being poor and on welfare. The morally valued role of self-supporting member of society was gone, replaced by the stigmatized role of welfare recipient. The role of citizen entitled to certain rights and privileges was put aside for the role of claimant: politically weak and solitary. As well, the personal sphere of what one could call one's own was considerably diminished. Some informants did not consider their benefit money their own—not having worked for it—and could not spend it without guilt or distaste. Even their homes were not quite their own, or their personal details, since both could be penetrated by the caseworker.

The high-profile public persona of welfare recipient they found themselves stepping into blighted their social identity, causing them to withdraw from others in confusion and shame. Nor did the marginal work-role give them the self-esteem, status, or purchase on the future that they lacked—rather it seemed the correlative of the welfare role, equally lacking in power and solidarity.

The Macrosocial Context

Government social assistance is, of all the forms of social welfare outlined at the beginning of the chapter, the most atomizing. The poor lack the self-enhancing forms of welfare available through the job, are unable to afford the middle-class tax shelters, cannot buy private welfare, and often are outside the scope of unions, benefit societies, and non-profit corporations. They are removed from a vast social machinery "of insurance and pension companies, of international corporations, of state institutions, which, biting upon each other in a massive interlocking of financial gears and their ratios, work to reproduce...structures of poverty and inequality" (Inglis, 1982, 153).

The only way low-income groups have held onto their small relative share of the national income is through an increased dependence on government transfer payments. For the 20% with the lowest incomes in 1983, 54.4% of family income and 67.9% of individual income was derived from transfer payments. To the vulnerable and dependent groups in our society—low income families, young people, single parent women, older women, the unemployed—government social welfare in its various forms is essential (Moscovitch, 1986: 90–91).

Yet, to the already multiplying deficits of joblessness and poverty, the government adds the burdens of under-funded and declining services and subjects people to stigmatizing social practices. Government social assistance does not decrease social inequality but adds insult to it. It contributes little to economic equality: after taxes, the unequal distribution of incomes is still very skewed in favour of more affluent groups, who benefit hugely from tax expenditures (National Council of Welfare, 1985: 77–79).

We can begin to discern a picture of the leads and lags of modern capitalism. The "concealed multipliers of occupational success" (to repeat Titmuss's phrase) have meant that the situation of those without employment is, in relative terms, even less well fortified than before. Dovetailing with the new synergies of the well-connected are the increasingly atomizing practices formulated by business and state for the poor. These new scripts for the economically disadvantaged are called, respectively, "casualization" and "erosion." Both casualization and erosion:

- Offered rationalizations for the reduction of responsibility of institutions towards individuals (economic competitiveness and a leaner state sector);
- Provided short-term work rather than long-term (part-time work and government projects);
- Fostered wider gaps in overall well-being between the full-time workers or tax beneficiaries and the marginal workers and transfer recipients.

Both business and government are formulating practices and institutional controls which structure people's action in a more individualistic, self-interested syntax—empowering some and crippling others. For all groups, but most painfully for the poorer, the severing of mutualities was the result. In an increasingly complex world, the poor and the unemployed were thrown back on state social security and the resources of the family.

CHAPTER SIX

Intermediate Organizations and Social Networks

Between the institutions of business and government, which offered a chilly and somewhat remote face to the unemployed, and the private spheres of family and kin, there lay a complex middle ground of social formations. They included: well-established organizations such as unions and churches; more precariously-funded community centres, associations, and self-help groups; and informal networks of ex-workmates and loose groupings of friends. Within this middle ground, modern urban life took on community forms.

Before presenting two key practices of the informants within this band of social formations, we begin with a brief history of the community response to the unemployment crisis.

Background: Community Response

With their antennae tuned to local happenings, London's community groups and social agencies responded quickly to the high unemployment of 1982–83. Churches stepped up their charity work for needy families and contributed funds to soup kitchens and self-help groups. New organizing and fund-raising expanded the activities of many groups, such as Womanpower (a job-finding and counselling centre for women), organizations for the over-55, and job-finding clubs. The United Way also encouraged and helped finance community responses to unemployment. Conferences on unemployment, sponsored by labour unions, King's College, or the Cross-Cultural Learners' Centre, brought together union leaders, the unemployed, community activists, and academics to exchange information and programming initiatives.

Out of this collective ferment grew three organizations in London targeted specifically on unemployment: the Unemployment Working Centre, the Unemployment Help Centre, and the London Union of Unemployed Workers (L.U.U.W.). The *Unemployment Working Centre* was formed by a loose coalition of community activists, church people, some trade unionists, and members of the public (employed and unemployed). From its early public meetings in November 1982 to the spring of 1983, its growth was astounding. The small volunteer board of directors found itself overseeing a large old building (leased cheaply to it by a religious order), a government grant of $150,000, plus support from the Catholic Church and the United Way, eight paid staff, and assorted volunteers. For the next two years, the Centre offered many services: a drop-in place for the unemployed to talk and have coffee, free child care, fitness classes, a skills exchange, seminars on job search and résumés, and counselling and advocacy on welfare problems.

The ideologies of the active group behind the Working Centre ranged from left to centre. Individual members supported political initiatives (picketing, protests at city council meetings) and they hosted the more militant L.U.U.W. within the Centre's building—but rarely organized political action on their own. The core group's leftism was tempered by its idealistic determination to be a *cooperative* organization, involving even the unemployed in its services and management. It also counted on broad support from throughout the community. That openness was a source of both strength—its tolerant, friendly receptivity to the unemployed—and weakness—the rather blurred organizational image it had in the community. As well, the board's energies were sometimes stretched thin over the various tasks that confronted it: managing volunteers, many programs, and fund-raising.

Gradually, the Centre became outflanked by the other two organizations, whose ideologies and programs were more circumscribed. The *Unemployment Help Centre* became the creature of the powerful, largely conservative London District Labour Council. While occasionally critical in its media statements, it chose to back away from political involvements and the cooperative movement. Conceived as an "agency," offering professional help on job search and social wage claims to unemployed "clients," its authority structure was not cooperative but essentially top-down: from board of directors to officials to clients.

The Help Centre and Working Centre became rivals, having different philosophies and ideological attachments. At one point in 1984, with funding sources tightening despite large numbers of unemployed, there were negotiations over a possible merger between the Working Centre and Help Centre, which proved abortive. The Help Centre could not abide the cooperative organization insisted on by the Working Centre and, once it saw that its funding from United Way was renewed, it abandoned the talks. With more solid support for its individualistic approach—by official labour, the United Way, and the local newspaper—the Help Centre hung on to survive its rival. The Working Centre's funding dried up in 1985 and it folded.

On the left, the *London Union of Unemployed Workers* provided a drop-in centre with job listings, and information/advocacy on unemployment insurance and welfare rights. But, beyond that, under its militant, leftist leadership, the L.U.U.W. quickly became vocal and determined in its view that the unemployed become a political force. In a series of collective actions, it organized rallies and picnics for the unemployed, marches in the style of the 1930s, pickets of Job Mart offices, and protests at City Hall. Its most controversial action, for which some of its members were briefly jailed, was the occupation of the Mayor's office to protest the withdrawal of welfare benefits from clients taking upgrading courses at the community college. While involving relatively few people, their sense of collective purpose was always remarkably firm. Though drawing on some trade union support, the L.U.U.W. actually saw itself as filling a vacuum created by unions' neglect of laid-off members and the unemployed-at-large.

Unions

Before touching on informants' experiences and views of unions, we should first note the complexities of the relation between unions and the unemployed. Unions, as organizations, are accountable first to their employed, dues-paying members: it is *their* wages and working conditions for which the leadership has to fight.

The unemployed—whether laid-off, dues-paying members with a possibility of being phoned back to work, or those further down the waiting list who are drifting away—are more difficult to parse in the union frame of mind. Over time, the unemployed members become too amorphous as a constituency, too diffuse in their needs, for the union bureaucracy to easily represent them. One informant called union offices and could not even find out how many laid-off workers there were in London. But even if the laid-off *were* monitored and organized, the union leadership would have to preside over two dissonant and unequal segments: employed and unemployed members. As well as being potential competitors for the former's jobs, the unemployed might pose a more general threat. The tendency of jobless persons to settle for lower wages and poorer working conditions over time might be seen to undermine an organization devoted to improving wages and working conditions. It was an uphill struggle to try to convince unions that it was in the interests of those members who might one day be laid off to contribute to bringing the unemployed back into the community.

The accounts of the informants who were actually involved with unions (about eight) suggested that, at best, the union apparatus was a sort of sluggish beast which would take the line of least resistance. It would act on behalf of the laid-off or dismissed worker only if the worker aggressively insisted on it. The more typical union response—especially at provincial and national levels—was to cut the unemployed member adrift. In some cases, laid-off workers went down to the hiring hall, got on the list (to avoid having to fulfill the job search requirement), and then waited. It turned out to be just one additional bureaucratic step in the layoff period. A few informants were helped by a union but, more typically, the union machinery failed to start up at all.

Three informants who felt they were unjustly dismissed thought their unions were useless. When MONICA, a single parent of 28, went to her union, in the course of being dismissed from a community college, they uncaringly advised her to take a leave of absence. The officials neither researched her situation, nor followed it up, nor counselled her adequately.

> *They could have gone to the registrar's office and said, "Look, this girl has been working for you very well in registrar's and in financial offices. You personally know she's a good worker. She's having problems with someone in her office. Can you hire her back?" The union sort of brushed off my suggestion.*

Also ANDREA, on Workman's Compensation due to a factory-related injury, was disappointed that the union would not help her with the claim, *"because I'm not working any more. I'm not important enough that they would want to do something for me."* Reminiscent of the critique of other large institutions, she added: *"Because we're not working, and we're not paying dues, we're not...there. There's a tendency to forget about you."*

If the unions' nervousness about the low-wage demands of the jobless may be partially justified, what problems did the unions make for the jobless? Many informants complained about the high-wage demands insisted on by unions. LAURIE thought that unionized workers at Canada Post had driven up the price of labour and made it harder for someone like her to compete for these unionized jobs. *"So the job is pushed out of reach."* The union drive for security for its members in such an unequal labour force had made the lot of the unemployed less secure. But this was not the fault of the unions, simply the inevitable result of a segmented labour market where the risks of unemployment fell unequally among its sheltered and unsheltered groups. The unions had not made the game, but simply were using the pieces available to them and *not* available to the unsheltered jobless. Following Ashton (1986), one can think of the labour market as divided into *sheltered* and *non-sheltered* areas. The sheltered segment can be defined as one that contains devices or organizational niches which protect jobs. A union is a shelter, especially for its more senior members. Professions which provide essential services and where recruitment and standards are internally controlled are sheltered, as are many government workers whose jobs are relatively secure. Craft or skilled workers' unions can influence their internal labour markets as can large firms, which lay out careers for their workers, or recruit internally for job vacancies. The *un*sheltered are those without these protective conditions; they are the unorganized, the working poor, the unskilled or uncredentialled, and those who, because of their age, sex, or race, are passed over by employers.

It was galling to experience the exclusiveness of unions first-hand. BERNARD wanted a job with Otis Elevators, who told him they only hired union members. The union, headquartered in Hamilton, would not take him in unless he was in the work force. *"They push you this way and that, this way and that."* The circuit he was looped into was similar to other "Catch-22" situations known to the unemployed: e.g. the requirement that to be hired one must have experience, which the young cannot get without being hired; or to qualify for welfare money one must have an address which one cannot afford without money.

As a result, some informants' views of unions could be harsh: they were seen as private clubs, whose members *"protected their own asses,"* were *"for themselves,"* who *"don't particularly care"* about those outside the fold. Their high wage demands were thought by some to keep Canadian industry less competitive and, by others, to increase the wage differential among workers. Other critical themes: their leadership was unaccountable to the rank-and-file and too highly-paid; their expensive dues kept the poor out; they offered more support to the older entrenched worker than to the young; their leaders were authoritarian. A few thought unions were too powerful; others thought they were not powerful enough.

Though the negative view of unions predominated, about a dozen informants were positive, arguing that unions were a necessary countervailing power to that of employers. Their very partiality to members' interests was thought to be a source of strength. They were lauded for protecting workers' health and safety on the job, for fighting against unfair dismissal or wage cuts, for arbitrating disputes with supervisors. A few recognized that, without a union, their lower-end jobs would have had lower wages and far fewer benefits. Some specific union accomplishments were singled out for praise. An informant claimed that his father's factory, Ford, had been greatly pressuring its workers to work overtime. One worker went berserk under the strain and began throwing tools around. In response, the union advocated reducing overtime from 10 hours to the regular shift in order to employ more workers. Other contracts, at General Motors and Fanshawe College, were also praised for trying to reduce the workload so that new workers would be hired.

Practices

With that background, we now consider two practices of the informants: "Organizing and Cooperating with Other Unemployed" and "Managing Social Networks and Friends," both of which are situated within the middle range of social formations.

Organizing and Cooperating with Other Unemployed

The informants' experiences and views of unemployment organizations will be presented as they bear on *individual* impacts, and *social* effects. We conclude the treatment of this practice with a look at *mixed and negative views*.

Individual Impacts

Among the 18 informants who participated in one of these organizations, there were those who were simply thankful for the opportunity to *"rub shoulders"* with other people. To those driven into a shell by repeated rejections by employers, these organizations extended an invitation to come out and reconnect. The hospitable atmosphere had a tonic effect. The staff's easy-going interest in people at the Working Centre, one informant generalized, *"helped the psychological well-being and self-esteem* [of the unemployed], *a step in the right direction."*

Apart from the child care, workshops, and the availability of typewriters and copiers, people liked the non-judging, sympathetic *listening* at the Working Centre. The counsellors did not set themselves apart from the clients. One informant was impressed that her counsellor had been unemployed herself, and thus could empathize with her situation. These staff persons were described by another as caring, having *"faith that you want to work and are not a bum."* In minimizing hierarchical distances and stressing common humanity, places like these often had a relaxed and expressive synergy. They formed, in LAURIE's words, *"fellowship communities,…good grassroots places I can go and get what I need. With that bonding, people aren't so isolated."*

The self in these collaborative community settings was neither as elaborately processed as in the state bureaucracies, nor as stacked up with competitors as at labour market sites. Instead, it found itself in a new social space where personal needs and their social handling were far more subtly attuned to each other. The personal facts of the self were not just grist for the official's or interviewer's mill, but were the very substance of a dual process of self-discovery and self-placement on a social map.

This seemed particularly true of the half-dozen women informants who were counselled at *Womanpower*. Unlike Manpower, Womanpower knew your name. While from the objective angle of logistics and responsibility the comparison may be unfair, it still carried the weight of personal experience behind it. Instead of the highly-structured role relationship at Manpower—in some cases to be "filed away" as a non-relationship—Womanpower offered a role relation whose content would thicken with personal detail. The facts of personal history were not simply to be coded or filtered out, but were a resource to be "mined" from the woman-client and applied to the job search. To draw from an older woman's diffuse experience of life in the home, or in unchallenging early jobs, those skills which could be formulated, then developed and presented, on job markets, was no easy feat.

The counsellors who tried to do this—at Womanpower, at some of the centres, or in small self-help groups—were forging new ground in the interaction of the individual and the social milieu. In a relationship at once role-disciplined and personal, the counsellor had to look the client and her "unprocessed" experience right in the face. These encounters required time, a relaxed ambience, an ability to listen to vagueness and silences. Most important, the goal was not to reduce "noise" and converge on one classification, but to *diverge* when necessary onto several paths where the personal and the occupational might meet. The role relationship between counsellor and client was intended to do nothing less than to transmute personal history to the idiom of public life.

Social Effects

Most often in these groups, this keying of the personal to the societal was not one-on-one, but collective. In self-help groups like the job-finding club formed at the Unemployment Help Centre, or the Over-55 club, the synergy was very compelling. For GAIL, the Over-55 club positively teemed with personal accounts. She was struck by the range of job experience among the members, which society seemed not to know how to use. She heard stories that taught her that age discrimination ran like a vein from the job market to the work world. A man associated with the club ran a department at Northern Telecom. The man he reported to was a *"whiz kid"* of 31. As he told GAIL (in her own words), *"I'm 45 and they are starting to look at me funny."* Meanwhile, she recounted, *"they are utilizing this man's experience and knowledge and the whiz kid is being made to look awful good. That to me is utterly ridiculous."* This kind of synergy broke down the self's island of self-regard and stimulated it to identify with and learn from the experiences of others.

Note how this generalizing procedure lifted the veil from the social order, bridging the gap between self and social world which unemployment widened. In these forums for the telling and handling of personal accounts, one's experiences were seen to occur on a more general plane, where they were elements and outcomes of complex practices and discriminations. The social findings learned so vividly with experienced others became conceptual tools of escape from self-blame. No longer a solitary sufferer, one was taking part in a slow, collective awakening to the social conditions from which many suffer. Out of these gatherings of unemployed was born a basis for new solidarities and understandings.

LAURIE's statement that *"there's a lot more bonding between the people"* might not have applied quantitatively throughout society, but it did say something about the qualitative enrichment of the connections which could occur in intermediate groupings. In these groups, practices changed from pure self-interest to the synergistic combining of self and others. Unlike the individualistic model of the marketplace where each person competed for scarce resources, here people *"look out for everybody else and pool their resources,"* according to KENNETH. He went on:

> That is, I think, the most effective way for the unemployed to deal with it. Letting people know where the food bank is, where the services are.... The more eyes you have looking for you, the more likely you are to get that job.

If unemployment organizations amplified individual actions to the collective level of mutual aid, so too did they increase the stature and credibility of the jobless before the social agencies. As advocates of individuals who had been wronged or delayed by the system, staff members themselves were surprised by how quickly individuals received attention when the organizational letterhead framed their inquiries. Even more, when staff members of the Working Centre or the L.U.U.W. went down to the City Hall welfare office with a client, that client felt more confident and sure of his or her rights. The advocate would challenge any discretionary move of officials that went against the client's interests. So when SIMON, 32 and married, was faced with a long delay in U.I.C. benefits following what he thought was an unjust dismissal, he appealed, with the aid of the Unemployment Help Centre. He did not know how he could have done this without professional advocacy assistance. In his words, he valued the *"help in just having the system explained to me before we actually did it* [as well as] *assistance in preparing two separate briefs."*

A handful of informants thought that the unemployment organizations had found the voice of the unemployed—*"We've got a voice,"* said one— and then projected it out into the community as a whole. One thought that to catch the attention of people amid the general collective din, it would have to *"holler and scream,"* alerting citizens and public officials. Some, like ERICA, thought the voice should be quiet and insistent. *"We could say, 'Hey,...we want you to know we are here.'"* A younger informant felt that *"They could put pressure on others, saying, 'Can you help us? Get something going for us?'"* These organizations, according to the informants, should educate the public to the plight of the unemployed, disproving stereotypes that depict the unemployed as "bums" who do not want to work.

Mixed and Negative Views

Approximately half the informants (37) were positive about the unemployed organizing; about a third of them were themselves involved. Nine informants had mixed views, and 17 either doubted its efficacy or held actively negative views. We will round out this treatment of organizing the unemployed by considering these less-than-positive views which offer useful insights into the social identity of the unemployed.

A few informants felt that these organizations constituted just another wasteful bureaucracy. Others thought that they were invisible in the community, or impotent, due to their lack of resources. "*Money talks,*" said one man. "*The unemployed usually go together with no money. They really don't have much power.*" People looked down on the unemployed, added another, "*I don't think people would listen to them.*"

Once together, what basis for making common cause would this heterogeneous group have? They had no positive social identity; they were an aggregate (not a group) who just "happened" to share the derived status of joblessness. University people, Grade 10 students, housewives, construction workers—what would they have to say to one another? The handful of informants pointing this out were relatively educated and middle class. One of them thought the existing organizations catered to "*another class of unemployed*" (she apologized for sounding snobbish).

Class distinctions aside, some informants wondered what would be gained by surrounding oneself with people whose common experience was misery and futility. As GAIL said, "*So many people have given up. In a group with all unemployed people, you are getting a lot of bad vibes and a lot of negative people.*" JANE doubted whether, "*when I'm dealing with my own struggles, I want to deal with other people's struggles.*" Several reactions to organizing the unemployed had this bewildered, defeatist tone. What could the unemployed do about their situation? Their condition was described by one as "*evolutionary.... The unemployed will always be around.*" AGNES put it poignantly:

> What can you do, short of a revolution? I mean, you're a victim. You can think all the thoughts you want, but what can you do about it? You can't do anything about it.

Another view, subtly expressed, held that the unemployed should organize, but not on their own. Alone, their limited resources and weak leverage in centres of power would make them ineffective. And who would be proud to wear the badge of the unemployed? Unemployment was a negative, derived status, often generated impersonally from the workings of the economy. As such, it had little sociocultural content and offered scant basis for organizing. As STAN, 30, an unemployed librarian, remarked:

> *I don't view myself as being a permanently unemployed person; I view myself as being a worker. People who are unemployed right now are still workers and should still have strong ties with people who are working.*

The unemployed union, he conceded, *could* catch those who fell through the union net after they had been laid off. But how much better to have the unemployed band together *with* the employed in cooperative organizations—how much more encouraging and less stigmatizing?

The few *specific* criticisms of unemployment organizations were directed towards the controversial L.U.U.W. Some informants found the organization to be self-promoting and publicity-seeking. So TRACEY, a single parent, charged that the union automatically fought for people whose gas was cut off without exploring the reasons, simply assuming that the utility company was wrong. The anger which the union seemed to run on and to direct towards political ends worried TRACEY:

> *There are angry people in there, angry people who can't find work. They are taking it out on all the other employers in London. Their attitudes are bad; you just have to hear them talk.*

She compared the London Union of Unemployed Workers unfavourably with the Unemployment Help Centre, whom she considered more "professional."

We may conclude by noting a few facts about the distribution of characteristics of those informants who supported organizing the unemployed and those who were against the idea. Generally, women, the poorer informants, those dependent on their partners, the older unemployed (having no peer group) and the longer-term unemployed were more receptive to the idea of organizing the unemployed—as perhaps one way out of a situation that resisted other solutions. Those who opposed such organizing were the young living with their parents, many males, and those unemployed for a short time. Perhaps some young entrants to the labour force and those unemployed for a short time had a common desire to see their joblessness as temporary, and not as part of a wider condition that was likely to last.

Managing Social Networks and Friends

Judging from informants' accounts, the meanings and syntax of relationships with friends and networks changed considerably with unemployment. The connection to *workmates and associates,* which we will examine first, became weaker and harder to sustain. The remaining friends began to be sorted perceptually into *"employed"* and *"unemployed,"* partly because one was unable to afford the reciprocated exchanges of a social life with the employed. We will then consider two models: *moneyed social relations* and social relations that *deviate* from the money standard. Finally, we will compare the social characteristics of those whose *socializing increased* with those whose *socializing was curtailed*.

Former Workmates and Associates

Particularly for those who were laid off, or whose temporary work project had ended, unemployment was often first experienced as a severing of ties, an exit from a significant part of the social world. Informants reported missing the camaraderie, the lunches with workmates, the flow of conversation. The sense of loss seemed especially acute for those informants (often women) who now found themselves in an unstimulating home environment. *"Oh, it's terrible now compared with before,"* according to MYRA, an unemployed housewife. *"I have almost no social life now. Before, my husband was working long hours and I would go out with the people at work. Someone would say, 'There's a show on tonight, let's go.' But now I don't get out at all."* For FRANCES, in her twenties and now home with her parents in a small town, the workplace was valued (and missed) largely because it was there that she made her friends. *"I rely a lot on work to meet people. I like people-oriented jobs. And I just haven't met anybody through work lately."* She added, significantly, that the short-term jobs she took, like telephone sales, did not allow her to develop close friendships.

When the termination of work was particularly harsh—e.g. a firing, or an abusive office situation forcing one out—the humiliated informants shrank from workmates. NORMA's dismissal from the bus company because of a prank left her so upset that she stayed away from her busdriver friends. *"When you hang out with people,"* she commented, *"you've got to pretend you're happy and all that. I just can't bring myself up to it."* She feared that her former colleagues would remind her of what happened or would pry into the incident. From another woman: *"I didn't want to see anyone, I was so down."* The workplace had changed from a zone of useful work with a taken-for-granted social network to a place which evoked positive memories and feelings of rejection. *"Oh no, I couldn't go back,"* said ERICA quickly, referring to a workplace which she had cared about and from which she had been expelled. The fact that the workplace was now seamless again, operating perfectly well without her, almost negated the memory of her time there. How could she recover her personal history in a place from which it had been expunged?

In one odd but instructive case, a female informant actually *was* in a position to sustain relationships with former co-workers. JANINE used to work with her father in his home repair business, even occasionally being put in charge of the workers in his absence. Forced to leave the work due to a pregnancy, now feeling trapped in her home, she described the change in relations with the mostly male workers. When she visited her father at work now, the men *"will look at me a little strangely."* They will smile but not in the lively way they used to. Whereas at one time they looked forward to her coming and would listen to her (especially when she took charge), that was all finished now. No longer a "worker" with status in the eyes of the men around her, she felt diminished. Even the bond with her father had lessened in intensity: *"he's not easy to communicate with now."*

Now outside the ready-made community at work, informants found themselves "losing touch" with former co-workers. These ties, never voluntary in the first place, were a social formation that grew out of, or against, the conditions of employment. The now-outsider had to work to *construct* relationships from outside this supportive framework. Not surprisingly, few informants found that their efforts at keeping up these ties were reciprocated by the insiders. From some of the longer-term and frequently unemployed, one even heard the claim that one simply could not make good friends at work. While undoubtedly true of their marginal work experiences, they might also be recasting those older bonds, diminishing them in retrospect so as to lessen the hurt of separating.

Employed Friends/Unemployed Friends

Informants were asked if most of their friends were employed, or unemployed, or somewhat evenly mixed. A quick sketch of the distribution of characteristics in these categories might be useful for the qualitative analysis to follow. There were 18 informants whose friends were mostly unemployed; 26 whose friends were mostly employed or in school; 13 who had a mixture of employed and unemployed friends; the remainder were unclear, had just moved in, were not answering, etc. (All percentages will be based on the 57 respondents to this question, not the whole sample.)

There was a significant relationship between *age* and the preponderance of employed or unemployed friends. The younger respondents (15–24) were more likely to have mostly unemployed friends (42% of them) than the 25–44 (25%) or 45 and over (22%) age categories. In contrast, the older age groups of the unemployed had mostly employed friends, thus having fewer friends who shared and (possibly) understood their condition.

Marital status (undoubtedly interacting with the youth variable) was also related: of those married or in common-law relationships, 19% had mostly unemployed friends, compared to 41% of the single informants. Of the married's there were 50% who had mostly employed friends, compared to 41% of the singles. The great majority of those with children at home reported that most of their friends were employed or mixed. There seemed to be a shift after marriage and childbirth away from peers sharing the same unemployed situation.

Finally, *social class background* was also related to the extent to which unemployment was shared among one's friends. Comparing the highest class background (I) with the lowest (III) [see Appendix A], we found 29% of class I respondents having mostly unemployed friends, compared with 50% of class III people. The proportion of each group with mostly employed friends was about the same (35%). When we related some of the indicators of *present* class status to the variable of "shared unemployment," the pattern held steady. Comparing those on social assistance with those on Unemployment Insurance (the former probably being more economically deprived than the latter), we found that 40% of social assistance respondents had mostly unemployed friends, compared to 17% of those on U.I. Of those members of families with no employed member (an economically vulnerable group, with many females), 44% of respondents had mostly unemployed friends, compared to 32% in that category for all respondents. Broadly, if we look at the class background and present socio-economic status of those respondents who share the condition of unemployment with most of their friends, we notice signs of class crystallization at the lower levels, a clustering of unemployed with unemployed.

In qualitative terms the unemployed person's movement into employed society was made problematical. Cut off from the "power grid" of work, money, and status that energized most urban citizens, he or she was the bearer of a stigma. A stigma is defined by Goffman as a significant defect or blemish which makes one's actual social identity different from the one expected by "normals." Certain stigmas were noticeable and discrediting, affecting interaction as soon as the stigmatized came into the presence of others. Other stigmas were concealed and potentially discrediting: the bearer had the task:

> of managing information about his failing. To display or not to display; to tell or not to tell;...to lie or not to lie; and in each case, to whom, how, when, and where. (Goffman, 1963: 42)

This latter, "discreditable" stigma (Goffman's term) was the mark on the unemployed.

How did informants manage their discreditable stigmas? There was always the risk of chance encounters with acquaintances, or old high school friends, somewhere in the city. One woman found it hard to run into someone she had known from high school. Sooner or later, out came the dreaded question: *"What are you doing now?"* She had to answer, *"Well, I'm...staying at home."* When called upon to announce one's social identity, one was at a loss. That this incoherence directly impacted upon *personal* identity was evident in this expression by young TERRENCE:

> *It's very hard for me to tell somebody, 'cause it's not like me.... I feel guilty in a way. I feel bad. Everyone has to do something in this world.*

He not only described the felt stigma of being unemployed in an affluent city; he also accepted the cultural bias against which the stigma offended, i.e. the link between the moral injunction to *"do something in this world"* with *employment*.

Some coped with the stigma by withholding themselves from the social round. SIMON commented:

> *I'm not quite so outgoing. I'm not so interested in meeting old friends because then I have to say, "Well, I'm not working." And then, "Well, why aren't you working?" And then.... There has been that negative aspect in my social life.*

Others concealed the truth by deflecting The Question in some artful way. Another tactic was to lie or shade the truth: e.g. to call oneself "self-employed." DICK, a young man, had mostly employed friends, which made him feel like *"one of the unfortunate ones."* There was something of the performance in his meetings with these friends:

> *They ask me, "Oh well, what are you up to?" I say, "Well, I'm unemployed, but I'm doing this and that." I say, "I do this and that" but I never really get around to it—'cause I got to make it sound good, right?*

> *"Oh no, I'm unemployed, so I don't know what I'm going to do now." You know what that's going to sound like.*

He was never sure if they "bought" this: *"It's hard to say what they're really thinking."*

DICK and other informants, ejected from the usual round of getting and spending, began to notice something about conversations: they seemed to be either "Discourses of Shop Talk" or "of Consuming." LORNE said of his friends: *"A lot of them have jobs, you know. It's hard. They'll sit there and talk about their work, and they'll ask you how your work's going. And you'll tell them. And they'll ask you how you get your money. And...when you say you get your money from Welfare, they really don't think too highly of you."* HEATHER found that her employed friends were not only busy, but were preoccupied with how busy they were. They talked about the things they did and the places they saw. *"And they're always chatting about people they're working with.... And I wonder if they're mentioning us to their friends. How she's only staying at home, how she's not working."* Having no work to talk about with her friends,

> *I withdraw from them. I don't say as much. They're going to think I'm boring, so I don't talk to them.*

A few informants reported friends who will nag at them, *"Haven't you got a job yet? Why haven't you found work yet?"*—as though urging them to make themselves alive and knowable in the contemporary idiom.

These questions and the "What Do You Do?" question suggested that "shop talk" was a key way of expressing modern social identities. GAIL made a point of taking an interest in her employed friends, listened sympathetically to their job gripes, tried to stay in the flow—even when she could not contribute much. Informants told how much they missed participating in the great outpouring of shop talk. DOROTHY, the partially-sighted teacher, suggested that unemployment withdrew the tools a person needed to become articulate within the culture.

> *The whole feeling I had...that nobody really understood where I was, what I was going through, what I cared about, what was important to me. Because I was no longer talking about my job as a teacher, in fact I wasn't talking about my job as anything. I had a very strong sense of not fitting in.*

DOROTHY's analysis took it down to identity: *"So much of what we do in our jobs seems to identify us, and sometimes we don't realize how strongly we identify with our occupations. We don't realize that until we don't have one anymore."* Constructing identity, then, with little help from society, becomes the unemployed person's burden.

The second prevailing conversation through which social identities were amplified and displayed was the "Discourse of Consuming." When MATTHEW had employed friends over, they talked about *"the rent they are paying,...the new cars, the movies, the restaurants they've gone out to. It really bothers me. They can't seem to relate to the fact that.... Where am I going to get enough money to get, you know, eggs, bread, for next week."* He has tried to talk to them but *"they don't really understand."* HEATHER, who wanted to keep a connection with her employed friends, steeled herself to listen to the excited talk about new purchases, a new home. Having material ambitions herself, she derided the slow progress of her own "consumption career" when compared with that of her friends:

> *Oh my God, they're going so much ahead of us, and here we are sitting back and...nothing's changing in my life, compared to theirs.... They're saying "We're doing this and that," and I'll think, "We're not going to be doing that for a while."*

Moneyed Social Relations; Dissent from Money

Of course, there was not just symbolic behaviour *about* spending; spending itself was integral to the expressive style of modern friendships. Having money meant being able to buy clothes that could be admired by friends, being able to entertain others, accepting an invitation knowing that one could contribute a gift or bottle of wine to the occasion, going out in pursuit of urban pleasures with one's friends. With money, choices could be made quickly; action was fluid and flexible. The unemployed, up against the moneyed dynamism of their employed friends, felt as though they were in quicksand. ERICA reported her friend saying, *"'Let's have lunch.' I can't afford to have lunch; I don't want to tell her that. They just don't understand that I can't go out and spend $5.00 on a lunch."*

There was a marked change in the syntax of practices as the unemployed tried to relate with their employed friends. Money had not only become part of the idiom within which urban social relations occurred. It was as though money had imperceptibly become the real subject in our social lives, and we had become participants in the life it conferred. Money so amplified and indulged the ego of the employed consumer that *its* enablements conditioned the direction of social life, rather than the conscious will of the person with money. This left the unemployed friend trailing feebly in the wake of the other's consumer drive. MARIANNE provided an instance: *"When Doris and I go out to dinner, which we haven't done for quite a while, I order the cheapest thing on the menu. I order a beer. She orders the most expensive thing, an exotic drink, you know [laughs].... I feel like a second-class cousin."*

The voice of action inescapably changed, slipping into passivity. In a culture where leisure was largely purchased, it was the possession of money (or at least freedom from worry about money) which gave people the confidence to take the initiative in friendship. For the unemployed, then, the active, self-initiating social life declined. *"If you can't pay your way, you don't want to go anywhere."* The tense of action for the unemployed person was very much in the present, oriented towards making ends meet. Even for those unemployed who *did* have adequate money, such as DOROTHY, money was not used to enhance a lifestyle, but to cling to for security. *"Were I in a different position financially.... I would be far worse off. Going out for a lunch or a dinner or to a movie as often as I do would not be possible. I think my periods of depression would be far more intense, of longer duration. Because I need that social life, I need that activity."*

Some informants found that their employed friends were understanding, up to a point. They showed empathy with the unemployed experience, supported political efforts to have more job creation and better social programs, and invited the unemployed friend to do things that did not cost money. One form of help, however, drew an aversive reaction. Often, employed friends paid the unemployed person's way, or offered to lend money. The informants, almost universally, recoiled from this generosity. Their words were blunt: *"If they pay, I feel bad." "They're always buying me stuff, I feel like a mooch, I hate that." "I feel guilty that they're giving."* This one-way giving violated the value of self-reliance at the core of our personal and social identities. As well, it was not good for friendship, which required reciprocity. As AGNES put it, *"You don't keep a friendship alive by being a recipient."* Most of all, it was to be invited to a game where one could not win.

This atomizing division between friends—those with money and those without—was often felt as a personal disjunction between the informants and their employed friends. GLENNput it this way: *"They're still my friends but in a way they're not, because I don't have money and they do."* The ties began to loosen. Once the symmetry of the relationship was recast, it became harder to freely approach people. BERNARD said that he hated to go to his friends now because they might *think* that he was begging, that he wanted something. All of this pointed up "the relative helplessness of people who have developed a life-style and value system around consuming and know of no other" (Fineman, 1987: 238).

Some informants could not take the lack of fit between their new situation and that of their employed friends, and totally changed groups. ALICE, single and 21, said, *"Now everyone I hang around with isn't working. I just changed my group. Because maybe I just don't feel I fit in with them anymore."* KENNETH, finding that his employed friends tended to blame the victim, now associated with the unemployed: *"We don't want to deal with that problem of being put down."*

Power relations tilted towards employed friends. Like some family members and caseworkers, they often patronized and stereotyped the unemployed. Some berated the unemployed for laziness; they said, "Take anything, your standards are too high." Those who were employed, single, and living with their parents had no clue, according to informants, how difficult it was to be poor while living on your own, or to be raising a family while unemployed.

> *They don't know what it's like to go to 17 interviews and not get anything from it…or to have a job that they hate and quit it.*

Employed friends inflicted petty humiliations on the unemployed person, as with DICK. DICK had a friend who called him up and suggested they go to Blenheim.

> *So he asks me, "Got any money for gas or anything like that?" I go, "Not much." "Well, how much is 'not much'?" I say, "Well, a few dollars." He says, "OK, I'll be down in an hour. I'll pick you up and we'll go…."*
>
> *So I wait an hour, and he wasn't around. Two hours, wasn't around. Three hours, wasn't around. So…. They sort of don't want to be bothered with you because you've got no money, right? Now if you had a job for $12 an hour, bringing $500 a week home. "Oh yeah, OK, we'll go to the bar, no problem, eh?" If you're unemployed, sort of push you aside, right?*

A potentially transforming element could be found in the informants' critique of social relations based on money, and their vision (and practice) of the *true friendship* which could replace it. Informants were critical of the almost mechanical reciprocity of "If I buy this time, you should buy next time." In a *"good friendship, you don't have to worry about it."* KENNETH found that, out west, *"just about everybody working wrapped his own little cocoon around himself, and nobody would reach out and help anybody else, until that recession hit."* As another described the employed's attitude: *"I've got a job, I couldn't care less about you."* JANE, an artist, lashed out at people for whom consuming was all-important:

> I'm not going to play in that league.... I refuse to be in the company of people who look down on me because I don't have material goods. I don't want their friendship anyway.... We don't have friends who are into owning houses and redecorating. No thanks.... And maybe in that sense I'm discriminating out of my best judgement.

Part of the force here might be her rejection of the rejecters, but clearly moneyed relationships disgusted her.

The informants felt that money should have nothing to *do* with friendship. It was too shallow, too exterior—like the "currency" of appearance on the job market. MARY counted on the visits from her employed friends, who liked her personality, what was *"inside her,"* and did not judge her by where she lived (subsidized Ontario Housing). BOB expected his friends to see his living self, not just another face in the jobless horde.

> They don't ostracize me because I'm unemployed—we went to high school together.... Anyone who would look down on their unemployed friend, that person's no friend.

Yet he did not want to do away with stereotypes, only asked that his friends exempt *him*.

> But you may look down on unemployed people in general. Like, "Why is that rubby not doing anything? He is in that position because he wants to be." Or those welfare people: "I cannot believe you cannot find any work whatsoever." I can find work, but I want to be with my wife and kid. People who are on welfare for 10 years are robbing the system. I can see you looking down on that. But a friend?

The informants' experience and vision of true, generic social relations was usually not as discriminatory as the above. Ideally, social life should be low-cost. The unemployed person should not be asked to do anything that costs money, which would be divisive. As ALLEN put it, *"We'd sit around and play cards, go out somewhere together; friendship isn't based on money."* *"Real friends,"* often sorted out from the others after the job loss, regarded one as still fully human, still part of the human community. *"They stood by me regardless, and were more anxious to help me than to find fault."*

Apart from some loyal employed friends and certain members of family, the people most eligible for this unadorned type of friendship were other unemployed people. The friends without work were valued by informants, particularly the young, for *"knowing the score," "knowing what you're going through,"* for being able to *"provide a support network,"* because *"we have the same struggle."* Unlike the employed who were *"all going in directions that are different,"* among the unemployed (as STEVE put it), *"You've got people doing the same thing beside you."* STEVE went further:

> You can understand when a person goes moody, you know why they're moody. You know whether to stay away, or come close and be supportive. You know whether to just hold them or just talk about what their problem is. Even just talking makes you feel better. You're in the same situation, but it helps.

Conversation was freer and less guarded. Friendship came out of common struggle, and there were no moneyed props or distractions to divide people. The human scale of friendship for the unemployed, though *feeling* smaller within the distorting mirrors of capitalist social relations, actually approximated a sought-after human ideal. Marx captured this ideal in a famous expression, at the end of the section on money: "Let us assume man to be man, and his relation to the world to be a human one. Then love can only be exchanged for love, trust for trust, etc.… Every one of your relations to man and to nature must be a specific expression, corresponding to the object of your will, of your real individual life" (Marx, 1964 [1844]: 193–194).

Particularly among older informants, however, who were less bonded to peer groups, there was the feeling that unemployed friends were not enough. A few informants even avoided other jobless people or because *"they get me down."* COLLEEN suggested broadening the choice of friends:

> Have people around you who are not all in the same boat, people that can give you hope, and have some people around you that are in the same boat, so you can discuss how things are going. You'll have bad days, and you'll want to talk to somebody who's been through it…and can give you advice on whether to take a job, or what to do in the meantime. Keep a well-rounded group of friends around you.

This suggested alternation of friends, however, was never easy. Monetized culture had so widened the gap between employed and unemployed friends that they seemed to inhabit different sensibilities, with different levels of effective energy. The ambitious unemployed person became a kind of marginal figure, kept by ambition from identifying with the jobless, and by economic deprivation from identifying with the employed. So HEATHER, for instance, moved from one set of friends to the other. When her employed friends talked about all the things they had done and bought, she and her husband became disgusted. *"I'm not interested in this, the way I should be…. I don't care what they've got."* Then they would *"fall back to people who are not as advanced."* But she recoiled from them as well: *"Oh my God, I can't stand being with people who aren't trying to do anything. Then I revert back to the other group of friends and climb the ladder of success with them."*

This swinging between sets of friends—already divided in the social order—recalled the distinction made by the anthropologist, Clifford Geertz (1968), between "models of" and "models for" social reality. He found that certain rituals of preliterate peoples presented "models of" the group's actual norms and beliefs while others suggested "models for" the group's adaptation to change. In the study at hand, the informants found that other unemployed people provided them with "models of" their present situation: understandings, tips, ways of coping—matters in which employed friends could not help. As for the "model for" moving ahead into the future, there was a divergence. For the older and more individualistic informants, it was the *employed* who provided the "model for" the future; whereas among the younger, more socially conscious informants, the way ahead was to be found in the human, non-materialistic relationships with their jobless peers.

Socializing More; Socializing Less

The informants were asked to compare their social lives now with the time when they had been employed: did they socialize more, the same, or less than before? Excluding those who did not answer or simply had always been loners (12), of the remaining 63:

- 13 had socialized *more;*
- 36 had socialized *less;*
- 14 had socialized the *same.*

Leaving aside those whose social lives were stable, what can we learn by comparing the characteristics of those whose social lives had expanded with those whose social lives had contracted?

SEX. Women (mostly single) were more likely than men to increase their socializing (25%) or to keep it stable (33%). Of the men, only 13% socialized more and 4% socialized the same, while a huge *83%* socialized *less* than before (compared to 43% of the women). This may have been due to women's greater connectedness to their community and kin network. It is also possible that men found unemployment more injurious to their social identity (involving a greater departure from the male provider role) than did women and thus held back from social contact.

AGE. Looking at the age groups, the percentage socializing more, declined with age. The percentage socializing less dramatically increased—46% of those aged 15–24 socialized less, compared to 91% of those 45 and over. Social networks thinned out with age. They began to cluster around work roles, and when these were exited, not only work associates, but employed friends were lost.

DURATION. Of those unemployed for more than one year, only 5% socialized more, where 74% socialized less—a really marked drop in socializing compared to those unemployed for shorter periods.

MARITAL STATUS. Of the single informants, about a third socialized more, a third less, and a third the same. Of those married, a remarkable 84% socialized less. Looking at the 16 married informants who socialized less, we note that many of them had children. Most of the divorced and separated with children also socialized less. As well, *all* housewives and househusbands reported socializing less. The married unemployed, especially those drawn deeper into the responsibilities of the family, withdrew from a social life outside.

POOR. The presently poor, as indicated by the absence of an employed person in the family household, and by the receipt of social assistance, overwhelmingly reported that they socialized less (75% and 69% respectively). Contrary to this, Mother's Allowance informants socialized more.

MOBILITY. Those very or somewhat mobile informants were significantly more likely to have reduced social lives than the immobile. The former groups have an average of 17% socializing more, compared to 26% for the immobile, and an average of 66% socializing less, compared to 44% of the latter. (It is difficult to know what is cause and effect between willingness to be mobile and amount of social life.)

Some general conclusions from this empirical sketch can be drawn. Taking social networks as that part of intermediate social formations in which we are freely drawn by others into wider community ties, the informants' participation in these networks became markedly unequal with unemployment. Those who were older disengaged from social groups at an even more accelerated rate; those unemployed for a lengthy period withdrew; and those who were forced more heavily into family responsibilities had less time for friends. Also, those who were poor and male curtailed their social lives. This cutting back of social life was the principle movement in the informants' relations with friends. A secondary, opposite movement towards a re-invigorated social life was also noticed among single women, the young, and some of the better-off.

Conclusions

The empirical idiom of intermediate social formations—with the exception of unions—was richer and more collectively orchestrated than the domains of job market and government agency. By and large the informants approved and often made use of the various organizations that offered a place to the unemployed. Relationships within these organizations had a fluid, flexible quality: at once looser and more personal than the ties to employers and governments, yet more objective and voluntary than the "hot-house" bonds of family life. They invited the unemployed to enter into practices which expressed and made thematic their personal and social identities—at a time when both dimensions of self were either under attack or in retreat from public life.

Taking the three unemployment organizations—the Unemployment Working Centre, the Unemployment Help Centre, and the London Union of Unemployed Workers—each had distinct inflections in the practices they formulated with and for their clients. The *Working Centre* linked individuals with others in cooperative groups. It offered to the unemployed person— through its contacts, programs, information—an abundance of synergistic possibilities. It embodied and encouraged self-help and placed the person at the centre of counselling.

The *Help Centre* tended to view people as individual clients seeking professional assistance—whether in résumé-writing, advocacy, or whatever. The counsellor played a directive role, but with the intention of activating the client—thus the voice could be described as passive/active. The counselling practice was keyed to a more competent interaction with employers—or government officials—but in the individual's interests.

The *L.U.U.W.* cast individuals as class agents, who shared interests with a latent class of millions of strangers, similarly related to the means of production. Its syntax was active-oriented, especially in its politics and counselling practices on behalf of the poor and unemployed. Its direction was outward, trying to expand its own small membership, and to form coalitions with or struggle against other organizations.

Yet the impact of these organizations on most of the 25,000 or so unemployed in London in those years was limited. Underfunded, lacking in political strength or strategic expertise, unable to offer employment—these intermediate groupings suffered from their own disconnections from the synergies of the city. Unlike other organizations, they had no professional credentials or independent power base—but depended on funding agencies.

There were other factors that weakened them. Social action as a response to a negative social identity seemed to occur when the following conditions obtain (Tajfel 1981, cited in Brown, 1986: 562):

- Personal movement is impossible;
- Group definitions are clear;
- The dominant power is perceived as not legitimate;
- The dominant power is insecure.

Many of the unemployed—especially those likely to be short-term and having no expectation of being discriminated against—sought and expected personal movement out of unemployment. As mentioned, there was no basis for a clear group definition. Finally, the dominant powers—employers, government—were mistrusted but not often radically questioned on their legitimacy. These powers had little reason to be insecure, given the individualizing and isolating impacts of modern unemployment.

As for social networks and friends, there was an ever more prominent "macro-author" joining in the formulating of practices. This was the *monetization of culture and community*. Partly stimulated by (and stimulating) the growth in services, urban Canadians had come increasingly to *purchase* their means to leisure and a social life. Social patterns and expectations changed: friends were expected to have cash and to be fluid and at home on the leisure markets of the city. Areas of entertainment and socializing that were *non*moneyed were looking somewhat shabby and unstimulating.

Marx wrote of the spurious enlargement of the person who has money within capitalism (Marx, 1964 [1844]: 191). "That which exists for me through the medium of money," he wrote,

> that which I can pay for,…that I am, the possessor of the money. The properties of money are my own (the possessor's) properties and faculties. What I *am* and *can do* is, therefore, not at all determined by my individuality. I *am* ugly, but I can buy the most beautiful woman for myself. Consequently I am not *ugly*, for the effect of ugliness, its power to repel, is annulled by money.

The necessary complement to the inflated powers which money conferred was the diminished value of the offerings of those without money. As an informant put it: *"I don't have anything apart from friendship to give back."* This devaluing of the unemployed under capitalism decisively affected their relations with friends. Work associations tended to unravel into non-relationships. The shared experiences were in the past tense; the voice of action started as an active attempt to keep up ties but the asymmetry of effort (*"I was always calling them"*) led to breakdown. Many employed friends came to be avoided, as one was cut out of the possibility of reciprocity with them. Social life was curtailed, especially as one became poorer, worn out, more involved with family, older.

Yet among those employed friends who kept the faith and understood, among those friends who were in a similar situation, there were synergistic possibilities that sustained social and personal identity. Within these solidarities was kept alive the vision and practice of a true community on the human scale—beyond anything money could buy or make possible.

CHAPTER SEVEN

The Imposed Practices of Daily Life

Unemployment is a lived experience in everyday life. Far from just a matter of job markets and labour flows, being unemployed affects how one sleeps and eats and goes about the daily round of tasks at home. To grasp this impact, it may be helpful to divide daily practices in two (Weigert, 1981: 198). When we make time—either for personal uses, or to connect our time with other people's—we are involved in "temporal construction." Yet we must also cope with external demands on our time, i.e. "temporal imposition." "Our biographies," Weigert writes, "could be analyzed as continuous overlapping processes of temporal construction or temporal imposition..." (1981: 198). In these terms the key question becomes: how did unemployment change the usual (i.e. employed) pattern of "constructed" and "imposed" practices in our informants' daily lives?

We asked the 75 informants many questions on this topic: how they organized their day; what they thought of various units of time (parts of the day, week, etc.); how they carried out and felt about housework, shopping, and other routine tasks. Their *constructed* practices—those which were chiefly personal and self-guided—will be dealt with in the next chapter. *This* chapter analyzes the practices *imposed* from the outside, especially from the fact of being poor in a cash economy and less mobile. The social practices under review here are two:

- Losing Ground;
- Economizing and Consuming.

Many other imposed practices could be mentioned, of course, including child care, division of labour between husband and wife, dealing with government officials, and so on, but they are prominently dealt with in other chapters. To avoid redundancy, and to expand treatment of the practices remaining, I have been deliberately selective.

Practices

Losing Ground

If one were to fly over a community on a weekday morning, each house and neighbourhood would seem almost like a centrifuge, dispersing its members to various centres in the city: to offices, schools, stores, factories, playing fields. From the view at the city's centre, all these bodies in motion appear to be pulled into convergent nodes of activity. Then at the end of the day, the "forces" reverse themselves: the city centres now almost fling their daytime occupants outward. The peripheral communities or suburbs appear to draw people inward: into their boundaries, streets, and homes.

The chief termini of this vast daily ebb and flow between the territories of the city and the residential zones are the home and the work-place, which are complexly related. Sometimes they are antagonistic: the work-place demands energies that strain the family, or life at home pulls the worker's interest from the job. More often than not, they seem to the modern person to be complementary. The work-place provides income, outside stimulation, and news, plus a kind of objective briskness in its activities. The home, on the other hand, refreshes the spirit, motivates, and renews the worker in the daily journeys into the work-place.

If the modern home can be considered a complement to the work-place, its history has given it a very different dynamic and atmosphere. In pre-industrial Canada, the family homestead was the site of family life and of production. Then industrialization brought society's productive work outside the home, into its factories, offices, mines, and so on. From the more bounded locales of the homestead and the local market, we have moved to a more expansive field of action: the modern city. The family, stripped of its productive role, has taken on new functions: developing social manners and consumption styles, and fostering personal growth.

The new field of action, the city, has expanded in scale and in the rate of mobility required to pursue its opportunities. We can define *"scales"* as spatial dimensions of varying scope within which people in a society act, and are acted upon. As indicated earlier, they include home, neighbourhood, suburb, city, region, nation-state, world. I want to add to this the concept of *"mobility rate,"* i.e. the rate at which space is experienced and moved through—a concept which embodies both space and time. When people own a fast means of mobility like a car, they have more control over their space and time than someone with a bike, for instance. They can reach any corner of the complexly-scaled society out there (control over space). They can also efficiently align their own schedules with the schedules of the institutions and resource-suppliers they need to reach (control over time). It should be added that these are interactive processes: the widespread use of cars *stimulates* and makes possible the expanding urban scale in the provision of services, work, entertainment, and so on. The car not only gets you there, it helps expand the there you are getting to.

Consider some of the spatial layers of the modern city:

CITY
SUBURB
NEIGHBOURHOOD
STREET
HOME

(A)   (B)

The (A) arrow refers to an experience of space which moves outward from the home to higher scales, where (B) describes an experience of space "down the scale" to ever more localized levels. (We have already sketched the daily movements of commuters up and down the scale.)

What spatial experiences of the community do the informants have? We look first at their *means of mobility*. We then chart the movements of a small number into *larger spatial involvements* in their community, i.e. up the scale (A). Finally the major movement (B) will be sketched: the *compression* of the unemployed into smaller-scale spaces, particularly the home.

Means of Mobility

Most informants, lacking a car, spent a good deal of their day on foot or on bicycle. With low incomes, and sometimes, children to consider, regular bus transportation was often unaffordable. People walked to look for work, to hunt for bargains, to visit friends, to check the Canada Manpower boards, or see their government worker. The disadvantages of slow mobility in a city were considerable. Being without "wheels" diminished the spatial scale they could cover. They were forced to shop or look for work within a limited area, thus reducing choice. Having to walk to several places in a day also reduced their productivity and made it difficult to control their time. One could not always estimate walking distances to opportunities that arose during the day.

While only a small minority owned cars, which were often quite old or in need of repair, many of the comments on transportation were centred on them. Influenced by the culture of the automobile, many informants talked of yearning to buy a car, trying to repair one, worrying that theirs would break down, or trying to use someone else's. There were informants who at one time *had* had access to a car and were now without it. They spoke of this loss in tones of mourning, as though they had been deprived, not just of a means of transportation, but of a part of their social identity.

DICK had done mostly seasonal and unskilled work. He had managed to buy a truck but was struggling to make the payments. Time weighed heavily on his hands and, apart from housework and TV, he worked on his truck. He spent four hours every few days cleaning it, washing every part of it, waxing it. But, unable to afford gas, he rarely was able to use the truck. Even for the unemployed, the automobile, cherished vehicle of mobility and escape in our culture, did not lose its attraction. Indeed, the relative *im*mobility of the jobless made the car even more desirable. Cleaning his vehicle did not just pass the time for DICK, but kept shiny a future hope of mobility.

The repossession of a car is a bitter experience. ALLEN, newly married at 22, had been working in construction and clearing almost $400 a week. While looking around a car lot, a salesman convinced the couple that they should buy a car. As construction was seasonal work, ALLEN was a little surprised (but pleased) when his loan application was approved by the bank. The loan was set for four years at fluctuating interest rates. Then two things happened to make ALLEN's car payments virtually impossible to bear. First, after quitting a job in Toronto due to what he considered to be intolerable working conditions, he had been unable to find work for 12 months. When his Unemployment Insurance benefits expired he was desperate. The second factor was interest rates, which had gone up to 19 1/2 per cent.

He went to the bank to ask them to renegotiate the loan over a longer term, since he could not afford to make the present payments. The bank had, after all, offered (several months earlier) to consolidate his few debts at a lower overall rate; surely they would agree to do it now. The bank said no. *"When it was good for them, they wanted to renegotiate,"* ALLEN commented. *"But when I wanted to renegotiate, they said, 'Forget it, you're not working, we're not going to renegotiate the loan.'"*

Two weeks later, ALLEN received a bailiff's card, informing him that the bank was about to repossess the vehicle. With the bailiff's advice, he opted for bankruptcy—in case, after the bank sold the car, they demanded whatever principal was still left to pay. The reflections of this young man, who became active in the London Union of Unemployed Workers, are worth quoting:

> *I can't understand the reasoning behind refusing.... If I'm unemployed, the money's just not there.... The worst part about it is if I hadn't made an attempt to do anything about it, attempt to renegotiate...I'd go on: "It was my own fault," and I'd be depressed about it. But I tried, I made an effort to meet them halfway, but they wouldn't go for it. So that makes me angry.*

*I like these commercials...the Bank of Commerce, when you see Anne Murray sing,
"The bank that cares, the bank that has the people in mind." I laugh when I see
these commercials.*

We now look at the informants' experiences of community space.

Expanding Spatial Experience

Many younger people moved more freely through the downtown area
than before. As STEVE put it: *"When I was working it was basically home to
work, home to work, home to work. Now it's home, downtown, floating around
the artistic underground."* Freed from the directional, linear groove from
"home to work," they could move laterally, against the grain. While inhabiting unconventional space and time, the informants' journeys turn
up surprises. GORD remarked: *"Yeah, I'll get on my bike and go downtown,
and I'll see things that I never saw in my car."* One day, he had biked down
to see the work on the Horton Street extension and discovered a nearby
children's centre. He met a woman working there that he had known
years ago and proceeded to renew the acquaintance. This would never
have happened (he felt) if he had not been on his bike.

Of course, people did not simply explore the city. They went to the
Employment office, hung around the youth centres, saw their welfare
worker. Few talked of meeting other unemployed, but in fact some did
go regularly to the Unemployment Working Centre or the London Union
of Unemployed Workers for a coffee or volunteer work. One man met a
group of "regulars" at the Woolworth's grill where they talked politics,
and learned about such short-term jobs as driving a rented car to Toronto. Some moved through the downtown area looking for bargains, shopping, or looking for work.

Apart from downtown—and the few dozen or so informants who used
it more than before—in what other spatial scales beyond the home did
the informants act? Many spent time in nearby parks and libraries, the
importance of which cannot be overstated. Parks and libraries not only
offered the fruits of nature and civilization, but did so in such a way that
money or class distinctions were muted. Of all public spaces, parks and
libraries were perhaps the least defeating for the unemployed and poor.

Most important in the interviews were reports of informants *reclaiming*
public space in their own neighbourhoods. They walked up and down
the streets of their working class areas or subdivisions. Some shopped lo-
cally. Being closer to home meant, for a handful of informants, that the
neighbourhood came into view, as though a mist were lifting. What once
was "ground," something to pass through on the way to work, was now
"figure." The small circumference around one's home, defined by the
limits of walking distance, did frustrate the job search. But it also circled

a potential community space, both familiar and unknown, in which neighbours "appeared" as potential members of community.

Two married women reported that, after they were cut off from work—and from work-based friendships—they "discovered" their neighbours. One was MYRA who plunged in and actively made contacts with neighbours she never used to speak to. The other woman, JOANNE, took a slower route. Very distressed at having to quit her job, she acutely missed the lunches and the *"gabfests"* with friends at work. She at first withdrew into her home: *"I didn't want to see anybody. I was so down."* She began to regret that she had not cultivated relationships in her neighbourhood, and that they could not take up the slack. Slowly she became involved in church activities in which she made friends who lived in the neighbourhood. Gradually, the potential community around her took on a dimension of depth.

A good example of seeing the local community with fresh eyes was provided by EVA. When asked whether she used different parts of the community now more than before, she replied:

> *Yeah, my own neighbourhood. I hang around here more. Because I'm not downtown, I'm not on the bus going to work. I'll spend time in my own neighbourhood which I never did before. We've been here for about four or five years, but you know, in the next block over there's this great house. And I'll just wander around. There's a coffee shop just up the street I didn't know was there. There's all kinds of things I didn't know about before.*

While not typical of the informants, there was a progressive content in this practice of rediscovery. Against the centrifugal flight from home and community, which our culture encourages and our expanding city scales require, there came this curious exploration of neglected ground—ground that should be inhabited, on which people would be happy to work. Though kept local against their will, the unemployed may instruct us on new uses of community.

The Compression of Spatial Experience

The predominant movement, however, is not (A), up the scale into wider contexts beyond the self, but (B), an imposed compression into tighter, more localized spaces. Though the local community *is* an important focus for the unemployed, many suburbs and subdivisions have few opportunities, little interesting society or scenery—and make the relatively immobile unemployed who live in them feel "stuck" or isolated. They have to take a bus to walk somewhere interesting.

The environment many of the informants felt trapped in was the *home*. ALLEN, after his car was repossessed, began to withdraw from social life outside the home. Not having worked enough insurable weeks for Unemployment Insurance, rejecting social assistance as unthinkable, he and his wife lived on her disposable income of $500 a month. Too proud even to ask his friends for a lift, they could not get to the beach or around the countryside. The home had become a virtual prison for him, from which he escaped by job-hunting and doing volunteer work with the London Union of Unemployed Workers. Anything was *"better than to stay home rotting.... There's nothing else to do, so you end up eating, eating, eating."* In the absence of meaningful work, "free" time at home could become un-free, under the direction of appetite.

Lacking transportation or resources, people stayed in much of the time. Some accepted this. Those who did not sometimes came to mistrust the people around them—as though these others were tainted with the un-freedom of the place. WARREN, living in poor circumstances with a wife and children, felt threatened by a social world which impinged on him so menacingly, controlling his life. One self-imposed limit on their social life was his feeling about baby-sitters in the area: *"You can't trust anyone, they'll screw you blind."*

Another informant, FRANCES, living in her parents' small town, partly against her will, expressed her alienation in a literary way. She described a freak character in Sinclair Lewis's *Main Street* with whom she identified:

> *The character in the novel always feels that the townspeople are watching her through their curtains. A paranoia. When she catches people watching, it's a real paranoia. And I'm going through the same things here.*

There is a element of projection here. FRANCES felt that her situation was strange—a woman in her late twenties with a Master's degree in sociology acting as a kind of live-in maid for her family. She assumed others in the town shared that view. A few other informants similarly imagined that the "generalized other" of the community was aware and critical—"watching" them even when they were at home alone.

There was something de-vitalizing about being at home when it was no longer a pendant to the work-place. A parallel between home and morning suggests itself. Just as morning is a promising time, the prelude to a gift of energy to the world—perhaps home is promising *space*, an anteroom to significant participation in the social world. But, with un-employment, the home lacks that prospective, outward-looking character; it becomes a shell encasing arrested development. More strongly, the home can become a vortex, drawing people in protectively, weakening their social impulses. One mother stayed home more in the winter, which depressed her, because she found it too much of an effort to bundle the children up. Listen to some of the other expressions:

I don't have the desire to get out.... I'm not as active. I get into a slump very easily, and someone will phone up and say, "Oh come on out!" but I just don't feel like it. (MARTHA)

Sometimes I just sit at home and mope. (EMMA)

I don't go out at all. I'm more stuck at home. I get bored, there's nothing to do.... I'd like to go driving once in a while, go out and do things. But now I don't have the money to do things anymore. (JANINE)

Not go out. I could spend four days not stepping out of that door. [When he gets a brief landscaping job for his friends:] *I feel very active. I want to work through the 24 hours. But when that job finishes, that's when I lapse into that, sort of...* (BERNARD)

The analogy of chess pieces running out of moves on the board comes to mind. The "squares" on the societal board lost to them were precisely those vital strategic spaces mentioned earlier: the offices, corridors, committee rooms, classrooms, and shops of the city. The final square for the informants, the home, was the stillest space on the societal scale. The motion was slow and bounded within four walls. It was pervaded by inertia, rather than focussed energy. Most of those who talked about being trapped in this way had been unemployed for over six months, many over a year. As affirmed in the last quote above, and others like it, people longed for their powers to be used, to attain to that active state which is natural to them.

Economizing and Consuming

The Informants' Incomes

For a community of between 100,000 to 499,999 (London's category), the 1984 low-income cut-offs were as follows:[1]

- An unattached individual $ 9,345
- A family of 2 $12,321
- A family of 3 $16,456
- A family of 4 $19,017

How did the informants' reported incomes compare with these figures?

Only about a dozen individuals and families in the sample had incomes *above* these cut-off points, adjusted for family size. But their incomes

---

[1] We will use 1984 figures from the Poverty Profile (National Council of Welfare, 1985). The basic poverty line is the Statistics Canada Revised Low Income Cut-offs (1978 Base). These are founded on recent consumer surveys which reveal that the average Canadian family spends 38.5% of its income on food, clothing and shelter—the basic essentials. Statistics Canada then adds 20% to that to get the low income cut-off point. So those Canadians who spend more than 58.5% on food, clothing, or shelter are judged to be living in straitened circumstances, i.e. are below the poverty line. Income figures at the cut-off points are found for families and communities of various sizes.

were modest, reaching at best, about $6000 above the poverty lines. Among the non-poor informants were unionized factory workers still on Unemployment Insurance benefits; a small number on substantial disability benefits; and, people living with and supported by either parents in financially secure homes or by well-paid spouses. For Unemployment Insurance benefit recipients, the hold on a non-poor income was often precarious and temporary—after 50 weeks, they would be cut off (or cut down to social assistance). These "exhaustees" formed a large part of the new poor in the 1980s.

About two-thirds of the informants were *poor*, with incomes well below the 1984 cut-off figures. We can look at the incomes of certain subgroupings within the sample.

The *sole support parents* in the sample, women with one or two children, made between $4320 a year ($360 a month) and $6912 ($576 a month)—giving them incomes of between 35% and 56% of the low-income cut-off for a family of two ($12,321 as indicated above). The *younger and older families*—especially those with only one earner, or those headed by workers in the service sector—were making between $6000 and $9000 a year, which is half to two-thirds of the cut-off figure of $12,321. *Younger informants* were paid from $270 up to $340 a month (the last figure if they were living alone).

When the more marginal workers of any age finally worked enough insurable weeks to qualify for Unemployment Insurance, their benefit levels—based on their poor-paying jobs—were very low. A gas station job yielded one man a U.I. benefit of $222 a month. *Long-term unemployed* informants with families, particularly if they had to rely on the spouse's income, found themselves far below the poverty line. So MATTHEW lived on his wife's part-time income of $8000. With four children, not even help from parents and a subsidized mortgage could keep his family solvent; they received food relief from his church. Older married women laid off from jobs, no longer able to contribute to the family earnings, were forced into dependence on their husbands' barely adequate incomes. Older women living alone after a layoff found that their Unemployment Insurance benefits were low, and there was only temporary office work and a small pension to look forward to.

These categories among the informants definitely reflected the new groups that were appearing in the ranks of the poor in the 1980s (National Council of Welfare, 1985; Shaw, 1985). The fact that many of the informants were receiving social wages (social assistance, unemployment insurance, and so on) in no way rescued them from poverty. As the National Council of Welfare study points out, for 1983: "Almost half of families whose major source of income is government transfer payments...were poor ..."

Beyond statistics, what were the informants' concrete experiences of poverty? A poor individual or family must spend such a large part (often 75% or more) of its income on necessities—food, shelter, clothing, utilities—that it must endure a whole series of *economies* which cut back its participation in the mainstream of society. One informant put it plainly: *"There is little left over once the bills are paid."* The various economies forced on the poor ranged from those in the least essential areas ("expressive" spending) to the most (food). Drawing on the interviews, we will look at each in turn.

Expressive Spending

If there was a little money to spend, LAURIE admitted, she would buy an article of clothing that would last, rather than a case of beer to bring to a party. Poor informants were often forced to abandon the expressive aspects of spending to make ends meet. But, in our moneyed culture, it is in the spending of *surplus*, not essential, income that social and personal identities tend to be expressed. It was this expressive spending that the informants seemed to miss the most.

People were pained, for instance, at not being able to buy gifts. JANINE commented:

> *Now I can't even afford to send a card for my sister's birthday…. It's really hard. Yesterday was my parents' 27th anniversary, and I didn't have anything.*

Another felt cut off from relatives and friends because she could not buy more things for them. Around Christmas people were sad that they could not buy many presents for their children. MARTHA expressed it exactly when she said that she found shopping depressing because she could not get what she wanted (she mentioned birthday gifts), but only what she needed.

Even in extreme poverty, there was a yearning for expressive spending. BOB used to spend his summers in Ottawa working as a computer operator for the government. Laid off in a Conservative government cutback, he had returned to London with his wife and child, and was attending Bible college part-time, as well as looking after the baby. His wife, now the breadwinner, worked in a shop for low wages. They were bankrupt, suffering such extreme poverty that they bought medicine on credit cards. Even with such severe deprivation, however, what he missed most from his employed days were the leisured moments he and his wife had enjoyed in restaurants and cafés. In their former town, they used to linger in a café over coffee and cheesecake for an hour or two. But now, *"you can't justify paying $10 for a coffee and a cheesecake. So if we want to have that, we bake the cake and brew the coffee."*

But doing it yourself at home seemed confining and too much like work. It lacked the *specialness* of a purchased experience outside the home. As BOB put it:

> We really valued those times, just to take off. We'd take her [the baby] with us, to a sidewalk café, park her there, sit, have a coffee, watch people go by. Just to get out of the house. We can't do that anymore.

A considerable experience was woven into that modest spending of money. There was the spontaneity of breaking away and doing something fun together in a different environment; the sense of well-being at doing something enjoyable beyond necessity, with the pleasure in each other's company which such occasions stimulate. These "necessary frills" of a relationship are increasingly things to be *purchased* not hand-made at home. Many of the unemployed are no less committed than the employed to these values, and acutely feel their loss in the condition of poverty.

Personal Effects

Unemployment and low-income seemed to stimulate a (partly) self-imposed austerity in certain informants. Mothers, especially, subordinated their own needs to the needs and wants of their children. MONICA always used her modest discretionary income to buy something for her child each week. Apart from making her feel better, it was a guilt offering: she was paying the child back for an earlier period when she was too busy to properly care for its needs.

Many of these mothers (and other women) reported neglecting themselves. People let their hair grow. Enhancements of feminine appearance—"*Little things...the things that give me pleasure, nail polish*," as one put it—were put aside. These "little things" were not trivial but were cultural furnishings of one's personal identity. MARTHA commented:

> I have had to come down, a lot, the way I dress, the way I spend money on...stupid little things like perfume and things like that,...which also in turn make you feel better about yourself.

Of course, some did splurge from time to time and treat themselves, but often with a trace of self-consciousness and guilt.

This guilt is worth pondering. HEATHER, a mother of small children, bought almost nothing for herself at all. She stifled her interest in "*nice things*" because she could not afford them. But, more than that, "*If I did buy it, I'd be so guilty that I'd be sick.*" This striking statement, at one level, indicated how people scaled down their aspirations to match their material condition, "making a virtue of necessity." HEATHER wanted what the cash society dangled before her, but she had evolved an ethic of self-sacrifice to help her live with her poverty. But, at a deeper level, note how subtly the responsibility for her poverty has shifted to her shoulders. A disturbing possibility exists that she could come to see herself as unworthy of material provision, as morally *to blame* for her condition. Self-sacrifice could become a kind of opiate of the poor, especially for mothers.

Home Furnishing

For the employed, the home and surrounding land can be shaped to express values reaching beyond necessity, to produce cultural images of harmony and beauty, and to affirm personal meanings. It is not just education but discretionary income which allows the middle class to turn the physical environment into an extension of its subjectivity. The *low*-income family, by contrast, must stock its home with shabbier furnishings—often whatever the prosperous "throw out." There is little impress of its subjectivity on its environment, rather it must passively accept whatever benefit or hazard the environment casts its way.

The situation of WARREN's is relevant here. He was one of the long-term unemployed (three years) informants, who was living with his wife and children on social assistance. His wife's income was too low to keep them out of a humiliating poverty. He described his own situation with emotion:

> *Right now we need furniture, we got a pull-out bed—I want to chuck that sucker out. And I want to get rid of the rug. My wife and I, we're sleeping on this pull-out bed 'cause we don't have any money to buy a bedroom suite. We got broken in and they busted it all up. They just trashed the place. took knives and just cut it all up....I need about $75 to $80 to go buy a bed. I don't have it.... At Goodwill, they have a box spring and mattress for $50. I can't even afford that.*

Not even the outside was within their control. Note the restless hostility, seeking an object.

> *It's the aggravation you have to put up with. You can't have nothing nice out there, flowers. Mary planted some nice flowers out there. Little bastards come along and they just pick your flowers, kick the dirt out…. Half those kids out there don't have fathers. They just don't give a damn.*

Rather than the anger fueling political or other remedial action, its direction was in towards the family, or changed into a suspicion of outsiders. Lacking political or economic resources to bring about change, the poor must learn to adjust. As WARREN put it: *"Just have to abide by it, just go with it. Not much you can do. My wife handles it OK: she's not a woman of needs."*

The poorer informants could compare their modest furnishings with the shacks of the Third World and know they come out ahead. But the real comparison they had to live with was the affluent society of London, Ontario, and the idealized material lifestyles displayed on TV. EVELYN, making $570 a month, looked around her small row-home with two bedrooms:

> *This is all I could ever get.... It's a lot better than a lot of people have in the world...but it's a little hole. I get all the noise from the pipes and the neighbours. My neighbour's been running the tap all week, and there's this high-pitched scream in this bedroom and the bathroom* [Child: "It's louder in my room."]. *I know it is, honey. So I've had battles with her* [i.e. the neighbour] *about trying to have it shut off at night. Because you can't sleep with this nnyyeeeahh whine.*

The poor must adapt to an environment which at any moment could erupt and bring them to their knees. The decaying material world around them was far from the field of personal agency that it was to the renovating middle classes; rather, it was a hostile master whose moods they must calculate and endure.

Clothes

Clothes were an area of major economy for the informants. *"Oh, heavens,"* sighed SILVIA who had been laid off, *"I haven't had new clothes for so long. Ahhmm!* [laughs, groans]." A few informants had not bought clothes for two years. Another one wore the same clothes she had bought last year, or borrowed from her family.

What made it a little easier was the availability of discount stores. There was Apparel Clearance (a cut-rate store for clothes that did not sell at the bigger stores), Bi-Way, Nabour, the Salvation Army stores and, *"the friend of the poor,"* Goodwill. COLLEEN pointed to her clothes: *"I paid 25 cents for these shorts and 75 cents for this shirt." "If it hadn't been for the Goodwill,"* added ANDREA, *"I don't know where we would be."* In today's free-wheeling fashions, she pointed out, one could do quite well from the discount stores. But a lot of time was consumed walking around the city, as these stores were widely dispersed. Ironically, the poorest consumers had to spend the most time on the marketplace. EVELYN commented:

> *The biggest problem is that you don't have a choice. You can't say, "I'm going shopping today and buy Becky a new dress, she needs something." You have to look around terribly, you spend a lot of time looking.*

To buy a quality piece of clothing was a big decision, and was long remembered afterward. ANDREA had purchased a $40 blouse several months ago. *"Forty dollars, whooo!"* She could have bought a week's groceries with the money. But psychologically it gave her a boost—a feeling of quality. On the other hand, paying the rent was often resented and not just because of the huge chunk of income it took away. It carried no thrill of entering into culture, of expressing a stylish detachment from necessity—while it took away the money that could.

Food-Shopping

Here also the informants "comparison shopped" for food in many places and did so more often than when they were working. The convenience of one-stop shopping was a luxury they could not afford. They visited the fruit and vegetable market, the No Frills stores, Valdi's and other discount food shops, Food City, A & P, and even food co-ops. While a handful grew some of their own vegetables in the warm months, most went to market, looking for specials.

Food shopping became far more deliberate and systematic than when one was working; impulse shopping had to be severely checked. A few informants memorized the prices of goods in the various stores. Some picked up and put down a favorite item like coffee five or six times. Especially near the end of the month, the food budget was carefully planned; each item was pondered before money was spent. Informants did a lot of "couponing" to take advantage of specials in food stores, occasionally enjoying the bonus of dining out at selected restaurants. The comparison shopping could be quite systematized. JOANNE made up an elaborate spreadsheet on which she arranged different items on sale at various places, allowing her to save between $35 and $40 a week. Before, if she wanted something, she went out and bought it. She expressed some pride in working the system in this way.

> *I would never have thought about going to Valdi's, Giffords and Food City.... And I've gotten fun out of it...the money, it's good to save. It made me feel good about me, too, to save the money. I have all these coupons. I can't believe I'm doing these things.*

The requirement for food was more inflexible than the previously mentioned items. But compared with rent and utilities like heat and electricity, food *was* quite flexible and formed one of the economies of the poor. A few informants ate grains and vegetables only, cutting out meat and fish. Many bought only the smaller cuts of meat instead of the larger economical ones, spending more per ounce than the better-off and eating significantly less. Some bought powdered milk. The young men on social assistance or low Unemployment Insurance benefits often ate little. HAROLD talked about how difficult it was to look for work *"if you couldn't afford a meal a day."* PAUL, living with his partner, said: *"We have Kraft dinner, we have bacon bits, and tabasco sauce. Let's see what we can do with it."* Before, he had not taken the hungry seriously. Now, even if he had no money, he would invite a poor man over for dinner. They could split a box of Kraft dinner three ways, *"instead of two."*

Two informants had been so impoverished that they had sought food baskets from their churches. One was MAUREEN, a 22-year-old single woman living with her foster father. She had left a child-care training program because of seizures, but was now healthy and ready to return. Her financial situation was grave, based on an income pieced together from baby-sitting, a small allowance from her indifferent foster father, and a meagre disability benefit. When she had run out of money for food the previous month, she had been forced to call one of the churches for a food basket. A man from the church came out to interview her to assess her need. His manner was nervous, which made her nervous and uncomfortable. She wished she could have avoided this painful encounter. *"I just wouldn't ever want to have to do it again.... I guess it's the price you have to pay if you want something from this guy."* The other informant, MATTHEW, a more regular food recipient, could not stand being in the house when the food parcel was delivered: *"It just bothers me too much. I hate taking charity."*

Cut out of production, some informants were virtually cut out of consumption. JANE used to shop at places where she could get clothes for $3.00. *"Now I don't have any money, so now I can't shop at all, except buy food and toiletries. I'm not a consumer right now."* A few could no longer take the rigours of stretching so few dollars in so many ways and they began sliding. ALICE, living alone, just got by on her social assistance cheque; her spending habits were in disarray. *"There's a little left and I go out and have a few drinks. And that's it."* A few younger men on welfare shoplifted. EVELYN, while she did not shoplift, understood the impulse:

> The frustration of being poor is that you have no choice.... I can't just move...into a house that I want to go into. I can't just go into a store and buy what everybody else is buying. It's very tempting to shoplift and do all kinds of stuff—I see very easily where people get into crime. I see very easily where people become alcoholics or do other things, like abuse their families.

Though cut out of expansive consuming, the informants walked through a public environment that was relentlessly commercial. As much out of a lack of anything else to do as due to the tempting displays, the informants often found themselves window-shopping. DONALD studied the objects in store windows, thinking of how to make such things for himself. But usually the window-shopping was more passive and wistful. The showcasing of unattainable material objects in the city stores, the leisure places that were off-limits, the people moving briskly to the next store—all this made the unemployed feel like tourists in their own city. GLENN expressed a feeling of estrangement, as though he were separated from the whole urban world by panes of glass—window-shopping on the social world, outside looking in. He walked down Dundas Street, seeing *"everyone rushing around, going to their jobs.... I just walk down the street. I have nothing to do, nowhere to go."*

Summary and Conclusions

"Losing ground" as a social practice stands at the intersection of two motions. First, the deprivation of employment (logical subject) robs the unemployed of usable space, truncating the scope of their action to the local setting. Then, in reaction, the individual (grammatical subject) withdraws social energy, in effect adjusting to the reduced "headroom" of the unemployed situation. Relationships with others begin to lose the savour of outside experiences. While active at first, the voice of action in the home gradually becomes passive and inertial. Left in the wake of an expanding urban situation, the experience of losing ground is atomizing. The unemployed become increasingly priced out of the city's synergistic possibilities, lacking the means of mobility to even make an approach.

Some informants, however, cultivated a practice that went counter to the centrifugal direction which the culture was urging. They developed a close-grained appreciation of the neighbourhood. This coming into focus was a first step in recovering the synergistic potentialities of the community close-at-hand.

"Economizing and consuming" was another imposition on informants' time. Being poor actually made them more of a consumer: taking more time to look for bargains; comparing notes with others on ways to save money; asking people to lend things which were not affordable. But without money, the self often shrank from others. The environment became not a field for personal action, but a threatening place that diminished the self. One developed an attitude towards self that could be quite ascetic and self-denying. One had to resist the attractive consumption items all around one: *"That's not for me. It would only make me guilty."* The syntax of spending for the poor informants tended to be passive and reactive. There was not the money for active intervention in the world, only enough to cope with crisis and necessity. Lack of money entrapped one in a contingent, precarious present. Acting necessarily in the interest of self and family, the unemployed person became atomized and estranged from the affluent community around it.

In words applicable to London, Ontario, Fineman writes of modern England:

> Money provides the only legitimate entrée to reciprocated exchanges that are the substance of social life. Symbols of worth—the car, furniture, particular foods, the pint of beer—are intrinsic to rituals of display, courtship, manliness, housewifery. But they are also symbols of employment. They reflect the proper order of things and are clung to, even in the absence of work (Fineman, 1987: 238).

It is with money, especially that income left over after the bills are paid, that most people buy into their membership in modern capitalist society, indeed define and express themselves. To be without that discretionary income was to be undefined and unexpressed in the important public idiom of visible consuming. Locked out of the hedonistic enjoyment of society's surplus, the poor and unemployed were nonetheless continually reminded of all they had lost.

CHAPTER EIGHT

Time and the Construction of Daily Life

The unified movement of an inevitable linear time characteristic of the capitalist age...suggests a sense...[of] a society in which all share the same time-scale and appreciate its careful warning pace. It tends to suppress a notion that *different social groups may have different times, or some no times,* or others attempt to pull time violently forwards. [emphasis added]

Paul Willis (1977: 134–135)

Everyday's the same. Days have no meaning.

ANDREA

I feel like, in the last year, I haven't grown up.... At the same time I feel 40 years old.

EVA, 23

The texture of daily life and the timing of its practices change considerably with unemployment. After all, full-time paid work and schooling exercise a powerful grip on how our days, weeks, and months are lived. When that grip loosens, for example, for a young person out of school looking for a job, or for a factory worker whose plant has closed down, one is suddenly faced with a vast amount of unstructured time. One British study tried to quantify this change (Fagin and Little, 1984, cited in Fryer and McKenna, 1987: 48–49). It took as instances of "structured time" such activities as preparing for and travelling to work as well as doing paid work itself, while "unstructured time" included such activities as socializing, watching TV, and sitting at home. The researchers found that the proportion of unstructured to structured time increased by about 20 times with unemployment.

This excess of unstructured time takes its toll on people. Qualitative studies from the 1930s to this day (Jahoda, Lazarsfeld and Zeisel, 1933; Bostyn and Wight, 1987; Fryer and McKenna, 1987) document the disorientation and suffering inflicted by the loss of the familiar time-structuring of paid employment. The person's own structuring of time falters, and there is a feeling of being caged in a boring, regressive present. While some unemployed manage to structure their days and find productive substitutes for employment, most experience negative effects. This is found across various industrial cultures and phases of the life cycle (Bostyn and Wight, 1987: 150).

How did the *informants* cope with this surplus of unstructured time? Having learned of imposed practices in the previous chapter, we now turn to those daily practices which were *constructed* and self-guided. Before introducing and analyzing the practices, however, a brief conceptual introduction is required.

Concepts

We all live in an un-interruptible stream of time. This flow is a raw material which society and culture "make" into meaningful forms. We make time as selves, interactants, and members of societies—which then form enveloping dimensions of time-experience. *Self-time* is a sequence "of I and me phases of self-experience and is...unique, personal and subjective" (Weigert, 1981: 199). The "I phase," incorporating Mead's (1964 [1934]: 228–233) notion of "I," describes the cutting edge of time at which the unique experiencing self moves. In an instantly-following "me phase," experiences become sedimented as material for the socially-constructed "me." Each act is a conversation within the self between the unfolding present and the inherited synthesis of the past. The self struggles to integrate both these experiencing and synthesized moments.

Interaction time is the making of time with other people. It entails the adjustment of the timing and duration of interaction among two or more persons who are present to each other, and is therefore only partly under the control of the self. Interaction time depends "on the actions of the other, as well as on the social definitions and rules for appropriately taking turns.... When actors cooperate to stage a common performance, like a family on a Sunday outing, they form a team and create varieties of 'team time'" (Weigert, 1981: 200).

A third (catch-all) dimension which I call *societal time* takes in the institutionalized, cultural, and historical frames in which we live as members of organizations, generations, classes, and societies. These form time environments into which we are fitted in various ways, and upon which we have little local impact.

The dominant conception of our own societal time is sketched in the Willis quote at the beginning of this chapter. Most members of capitalist-industrial societies believe themselves to share the same time-scale. An example of this can be found in the message of self-improvement books on time management: "We all share a 168-hour week, so how can we effectively achieve our goals within that framework?" An added element is the *ethical* prescription about how we are expected to fill this time. There is a requirement that people should be either "engaged in, preparing for, or supporting those in paid employment" (Bostyn and Wight, 1987: 150). Having employment—and spending its income—are held up (in the dominant ideology) as the exemplary means to further the progress of the whole of society. It is *this* cultural environment within which both employed and unemployed are socialized.

The experience of the three enveloping dimensions—self-, interaction, and societal time—within the constructed day of the informants is the topic of the chapter. The first practice, "Self-Timing," refers to the ways in which people "periodized" their unstructured time. We follow with a grouping of social practices in which the self "Engages in Goal-Oriented Activities," involving societal or interaction time. We conclude with a cluster of practices in which the self, unanchored to objective time, struggles to get through a formless time which has become external and alienating—"Killing Time." We will explore the more general possibility, sketched in the Willis quote, that the unemployed have an *alternative* conception and experience of time, following from their ejection from the mainstream of society.

Self-Timing

If employment shapes the experience of days, weeks, months, and so on, how did *un*employment affect the informants' view of and participation in these units of time? On certain units (e.g. the month, seasons) the material was sparse. Within the month, there was some excitement around the arrival of the benefits cheque. As for seasons, the dreaded time was winter, which forced people indoors and curtailed their already limited mobility. The richest accounts by far were concerned with times of the day and week.

Times of the Day

Pierre Bourdieu's research in Kabylia presented the traditional meanings of morning and night (Bourdieu, 1977: 143–153, cited in Giddens, 1984: 133): Morning, or the opening of the day, is a time for people to stream out of their houses to work in the fields. "The morning is not just 'daybreak' but a triumph in the struggle between day and night; to be 'in the morning' is to be open to the light, to the beneficence that is associated with it..... It is not just a transition in time but a keying of events and practices" (Giddens, 1984: 133). Night, on the other hand, is the endpoint of the waning of the day, and forms a central metaphor for various sorts of decline and decay.

Morning

For the informants, the morning was a significant time (night also, to be discussed later). As a prospective time, renewing energies for some promising pursuit during the day, it evoked from informants (whose prospects were not promising) a mixed, even divided, response. There were those who *faced* the morning, calmly or anxiously, and those who *negated* it by sleeping through it. We will examine each broad response.

The first group included those who either said they liked mornings or simply reported that they rose at an early hour. That it was a difficult, pivotal time, even for these, was borne out by the few positive things said about mornings. Only one person explicitly called herself a "morning person," and even she—DIANE, a 25-year-old social services worker, jobless for six months—seemed tense and compulsive about her early rising. She was determined not to *"let that slide..., [did not] want to start sleeping in till noon."* Elsewhere she expressed anxiety about falling apart, or drifting into an almost irrecoverable malaise; against this, rising in the morning was a fortifying act of will.

The morning held the promise of the first delivery of mail. MATTHEW felt that *"In the morning, there's always hope, because the mailman hasn't come yet. There's a possible chance...letter...that they may want to see me or talk to me."* The morning was a busy part of MATTHEW's day, spent in looking for work, going to the unemployment office, sending out résumés. But, *"after the mail has come, after twelve o'clock or one, it's just another day. It's another day, and that's when it gets bad."* ANDREW indicated a similar shift in intensity at two points in the day: after the mail had come, and after 4:30 p.m., after which no one would call. These were only the earliest examples of how the rhythms of societal time reverberated in the informants' day.

Mornings were acceptable *if* there was something to get up for—typically, either paid work or some absorbing activity. Many had to fight the temptation to follow the line of least resistance. Hence DOROTHY: *"If I get up in the morning, knowing there's nothing that has to be done that day,...or I don't have to go anywhere, there's a temptation to say why bother to get dressed, why take a shower—but I do anyway."* The resistance to rising came, she thought: *"when I don't have any purpose in the day, and it's difficult to create a purpose."*

What looked like laziness was, in many cases, an internal debate while lying in bed. Two strong but conflicting tendencies operated on the recumbent figure. "I *must* get up," was the voice of the work ethic. "But I have nothing to get up *for*," was the answering call of the self, shrinking from the task of constructing its own time. There were those who, unlike single DOROTHY, had children whose needs inscribed a routine in their lives. So MONICA overslept immoderately in the summer; but when her child was back in school, she gratefully adapted her day to the child's routine.

For many informants, the self could not cope with the constructive rigours of morning. They expressed hatred of getting up, or simply slept in. As NORMA put it plainly: *"I hate mornings because there's nothing to get up for. When you're working, you get up and go to work....*[When you're unemployed] *you've got this whole day ahead of you and it's going real slow. What am I going to do today?"* Many tasks were judged insufficient to get up for in the cold light of the unemployed's day. The housewives and househusbands dismissed housework as anything "pressing" or structuring enough to get up for. Many other domestic tasks, robbed as they were of status, influence, or transferability to the outside world, were similarly demoted subjectively. *"Now, there's no reason for me to get up,"* was a common refrain.

If we compare the characteristics of those who faced and accepted mornings (15 in number) with those who did not (23), further generalizations become possible. Seventy per cent of the negative group were "middle" and "long-term" unemployed (seven to twelve months, and more than a year, respectively), which compared with 56% in the sample and 53% in the positive group. The negative group were more likely to have a less advantaged class background than the positive group. As well, in the positive group there was a significant over-representation of people who were well supported by their families—whereas such people were under-represented in the negative group. In sum, one is less likely to energetically pursue opportunities the longer one has been unemployed, the weaker the family support, and the less one has been surrounded by models of occupational success.

Afternoon

The informants' views of the *afternoon* were more ambiguous. Afternoons rarely delivered on the promise of morning so, especially for the "morning people," there was a downward turn. For some, afternoons were perceived as *"slow," "draggy," "boring."* For a housewife with children like HEATHER, the hours between three and six formed a kind of hiatus between the fast-paced morning and the more sociable evening. "Interaction time" was in a lull, with no one making demands, and the children occupied. In this quiet time, she was tired, yet not able to relax, because supper was coming up. For single parent EMMA, who found afternoons *"like two days in one": "the brightest part of my life is when my daughter comes home and says 'Hi Mom.'"* For men and women who were in the home all day, the onset of interaction time in late afternoon was a welcome deliverance from the surplus of self-time.

The afternoons, and daytime generally, were noted by some of the informants as the time when most people were at work. They reported a consequent feeling of strangeness, like a child home sick from school. *"During the day,"* said KATHY, *"you sort of feel you should be doing something."* There was a feeling of guilt, especially as five o'clock neared: other people were finishing work and *"my day isn't even half-over"* (EVA). Many, reviewing the day in the late afternoon, felt *"dissatisfied"* or *"self-defeated"* because they had not done anything useful. The echoings of societal time were heard by the unemployed, making their own lives seem, in comparison, stretched and ill-defined. As E.P. Thompson wrote:

> In mature capitalist society, all time must be consumed, marketed, put to *use;* it is offensive for the labour force merely to "pass the time" (1967: 90–91).

Evening

There was a slightly more favourable response to evening. If daytime aroused guilt for not working, *"at night,"* as PAUL commented, *"I feel less guilty for not doing anything."* Or, in KATHY's words, *"In the evening, you know you really don't have to be doing anything."* With pleasure and relaxation legitimized, evening, for many, was a time for creative pursuit. A few artist-informants took a perverse pride in working late into the evening while the rest of the society relaxed—turning the societal rhythm of work/rest on its head. Most, however, liked the more interesting interaction time the evening afforded. People were home from work and school, visitors might drop in, outings were embarked upon. The television viewing was more stimulating in the evening and more likely to be shared.

The negative view of evening expressed by only a few had to do with the accumulated resentments from the day. MATTHEW's wife worked evenings. Alone with the children each evening, he would get depressed. He would become abrupt with his children, even flying into rages. *"Then I'll say, 'Why did I do that?' It's just because of all these things building up."* PAULA tried to express why she disliked evenings.

> If you went to work, at least you're coming home in the evening. When I'm home all day, I feel as if I should be coming, and then I get confused. My whole metabolism's gone crazy, because it's, like, I'm coming back from…where have I been? Or I've gone and I'm still waiting to come back.

To interpret this is difficult, but she seemed to be expressing both harmony and estrangement. Home was the natural resting place for the outside self which had spent its day in the productive realm: it provided for the reconciliation of two parts of the self. But her present self, which was at home *all day* and *evening,* lacked its natural outside complement and felt bereft. Or, more distantly, she imagined herself as the outside self "waiting to come back" to be grounded in the private realm. There are images here of both *rupture* of the links between private and public roles—the person homeless in the labour market, the person mired in the home—and a premonition of their *reconnection*.

Times of the Week

The time patterns of the informants were often unsynchronized with the schedules of employed people. Some thought this positive, others negative. For a few young people who had relatively secure social support, going against the grain of masses of people was a liberating experience. They chose to go to the beach in the summer during the uncrowded week days rather than the weekends. One informant was pleased at avoiding the predictable devices of the employed, such as *"sneaking out a couple of hours early from work on a Friday or whatever...to have your leisure time."* A few informants, having funds, preferred the uncluttered shopping on weekdays, with the extra attention given by sales staff.

A *negative* feature of the lack of synchronization was the difficulty of meshing energy levels with employed friends or partners during the working week. One man found it necessary to schedule badminton games with his working friends on the weekends; after work during the week, they were simply too exhausted to play. The young househusband, TONY, used to burden his wife with his excess energy and desire to go out when she returned from work. Recognizing this as a problem, he was looking for ways to expend more energy during the day. Often the unemployed wanted intense social interaction with their employed friends during weekday evenings, when the energy levels of the latter were low.

Weekdays

Without the time markers of institutional experience in schools, factories, and offices, the informants' week became a featureless blur of days. SUSAN, a married woman of 28, had to stop her housework and ask, *"Is this Thursday?"* People lost track of whether the days were weekdays or weekends. ANDREA took a trip to a huge mall in the area, only to find the doors closed. She stood there until she remembered that it was a holiday: *"You know, you have no perception of holidays."* It was as though, standing there, she were trying to remember the "tune" or rhythm of societal time, from which she had been excluded.

A chief rhythm of the societal timing of the week was the alternation of weekdays and weekend. Society worked, rested, worked, rested—like the contraction and dilation of the heart. In this satisfying pulsation of work and leisure, each enriched the other. But this was taken from the unemployed. For many of the informants, in the words of one: *"The whole week is a weekend."* Deprived of societal work that offered a *rationale for leisure,* the unemployed found their leisure time devitalized and pointless. Without a working week, the weekend was a rest...from what? For what? ALLEN spoke of weekends when he was employed: *"I used to love 'em before.... [Now] it's the same as any other day, pretty well." "When you're working,"* said CRAIG, *"weekends seem like a rest. I rest all week, everyday."* Perhaps GORD best summed up the meaning of the weekend when employed as compared to now:

> *I used to have a feeling of elation, eh? Well, that's gone. For better or for worse. Maybe it's just as well. One day is the same as the next. It just seems to go on.*

GORD's statement was a grieving one: he was not just saying goodbye to work, he was saying goodbye to *leisure*—in perhaps its highest form. He also described the subjective feel of what was *left* of leisure: undifferentiated, characterless, *"it just seems to go on."*

Weekends

For those who no longer looked forward to weekends—who saw them as blended into the *"mishmash"* of days—the sense of estrangement could be quite sharp. For BRIAN: *"I get a little fed up with people saying, 'Well, isn't it great the weekend's coming, Friday night, what are we going to do?' I can't see that Friday night is any different than Monday night, or Tuesday night or whatever."* His working wife unwittingly *"rubs it in"* by being quite zestful when the weekend arrives: *"She says 'Let's go here,' 'Let's go there.'"* A similar antipathy was directed to *holidays.* BRIAN found holidays had no special meaning for him: Christmas could as easily be in July, when it would be more convenient anyway. *"I think they should do away with Christmas and Sundays,"* he laughed. Having been locked out of a vital rhythm of societal time, he wanted to flatten *its* time. This resistance to "special days," which are gifts of repose for a working community, seemed to derive from a bitter sense of exclusion from the community. The specific resistance to Christmas could, of course, also be traced to the pressure on people to celebrate their family bonds with items of consumption—pressures which low-income people find almost unbearable.

Weekends, especially Sundays, were difficult in other respects. The relatively loose (societal) time-structuring of the weekends meant that there were even fewer time "pegs" than usual for the unemployed (especially single persons). There were no courses, no job interviews, few meetings of clubs or voluntary associations. On Sundays, public establishments were closed, and the buses ran less often (making visits with friends more difficult). Thus the burden on the self to *construct* its time was greater. For a jobless single woman like DIANE, who moved into the area a few years ago and had few friends, neither societal nor interaction time took up the slack. She remembered how the self was overwhelmed in the early weekends: *"I used to loathe weekends.... That used to be the time I would fall apart most."* Gradually—by making friends, going to parties, movies, and working out—she pulled herself back from the drift into de-structured, collapsing time. She now carefully planned each weekend; though without enough money to entertain at home, she cut corners to make sure she could afford to go out with her friends.

The informants who *liked* weekends pointed to the more interesting interaction time it offered. Partners were home on weekends and had more time for the unemployed person. People moved freely about—relatives, visitors, friends of family members—forming a welcome contrast to the monotonous, lonely weekdays. In the opinion of CONNIE, unemployed for two years, *"One of the big problems of unemployment is isolation."* She looked forward to weekend visits to her parents' home. The informants could see their friends without feeling they were a bother. For women burdened with housework and child care during the week, weekends could be a pleasant change: routines were relaxed, there was no extra baby-sitting, a night out might be planned, and adult voices were heard in the house.

The findings here of an overall divided response of the unemployed to weekends—some finding them unpleasantly similar to weekdays, others liking the variety of movement around the house and neighbourhood—seems to correspond to a deeper division in the general response to unemployment. A recent study of the unemployed in the north of England (Fryer and McKenna, 1987: 62–63) revealed that the people who found weekends the same as weekdays tended to be less happy than the others. While cause and effect may be blurred here, we *can* say that the fading of time markers which unemployment brings is a major dislocation for people, one that surely is at the heart of the social reality of unemployment.

The Qualities of Time

Generally, "good time" for the informants was fast-paced and preoccupying: doing art, housework, solving math problems in a correspondence course, baking, composing music, devising a diet program on a home computer. As one put it, *"When I'm busy doing something, time just goes zip, zip, zip."* When the task was prolonged and involving, there were not enough hours in the day. Self-time became "good" time when human powers were fastened to the demands of the objective world, issuing in some craft or work. Self-time became even better, for some informants, when its activities were also exchangeable with some future state— whether it be employment or a higher form of action or self-development. "Good time" also included *interaction time*. The informants liked *"very perky social occasions, seeing people you like, doing things you like; the time goes fast."* Time quickened during social visits; the presence of others prompted one to respond smartly to the objective stimuli of action and conversation.

By contrast, *"bad time"*—a label often applied to Sundays or the time just before going to sleep—was time devoid of event and variety. It usually entailed inward-looking self-time, i.e. time unfolding within the reference system of the self and its subjective memories and time-markers. "Bad time" lacked external contact with either a resistant reality or other people. Time became palpable and slow, you could almost *see* it. Not just a void in itself, "bad time" voided or negated the energy and tension of other practices as well (expressed as *"feeling lazy"*). This will be elaborated in connection with specific practices. Not all informants, however, accepted these equations. Some of the younger, artistic informants considered good self-time a *release* from a societal or job time they felt was oppressive. Far from the job being a redemption from unemployment, the reverse was true: their art and way of life while unemployed delivered them from what they judged to be the chilling straitjacket of the "nine-to-five" world. The most articulate example, worth exploring in a little detail, was VINCENT's. Unemployed for seven months, he roomed with another fellow in a vacant warehouse behind a taxi depot in east London. Since finishing Grade 12 in commercial art and also some academic subjects at a local high school, VINCENT had picked tobacco, washed dishes, and delivered papers. He lived alternately with his mother (where he saved enough to pay the first and last month's rent at a place of his own) and in a succession of poorly-heated flats. He had even squatted in a vacant house in the inner city for some months.

Partly due to the stresses of poverty and marginal work (he felt), VINCENT has had psychological problems for which he has seen a counsellor. While in school he was found to be dyslexic, which affected his grades. Living on welfare, having a difficult but sustaining relationship with his mother, VINCENT has managed to retain a positive philosophy through it all.

His "work" was his art and he created best in the course of a free-flowing day. For VINCENT, time should be variably paced: he liked the way it sped by when he was "executing" a work, and then slowed down while he was resting or contemplating. *"I'm a bit of a dreamer, and a bit of an idealist...[and] a philosopher."* While he did not like unemployment, he preferred it to mindless work. *"When I'm not working, my mind's working and my being's working, eh?... But when I'm working at this kind of thing* [i.e. dish-washing], *my mind just goes dead. And I'm just trying to struggle for air."* His art suffered and the whole quality of his life and ideas went downhill: *"I just kind of slide into my little hole and just sort of...fall apart, until the clock goes off again."*

What did VINCENT really want? *"If I could get a job, you know, that's...mind-invigorating, plus has an income too...the two sides of the coin, it would be great. Some people find dish-washing great, and I say great for you. But I've got bigger ideas in my head, and things to explore."* There is probably a creative minority in any group of people, employed or unemployed, for whom silence and solitude are not vacancies to be filled but are welcome conditions for personal work. For people like VINCENT, societal time is a martial rhythm which threatens to drown out the private cadence cultivated within self-time. This does not mean that VINCENT was not harried and distressed by his poverty—the cold nights shifting the space heater from head to foot—or that he was never bored: simply, that not every unemployed person sought essential fulfillment within the societal time of paid employment.

Engaging In Goal-Oriented Practices

One way of organizing informants' accounts of daily activities is to range them along a continuum, from *goal-oriented* and focussed on the one end, to *non-goal-oriented* and unfocussed on the other (i.e. *killing time*). We deal with the former grouping first, which includes:

- Taking Courses;
- Doing Volunteer Work;
- Carrying out Hobbies, Reading;
- Doing Housework.

Taking Courses

Taking courses helped to redeem time from the endless present. An involvement that offered its own satisfactions, it also held out the promise of being exchangeable against some future condition of employment. A handful of informants were taking a course in upholstery-making at the local community college, with Manpower's assistance. None of them expected to open a thriving business right away, but they *were* turning more modest possibilities around in their heads. Many intended first to do work for relatives and friends, through which they would build up a clientele by word-of-mouth.

The student-upholsterers took satisfaction in learning something concrete and useful that would be appreciated in every home. Comments about other courses, especially by women, revealed a similar confidence in skills that were solid and objective, having real uses. SUSAN, a former bank teller, wanted to find a job repairing electronic equipment, for which she was taking a Women in Trades and Technology (W.I.T.T.) course. She utterly rejected banking work. Some other women, enrolled in the same program, also rejected their former occupations in the "female ghetto" (in this case, secretarial work). Their courses were freighted with their hopes for change and a different future. In SUSAN's case, the course would be a vehicle towards financial independence which, among other things, would enable her to leave an unhappy marriage.

Courses structured time, putting people back into a system, *"back into the mainstream of everyday life."* They built self-esteem, and provided content to one's life. EVA used belly-dancing and exercise classes to get rid of her excess energy from being at home. But also, belly-dancing was *"kind of cool. It gives me something to talk about; people would say, 'Hey, that's interesting.'"* At last, she would have an answer to that tiresome question: *"They say, 'What do you do all day?' Oh, I could strangle them! Because there are so many things you've got to do all day."*

Doing Volunteer Work

About 30 informants from various backgrounds were doing or had done volunteer work. The groups under-represented in their number were men, the long-term unemployed, sole support parents, and housewives with families. The variety of this work was large, as can be seen from this partial list of their involvements:

London Union of Unemployed Workers	Ploughshares
	Lunch supervision at school
Central American group	Teaching English as a Second
John Howard Society	Language
Food and housing co-operatives	Sexual Assault Centre
Women's Resource Centre	Women's study groups
Scatcherd Centre (Downs Syndrome children)	Senior citizens groups
Cross-Cultural Learners Centre	International Youth Year
Tenants' Associations	Crouch Community Library
Victoria Hospital	

Of course, the intensity of involvement varied among the informants, but this remained a significant social practice. What functions did volunteer work perform? What value did the informants hope to receive and generate in these community involvements?

There was a mixture of motives. A minority of informants cited self-interest: volunteer work was a way of being noticed or of gaining job-oriented experience. One person believed that volunteer work at Victoria Hospital would look good to an employer. Another, GAIL, was helping a friend start a business in return for past favours. If the business took off, she would have a place in it. As well, in her calls to companies for her friend's business, she kept an eye out for possible openings for herself. People looked to volunteer work—so often people-oriented—to help generate a network which might lead to employment.

The purely self-interested motive for doing volunteer work only scratched the surface, however. People spoke of their pleasure at being valued by the community. JANE put it this way:

> *Getting involved in the community…has value. Where I've gone is feeling like I'm not needed to being needed. I wasn't feeling like I didn't have anything to offer anymore.*

Young KIM, lacking school success or job experience beyond baby-sitting, was doing volunteer work at the Crouch Library. First, she went out and got the "job" all by herself: *"I wanted to go out and see if I could get myself a job without nobody's help."* But, beyond that, it gave her a role and increased her sense of self-esteem. *"It makes me feel like I'm wanted somewhere. Because most of the time I'll do something and nobody will say, 'Well, OK, you did a good job.' But here, everyday when I'm here, they say you answer the phones good, and are doing a real good job."*

Many informants had a very deep need to *give to society* instead of just being a passive recipient to which unemployment had reduced them. ERICA, back in the household after years of work, was asked what she would do if she won a lottery. She stated categorically that she would not work for money—as though that were of a lower order—but would do volunteer work.

> *I love to be part of a team. I love to be of service. I love to be needed. Oh, yeah, I like working.*

But, as much as volunteer work attracted ERICA, *"my husband won't let me. He says there's no way you're going to give it away, if you can't get paid for it. I feel it would be good for me to do volunteer work, that it may be a way of getting a job."* Given the scarcity of money in their family (and that she had not won the lottery), ERICA was bound to the wheel of the job market search. But beyond that practical necessity lay an orientation to the community that was profoundly giving and synergistic. Hers was a vision of work that transcended the necessary link to income, that was beyond employment.

Volunteer work performed many of the same functions as employment. It got people mobile, put their minds to work, set them on a schedule, and provided, in short, a much-needed structure to their lives. People used volunteer work to pull out of depressions or to extricate themselves from an unstimulating home. For women with children, it brought them into the world of adults. SUSAN noticed that her confidence rose when she was involved outside the home (taking technical courses, for instance) and fell again when she returned to the home full time. Needing to be out and in contact with adults, she founded a women's study group in her home town. She helped organize talks, films, and consciousness-raising sessions on the theme of women and economics. As vice-president and the person in charge of advertising, Susan felt that it was something she really needed at the time. Volunteer work of this sort had the added virtue of drawing people of similar interests together—something a job often failed to do—as well as affording opportunities to make friends.

Several young informants were involved in volunteer projects organized under the auspices of International Youth Year. Art and design displays, photography, and music projects stimulated exciting synergistic action among the young, e.g. forming a business to promote artistic projects. The most enthusiastic supporter of International Youth Year was STEVE, who eloquently captured the positive aspects of volunteer work:

> *It's been extremely positive for me. It has opened up corridors to follow out and to go down that I didn't realize were there all the time. [Such as what?]... Exploring artistic photography and making a good living out of it...in Toronto, Montreal, and New York.*

> [What else has Youth Year done for you?] *It's given me some confidence in myself that, when I lost that job, I didn't have. It was my fault. I had made some mistakes in that job. When I got involved in International Youth Year, I thought I would make the same mistakes again. They haven't occurred.*

It gave him the valuable experience of successfully finishing a project.

> *For the first time I have completed a project...to the best of my ability, and had people recognize it. Recognize me for doing it. And pat me on the back, which is a very pleasant feeling. Working without any restrictions, without people telling you it has to be done this way, you cannot do that. Because we as a group did things that people said could not be done.*

A few criticized Youth Year for pushing design and fashion ahead of the other arts, but the principal point holds: volunteer work can allow people to exercise their powers with others on significant projects. For the young, particularly, it can sustain the continuity of learning and developing during the transition from school to paid employment.

Along with volunteer work's practical advantages were some practical disadvantages. As a relatively fixed involvement, it took away time from the job search and could reduce flexibility in taking on work. As MAUREEN put it, volunteer work was fine when she was going to school, but from her present position in the job market, it was too inconvenient. If a job came up, people did not want to be tied to an organization and have to walk out on it.

A touch of cynicism and frustration about volunteer work was apparent in some responses—a feeling of being used. KENNETH did volunteer work in Edmonton with a church group whose program was called "People for Employment." "*It was a bit frustrating: I could help them get work, but I couldn't help myself get work.*" In a secure context like schooling, solid support from a spouse, or employment, volunteer work made more sense; for someone vulnerable and exposed, it did not. The informants were well aware of its lower status relative to paid work, its lack of income, and the fact that it did not count as experience to employers. For DEBBIE—a poor, unattached woman, who had been laid off from her lab technician's job—community involvement and volunteer work had always seemed natural to her. But, laid off again, and braced for hard times, she had decided not to become the *"universal volunteer."* She would make room for things she wanted to do. She vaguely felt that people should get paid for volunteer work.

Whatever the functions of volunteer work for individuals—for the informants, mostly positive—in a societal context, it may not be progressive. As a widespread social practice performed mostly by women within a changing political economy, it may be used as an exploitative force. Moscovitch's (1986) analysis of the erosion of public benefits in Canada since 1975 places volunteer work squarely within this new development. Both state and capital have attempted to shift the services and benefits once provided by state welfare over to charitable institutions who use mainly volunteers. Not only does this restructuring degrade these services, it is also anti-feminist: "Since women constitute the majority of both workers and volunteers, the implication is that women can and should be induced to work without pay, and that their training means little because the work they perform is an extension of their maternal role" (1986: 89). We have the divisive result of women volunteers being placed unwittingly in the role of undercutting women public service workers and unions who have fought hard for their place in the Canadian public sector.

Carrying Out Hobbies; Reading

A vast range of pursuits, from small ritual practices to full-blown avocations, could be loosely grouped under "hobbies." At the serious end, there were the artistic pursuits of mostly young people who were seeking a lifework. HERB's creative project, coming out of Youth Year, was scene-making and make-up for artistic projects. Living with his parents, he (like VINCENT) loved the open-ended freedom of the jobless day. *"You are not in this routine where you have to stop at this point in time because you have to get ready and go to work. You can stop when you feel like stopping. Or you can work straight through the day."* All he needed was some financial provision so he could pursue his work with the flexibility it required.

Hobbies gave the informants small experiences of mastery in a familiar terrain. WAYNE, dislocated from job and family, living in an unfamiliar part of a city he did not like, sat in his room after his upholstery course from 3:00 to 11:00 p.m. Knowing no one in the city, he worked at his hobbies. The chief one was his ham radio: "*I sit for hours and listen to…the guys talking all over the world, and it's fascinating, really.*" The problem was, at the time of the interview, it was at the repair shop and "*it was driving me nuts not having it.*" He worked for hours on his models, spending a very long time on the one at hand, because he could not afford a new one. Plainly, these were more than just hobbies for WAYNE. In a bare flat, without so much as a picture, without family or friends nearby, they were a connection to his personal world. Working on his models gave him not only a means of filling time, but re-created a familiar environment of action in a strange setting. They were also a principal means of self-control: keeping the self occupied with external tasks saved WAYNE from his inner rage.

Economic reasons forced informants to drop many former hobbies and sports: tennis, skiing, figure-skating. As MONICA wryly commented: "*I have time now for the hobbies but not the money. When I was working, I had the money but not the time.*" Informants took up simple hobbies, such as cooking, exercising, knitting and sewing, jigsaw puzzles, calculations, singing. These activities were sometimes tinged with *guilt*. CONNIE, who liked caring for plants, began, after 18 months of unemployment, to feel guilty about it. "*When I find myself doing things that I would not really have found time for when I was working, I get the feeling that I'm avoiding…getting out there and finding work.*" From TONY, who enjoyed writing songs and playing guitar: "*Sometimes I feel guilty about it but not very much. I guess pragmatists would see it as a waste of time, but that's pragmatists.*" Creative people sometimes felt the need to defend their occasionally rich enjoyment of unemployed time, as though being aware of a disapproving generalized other. Hence VINCENT's defensiveness: "*Some people with a set mind about the way things should be probably would say, I'm just taking a freeloading vacation, right? Whatever I do, I do with a purpose and I take a certain pride in what I do.*"

The most common diversion was *reading*, with most informants indicating that they read more while unemployed. Many read for escape, to fill otherwise anxious time. "*If I'm in a period of great anxiety,*" STAN commented, "*I will disappear in books.*" The type mentioned most often were nonfiction: self-improvement, history, philosophy. Fiction was low on the list (probably under-reported), partly due to the guilt attached to a literary form more associated with holidays or leisure than employment. One woman "feared" novels because she would sink into them and lose track of other things.

The norms of the work world seemed to reach even into private pursuits and hobbies. At best, hobbies allowed for personal mastery and the engagement of a self-under-pressure in calming, external tasks. But more often than not, there was guilt or defensiveness in engaging in pursuits so unconnected to the ethos and instrumentalism of employed society.

Doing Housework

For many informants (as we have seen), housework was an *imposed* practice which unemployment made even more of a burden. Especially for the poor, who could not afford many labour-saving devices or processed foods, work at home was often time-consuming. So MARY numbered among her tasks: cooking, sewing, housecleaning, and more. *"When you're poor, you do a lot of your own cooking, you prepare a lot of your own vegetables, a lot of your own sauces."* As well, she chauffeured the children to scouts, air cadets, and school functions.

What made housework a *constructive* activity was the informants' stretching of it to fill in an otherwise formless day. This stretching procedure was not always consciously directed, as in MARY's case. When she was employed, she contained domestic work and did it efficiently.

> *I find when I work, you put things in a different category, even emotionally. You could sort it out faster, it doesn't build up. At least then, you went somewhere, you were going to work, and you worked the rest of your life in after that—whether it was my cooking, my sewing, or my housecleaning. And it all fit in, and you were accomplishing something. Now, ohhh, I find this wasted time....*

Her more efficient personal structuring of time at home while she was employed was partly because she had less time in which to *let* things expand. But, also, employment seemed to have given her a demonstration effect of how generally to channel time more effectively. Without that exemplary discipline of outside work, the channelling and sorting of domestic labour wore down and the tasks "spilled over" throughout the day. Among the capacities overrun by this undisciplined sprawl of domestic work were the busy person's self-imposed *limits* on this or that activity. Like other informants, MARY found it hard to set bounds on what she did, to say "no" to others and to her own time-filling urges. In her words, "[you take on] *stupid little stuff* [to] *keep you busy."* She would do more things for people, tie up loose ends, put a shine on things. Partly unwittingly, partly deliberately, MARY's domestic labour expanded to fill her time but not to master it. She was left with faint self-contempt.

Other informants were very purposeful about expanding their housework to fill time. Some cleaned closets, basements, cedar chests; *"just stupid jobs that seem to take so long, but don't really need to be done,"* as EVA put it. EMMA sheepishly admitted: *"Yes, I'm always cleaning the floor* [laughs]. *I'm going to wear it off!"* People rearranged their homes. *"I find when I'm bored,"* said house-bound HEATHER, *"I change the furniture around. I think I've changed the living room around four or five times and I will thoroughly clean everything behind it."*

DICK, a distressed young man on social assistance, waiting for his first real job, was asked what he did all day.

> *Do dishes. Vacuum the carpet about two or three times. Probably tomorrow, I'll*
> *wash the floors—all the floors. I'll just take my time. It takes me about three hours.*

While sitting, he might notice a bit of dirt on the rug, and would promptly set about cleaning the whole carpet.

In DICK's case we begin to see the cost to the *self* of this "make-work."
This sort of practice, though it helped get him through the day, turned
into a negation. His action did not positively extend the self but was a
"going through the motions." This made the action puppet-like; the self
was absent. When DICK was doing dishes or vacuuming, a strange feeling came over him. "*It's not me, you know…. With this unemployment, you*
sort of change your habits. You do, you know." Many of these domestic tasks,
when untied from work or devoid of a social purpose, were hollowed and
hollowing. They did not mark the growth of an identity reaching into its
social world; they did not earn an honourable living or status; they did
not convincingly structure one's life. For some informants (not all), they
were touched with a spreading blight which unemployment imparted to
many daily activities.

Limited to a small sphere of work in the home, it was not surprising
that housework was freighted with psychological and expressive contents. It could be a safety valve, or sublimation, for hostile feelings. WAR-
REN could not be more frank:

> *When I get super pissed off, I'll clean that house from top to bottom—wash the*
> *floors, vacuum, do the dishes, clean the house up…I feel better….I come home, she*
> [his wife] *knows, I go to apply for a job and I see some fuckin' goop that's got my*
> *job that I should have, I come home…. She says "You have a look on your face,*
> *something happened, and I won't bother you for a couple of hours."*

The home was where the violence of the exclusion of the unemployed
finally worked itself down—whether sublimated or direct.

Housework had for many a positive, therapeutic function; at the very
least, it took their minds off their troubles. Even JOANNE who disliked
housework had to admit: "*I like the results."* The production of a clean and
ordered home formed an image of harmony which calmed the distraught
mind. In the small mastery over the environment which efficient
housework (and other tasks) achieved, there was a purging and a heal-
ing, as well as distraction. As SILVIA expressed it: "*If I start feeling sorry for*
myself, I can really pitch in and it's the only way I can get rid of that feeling. Tear-
ing a room apart or a cupboard or whatever. Oh yeah, I do more housework now."

For the longer-term unemployed, housework—ever the indicator of internal states—tended to deteriorate. MARTHA felt that her general lack of
motivation to do *anything* was reflected in her housework. It took a large
effort of will to do a laundry or put the coffee on. If she desperately had
to do a wash, she would do it but not before. Others reported being too

depressed or dragged out to do housework. *"When I was working,"* said PAUL, *"I thought 'I don't want to look at a dirty house. I want to clean it up.' I had a lot more ambition to do things."* Now he disliked housework, *"because I'm there so much more, and you get so much more lazy."* COLLEEN put it concisely: *"The more bored you get, the more you don't want to do. I spend less time doing housework now than when I went to school."*

Compared with those who did housework more—who still had hope, or who had imposed responsibilities—those who did housework *less* could no longer sustain the busy pretense of make-work. The ever-present temptation was to drift into a formless day where one's time was truly negated. To describe this, the word "lazy" kept cropping up in the interviews. *"I'm so downright lazy,"* said BERNARD, jobless for eight months. "Laziness," as a convenient catch-all label, obscured the content of what was surely a *social*, not a mere individual, impotence. Being cut off from others, from an honoured work role, from a commitment to a future, from worthwhile freedoms—*these* were the ingredients of this self-described "laziness," especially for the long-term unemployed. Laziness was a social construction, a reaction to unemployment, covering behaviour symptomatic of a lack of freedom and power.

Killing Time

A number of practices were not carried out to achieve a goal—whether for external or internal satisfaction—but were actions (including *"inactions"*) of a self *killing time.* "Sleeping" fell into this category, but has already been dealt with earlier. The others were:

- Watching TV;
- Drinking;
- Doing Nothing.

Of course, each of these practices *could* be purposefully carried out: people watch television, sit idly, even drink, in self-guided, intentional ways. In *unemployment*, however, the accounts suggested that something happened to them. They were assimilated to a more general need of the self, namely, to solve the problem of unstructured time. As such, they joined other practices in a shift towards the non-goal-oriented, unfocussed end of the continuum mentioned earlier.

Watching TV

For much of the informants' time, the self was unfettered, knocking loosely about in the day. Self-time was dominant, as the person tried to get through those long intervals between the fixed points set by societal and interaction time. Television, being continuously and easily available to fill just those intervals, was a most significant medium (for those who could afford one). It was the object of complex emotions: liked, depended on, held in contempt, loathed. About half the informants watched more TV while unemployed than when they were working; the rest watched the same amount or less than before. Whatever the pattern, few were indifferent to TV.

The informants who watched *less TV* than before reported this emphatically, with pride in their voices, as though they had survived a struggle with the medium. *"I discipline myself not to watch too much,"* said NANCY, 28 and single. Like not sleeping in, resisting the temptations of TV was a small act of mastery. A few felt that the "tube" made you one-directional, and failed to develop your mind. A small number explained that they watched it less because the context for watching it had changed. When they were working, they were too tired to do anything but *"veg out"* in front of the set, watching whatever was on (*"mindless TV"*). Now they had more energy and were more selective.

Many informants watched *more TV*. The reasons for it, and the emotions attached, were complex. For one thing, TV was *company*. *"I watch TV a lot; that's my only company,"* said DESMOND, a 28-year-old married man. MONICA kept the TV on because she heard her son all day long, and *"I want to hear adult voices."* Even FRANCES, who had a Master's degree and liked books, drew close to the television, where people could be seen and voices heard. *"Where it's noisy. I like the noise; the deathly silence of the house begins to get to me."* A few kept the radio and TV on, uneasy about the silence.

Many gravitated to the TV as a form of *escape:* it took no effort, presented no challenge. *"I plant myself in front of the TV; I find real escape in television"* (COLLEEN). This practice was especially prevalent for the longer-term unemployed. ALICE, jobless for seven months, slept through most of the day and then watched TV until it went off. Asked when time went slowly or quickly for her, she replied: *"As soon as the TV goes off the air, it goes slow."* Informants who were particularly distressed and dragged out talked in terms of *"addiction,"* of falling asleep in front of the TV at four in the morning.

TV seemed to operate like a magnet for the depressed or drifting. It had the virtue of asking nothing more of an already overburdened self. Informants spoke as though they no longer exercised choice in the matter. *"I do it because I have to do it,"* was DESMOND's striking statement. PAUL put it this way: *"I'm at home a lot, what else it there to do?"* Even those critical of TV could get drawn in, as ROSS commented:

> I abhor TV but, being at home, my parents have all the Pay TV channels, big colour TV—I can get psyched into it.

TV was less a chosen medium than a "ground" for the surplus energy and time of the self at home. While particularly affecting the long-term unemployed and certain of the isolated young, it could serve this function for anyone. Here is a comment from well-supported TONY, unemployed for only a brief time:

> *I try not to watch it when I'm alone.... The biggest reason is that you can sit there and watch it and watch it and watch it and watch it, when no one's around. I don't like TV very much, to tell you the truth.... Sometimes I'd just like to...kick it out the window, and at other times, I really enjoy it.*

Perhaps the source of the ambivalence this man expressed (common among the informants) was a vague sense that the TV was a rival to the self. Or, better, not so much the TV itself, but the practice of surrendering autonomy to a part of the environment that sucked up but did not redeem unstructured time. We are beginning to look at practices whose syntax is imperceptibly shifting. Self-time may be dominant, but the self is no longer the active organizing centre. Rather, the self has capitulated to the inducements of appetite and its environment, which, so gratefully seized upon, become vortices or time magnets.

Drinking

Most informants did not consider drinking a problem or a significant social practice. Many reported drinking less than when they were employed. Looking back on that period, LAURIE commented: *"You get out in the wide world and there's a lot of drinking going on, just socially.... There's a lot of glamour attached to it. If it's winter, what else can you do?"* Being out of those circles, and having less money, drinking was a scarcer practice.

But those informants who did report drinking more or commented upon it outlined some of the functions which drinking served for the marginalized. Five informants were either alcoholics at one time or had serious drinking or drug phases. The most recent problem was that of BERNARD's. After being laid off, he began to drink seriously: *"trying to drown my problems.... At first you feel someone might help you find a job. Then it gets into, 'Oh, hell, nobody will help me.' So what,...you start drinking seriously."*

Three informants in their late teens—all unemployed for significant periods of five months or more—were not coping well, and they welcomed drink as an escape. For two of them, the big change was not so much quantity of drink but motive. *"Before it was just the cool thing to do,"* said HAROLD. *"Now I just drink to escape.... It's kind of a break from reality."* GLENN put it more graphically: *"When I was working, I didn't drink to get as drunk as I possibly could. I drank to have a good time. Now I drink to get as drunk as I can and forget everything."* When LORNE and his friends get together, they get drunk and happy, forgetting all their troubles for the moment. When asked what he would do if he won the lottery, he replied, *"I'd just sit around and get drunk and do nothing."*

Other informants would drink if they could afford it. ERICA pathetically indicated: *"If I could afford it, a couple of good drunks would be great. Yeah, I often think I would like to stop in a bar but...I don't.* [Would you drink more if you could afford it?] *Oh, yeah. You know, there's not much to life right now.... I would go out and get plastered a couple of times."* If excessive sleeping shortened the unbearable day and TV-watching lightened the burden of constructing one's time, perhaps alcohol offered some deliverance. For a moment the self was eased of the strain of clear-headedly facing its sober reality.

Doing Nothing

The informants' sense of the working society's attitude towards idle time was neatly conveyed by the practice of 56-year-old MARK. He was an ex-alcoholic living in the underside of the city, deriving income from welfare, the odd job, and from bottles picked up off the street. After a brief job search in the morning and a bite at the soup kitchen, he sat in the park. This for him was a peculiarly self-conscious practice:

> You look quite dumb sitting out there, old bum, nothing to do. So I'll sit there for about an hour, and I'll go home, have a snack, pick up a book, then come back to the park.

Whatever moved him off the park bench after an hour—whether it was the fact that people looked blandly at him, or just the awareness that he was doing something of which society disapproved—his "doing nothing" was not simply a negative but a *practice*. As well, it was not only a solitary but a *social* practice, i.e. being in relation to others and the cultural climate. By sitting there too long, he was violating an ethic which has permeated mass consciousness: that one's time should be spent in purposeful activity and not wasted.

The experience of idle time was variable among the informants. Some structured their time well and had little left in which to just sit around. A few enjoyed the introspective moments given them. The majority, however, spoke of the pull of idle time and their countering motion away from it. A significant minority, especially the long-term unemployed, were oppressed by it. In short, doing nothing constituted a significant, perhaps pivotal, practice for many informants.

When asked about idle time, some informants betrayed an attitude of fear. *"I don't like doing nothing. It frightens me, so I try not to do that,"* said BETH, a 30-year-old woman. What do they fear? DIANE had a troubled past, with broken relationships, illness, and poverty; when she was idle, she had time to think of *"the last three years of my life, wallowing in self-pity."* Her life was in danger of being dragged into memory, repeating itself compulsively, like a broken record. She wanted to move ahead, or *be* moved ahead, out of her subjective culture.

Under the surface of "doing nothing" a good deal went on. People not only spoke of feeling guilty; they felt a tension like that of a caged animal. TONY was articulate on this theme:

> *I feel guilty about doing nothing.... I really try not to do that. If I was working, I think I could get away with it. But I am so afraid, that if I don't stay productive, that I'm going to get this sort of restless, lazy feeling. I don't want it to get the best of me.*
>
> *People who are unemployed feel* restless and lazy at the same time.... *I don't know why people feel this way.... I just accept it, because I've felt it before and I've seen other people go through it and so, my way of not feeling that way is to stay busy.* [emphasis added]

According to TONY, while idle time voided *some* of the energy to be active, it also wound up an unfocussed internal energy. Monotony was experienced by the informants as stressful. As KARL remarked: *"Usually when I am doing nothing I'll sit around and get really tense."* PAUL: *"I hate it when I have nothing to do. Pace the floors, just thinking: 'What am I going to do?'"* People spoke of going *"buggy."* JANINE put it vividly:

> *We'll be sitting around and I'll say, "Let's go do something." And he'll say, "What do you want to do?" And I'll say, "I don't know! Anything!" Then we'll go out for a walk.... I got to do something, just can't sit in one spot.... Most parts of the day I hate is when I don't do nothing.... I'm a very energetic person. I like doing things. And when I'm not working, I feel lazy. When I got to go to work I feel more alive.* [emphasis added]

Outside the context of meaningful work and *in* the context of killing time, practices became somewhat lifeless, as though "doing nothing" was a paradigm for the rest of their actions. A faint contempt or patronizing attitude was shown towards other acts, as in FRANCES's case. When employed, she did her knitting and sewing with efficiency and enthusiasm. *"Now it's just, 'Oh, I don't have anything else to do, let's just go sew a bit.' You trundle the portable TV into the sewing room, stick it on—it's just there for noise—and you sew for a while."* FRAN, single and 32, commented: *"Can't say I spend a lot of my day doing nothing, and yet, sometimes you wonder where your day went and what you did with it."* These other practices were not doing nothing, but somehow felt like it. MYRA stated it forcefully:

> *I feel like I'm wasting time. I feel like I'm not accomplishing anything. I don't really feel like I'm contributing to the marriage, to society, or anything like that.*

While the majority of informants did not like idle time—trying with varying success to fill it, escape it, or shorten it—a small number were overwhelmed by it. They tended to be medium- and long-term unemployed, without substantial social support, and they were all depressed. Two had been in the hospital for treatment of their depression. The following descriptions, while untypically severe, in a sense bring us to the logical endpoint of what it can mean to be crushed under a surplus of self-time. They also reveal aspects of the informants' *depression*, which was like a culture that thrives in the medium of unstructured time.

The two cases where therapy had been involved were moving, especially since the people were so articulate. SALLY, 30, was trained as an RNA, but had had a breakdown during her first job. She eventually found work at a local college library. There, she was, according to her account, wrongfully dismissed due to the suspicion that she had mismanaged the distribution of a film. Suffering from a lack of self-esteem, she had been hospitalized several times. At the time of the interview, SALLY's life was structured by her technical training courses, and her boyfriend. The empty time between courses was painful to endure: *"You're sitting there for hours on end and it seems like there's no end. And, is it time to go to bed yet? ... It really makes things kind of hopeless."* ANDREW, who had also been treated for depression, was a 35-year-old former journalist living with his parents and had been unemployed for 16 months. He was a loner, who hinted at suicide, but was also passionately revolutionary in his attitudes towards the establishment. He was embittered by being dismissed from his newspaper jobs for political militancy. Sometimes he just sat distractedly at his typewriter and did nothing. *"I feel in a sense that I'm cursed, that whatever I do, it's going to work out wrong. I have a very hard time motivating myself to do anything."*

MARTHA was 44, divorced, with two teenagers at home, and had been out of work for ten months. After being duped by an unscrupulous travel agent into working for six months with no pay, she was at a loss as to where to turn, or what her future was to be. Her personal structuring of time was in disarray. *"I've got nothing to do in a day... I really have to push myself to do anything, the laundry, going down the elevator.... For myself, when I'm busy, I'm super-super-busy. But once you start dragging yourself down, it's an effort to even...put a cup of coffee, you know."* When asked about hobbies: *"I don't do anything now. Just lost interest. [Any reasons?] Just because of my lackadaisical depressed state."*

Sometimes the engulfment in this voiding time was not given the name "depression" but had a similar torpor and self-absorption. DICK had never held a permanent job. His girlfriend was at college and he was alone during the week. *"Every day of the week is just like one day after another. There's nothing really you can plan. I take one day as it comes.... My girlfriend*

comes in and wakes me up. I say, 'What do you wake me up for?' I've got noth-
ing to do. What's the use of getting up from bed? You might as well sleep till two
or three in the afternoon, do your work, watch a little TV, eat supper, watch some
more TV, then go to bed. And do the same thing over again.... I sit on the couch,
go to the window, look outside and...nothing, you know."

DICK was living with a negation, his time had been "killed." All the
others who fought the void that beckoned to them in unstructured moments sympathized with DICK and the other sufferers. Wrenched out of
societal time, they had been pressed into ever-diminishing time scales.
Forgetting plans about careers, or what the next few years will bring, it
became: Get through the month; Get through the week; Take each day as
it comes; Count the hours. Then, the final compression into consciousness
of minutes, the ticking of the clock.

In the final analysis, "killing time" and "losing ground" were deeply
linked. The intense compression of the unemployed into smaller and
smaller units of space with its terminus in the home had its counterpart
in the intense compression of the unemployed into smaller and smaller
units of time.

Conclusions

The constructed activities of the unemployed at home and in the community had a markedly varied syntax. Goal-oriented activities in the community were synergistic and enriching involvements away from home.
Relations with others in volunteer work, or in classrooms and training
shops, restored a sense of connection with other adults who could be considered equals. There was the active pursuit of artistic work and hobbies,
where one was the subject of one's action and worked in the future perfect tense.

The danger was, however, as unemployment became entrenched, that
public involvements would dry up, and one's practices would become
atomized evasions of unstructured time. Activities in the home would slip
into the passive voice and an oppressively real present tense. The unemployed person may have been nominal (or "grammatical") subject of
his or her practices, but the self would begin to cede initiative to any
stimuli that could promise deliverance from the task of organizing the unstructured day.

Judging from the interviews, idle time was like a dry rot undermining
the social construction of human activity itself. Especially in the disabling
context of unemployment and poverty, idle time sucked energy from life,
collapsed plans, postponed action, left one prey to appetites, fantasies,
regrets. For many of the informants, then, it was not just a void but a *void-*
ing force. The phrase "killing time" should suggest a conjunctural prac-

tice, indeed a "multiple killing," at an intersection in the relation between society and self. First it is society that "kills" the time of the unemployed by refusing to buy labour power which is surplus to the requirements of capital's quest for profit. Unbought, unwanted, their time has been placed "on the shelf." The second "killing" is the voiding or negating influence which idle time exerted over other parts of the day ("killing" is here used as an adjective). The third "killing" comprises the ways the unemployed themselves reactively try to "get rid of" idle time.

CHAPTER NINE

Family Relationships

We have learned that being involuntarily deprived of work in our society pushes people out of the public realm and down into microsocial settings and relationships. A key social formation then is the *family:* not only does it share the burdens of its unemployed member, it also (in many cases) mobilizes to protect and sustain that person.

It may be useful to make a familiar distinction at this point between "families of orientation," i.e. the families that make us, and "families of procreation," i.e. the families which we (some of us) make. In our society these family types live apart, do different work, and often carry on in different lifestyles and social worlds. For adults, each type tends to have its own distinct kind of "we-feeling." In our family of procreation, emotional depths, and even dependencies upon the relationships, arise from extensive mutual involvement in daily life, shared resources, and life plans. At its best, this family type sustains and confirms the identity of its members, and offers love and the opportunity to love. On its more negative side, the family can inflict abuse and reinforce inequality in a more thorough and intimate way than any other institution.

The family of orientation, on the other hand, is also, especially in the early years, the object of deep attachment. But as we move into adulthood, these bonds lose their existential urgency and are kept at an emotional, and spatial, distance from the family of procreation. A Canadian adult will often relate less frequently with parents and siblings than with friends. The nuclear family tends to want to walk its own path to its own future engaging selectively with members of the earlier family out of voluntary choice, not compulsion or need.

The purpose of the chapter is to describe and analyze how the informants' experiences of unemployment entered into this "normal" (and normative) pattern of Canadian family life. The social practices under review have to do with relationships with the *partner:*

- Being Supported by and Depending on the Other;
- Being Impinged on by the Other; Chafing;

- Dividing Domestic Labour;

with *children:*

- Caring for Children;

and with *parents and kin:*

- Re-intensifying Bonds with Parents and Kin.

The Partner

Being Supported by and Depending on the Other

There were 15 married informants and eight living in common-law arrangements. Some of the others had relationships with boyfriends, girlfriends, or talked about ex-spouses. Generally, the talk about relationships dwelt on difficulties rather than satisfactions. This undoubtedly reflected real-world strains imposed on couples by joblessness; but, additionally, it may be that the positive underpinning which committed relationships gave to people's daily lives was taken for granted or could not be easily verbalized.

The unemployed person's partner, in his or her comings and goings, provided structure to an otherwise rather shapeless day. Helping them get off in the morning, preparing supper for their return, spending time together during the evenings and weekends, going shopping—these prosaic events formed parts of a scaffold on which the unemployed person's week was built. DESMOND's wife rose at six a.m. for work, and he struggled hard to get up with her. After that,

From eight a.m. on, I'm just here by myself, and when they [i.e. his children] come back from school and when my wife comes back from work, that's when I have company. This releases my tension a little bit.

What he did in the evening depended mostly on what his wife wanted to do.

The negative side of this was that an emotional need or craving for the other arose in certain people. The lowering of confidence and self-esteem caused by unemployment intensified the need to be loved and respected. It was as if the person had become an empty vessel which needed to be filled by the other. DIANE, who had just broken up with her boyfriend, explained:

Because I'm in this real down right now—you can't be in a relationship unless you like yourself, unless you're happy with yourself, feeling you have something to give. Well, when you're unemployed those things seem to go down the drain, you know, your self-esteem, confidence.

...It's helping to break up this relationship more than anything. I think if I was working I would be so much happier with myself, I would feel like I was doing some-

thing—I would have interesting things to say. It would just be so helpful and I wouldn't miss him as much if I had more in my life, and we weren't going to be able to see each other that often.

The women tended to be more expressive about this dependency. KATHY waited for her man to come home from about mid-afternoon on. The only times she enjoyed, it seemed, were the weekends and evenings when he was home. The rest of the time she was in a kind of depression, not even able to read: *"When he wasn't there, it was awful."* [This was an untypically severe reaction]. MYRA, the former nutritionist, had an intern-husband who left at six a.m. and often would not return until eleven p.m. or later. She expressed her situation movingly:

And often I am waiting and waiting. And often he can't get to the phone and call me. And this is why I think if I were at work, I would have things to do in the day, and things to do when I got home, and wouldn't always be waiting and waiting for him to come.... Having him be the answer to...whatever. [emphasis added]

As with the other vortices in the home, discussed in the previous chapter, the *relationship* could subtly change its syntax to the passive voice. She was not the active participant in the relationship, but the one who waited, passively. The other had become the *answer* to a generalized need of the self.

The partner came into the home fresh from the outside, importing what seemed to be a different, more bracing sensibility than that of the unemployed. The informants appreciated this brisk objectivity, the sense of events having transpired, a real-world confidence that difficulties could be overcome. Yet, when it come to their own chances of being employed, some informants mistrusted their partner's optimism and robustness— feeling that their cheerfulness was somewhat obtuse and even constituted a denial of suffering. While the buoyant optimism was appreciated as an antidote to a depressed mood, one never knew whether it was well-founded in fact, was just a pep talk, or was an evasion of the sheer depth of the unemployment experience. JOANNE spoke of this:

I don't really know if he [her husband] *is trying to instill confidence in me by not worrying or...if he's just not worrying because he's not worried.*

Sometimes it's a little frustrating. Because I will want him to see that I am feeling this anxiety, and he will say, "What are you worrying about? You'll find something." And I want to talk to him, and I want him to reassure me more—but he doesn't have that to give, I guess.... Or just, truly, he's just not worried! Maybe he's got supreme confidence in me. [laughs]

She wanted to go along with his jaunty outlook [*"If he's not worried, why should I be worried?"*], but also wanted to show him the depths in her life experience than he had so far evaded.

Apart from listening to the unemployed person and helping build self-esteem, partners and lovers were consulted during those crucial moments in the job search when human agency and freedom were on the line. COL-LEEN was a recent psychology graduate who had worked for years at minimum wage in grocery stores and out in the fruit fields. She desperately wanted to use her education in the area of child development. Then she was offered a day care position, during a particularly job-hungry time. The position involved 45 to 50 hours per week and paid only $8000, which would not even allow her to pay back her student loans—nor was it a direction she wanted to take with her psychology degree. Yet her family, and her partner Jerry's family, urged her to take it; it would pay the bills. Even Jerry supported their position at first. He had worked as a cabby and a tobacco-picker in the summer and was just beginning university.

She explained to him that she felt she had to hold out for *"what would let me work the way I want to work."* He thought it over and then reversed his decision, telling her (in her words): *"You can't really sacrifice everything you want because you have to have a job. There are limits to what you should take."* Jerry had perhaps caught the importance to COLLEEN of this decision; of how her sense of will and purpose, even self, required her to go beyond passively accepting whatever the market threw up, into the realm of autonomous choice.

For many others as well, the support of a partner meant that one could more effectively exercise human agency in the marketplace. TONY thrived on his wife's support. After a brief government work project, he conducted his search in a slow deliberate manner. His wife totally backed up his refusal to take just anything. After selling books in offices for a week, a job he hated, he simply quit. *"Her reaction to that was I'd rather be poor and happy than have money and be miserable. She's great, really supportive."* Having had many jobs that she did not like and now with a good job, she seemed to respect his decision to wait it out. Asked whether he felt jealous or resentful at his wife's work, he emphatically said no: *"She understands, has gone through it all. She understands when I say that I don't want to sell books."*

Not all partners provided that key support for self-affirming decisions. JOANNE's difficult but necessary decision to quit her abusive office job greatly improved her marriage. But her husband, rankled at the loss of income, told her once: *"Maybe you shouldn't have left that job,"* and it stunned her. She rationalized this unempathetic remark by claiming it was made in anger. Her (perhaps excessive) need for reassurance from her partner is evident in this excerpt:

> *He must know as I do that things are much better between us, since leaving there. I have been a much happier person.... Basically, at the bottom line, I knew I had done the right thing. To remove myself from that atmosphere. I knew I was right. I*

don't really need anyone to say, "You did the right thing." ...But like everyone else, I need some reassuring, I need some stroking too.

The husband's remark had cast doubt on one of the more self-determining moments in his wife's life.

Being Impinged on by the Other

If the occasionally absent partner was a magnified object of dependence, the constantly *present* partner became a diminished figure in a shrunken world. The lack of stimulation from employment in a mobile, cash-oriented society eventually worked itself down to intimate relationships. *"Not having...outside stimulation does affect your relationship,"* commented COLLEEN. *"You're constantly around each other all the time. Instead of having your own world to go to, and then come home...something that interests you as well. It strains things. Money's tight and there's no way for you to go out and do something on your own."*

What world *was* left to the unemployed (or underemployed) couple? Unemployment, with its negative status, had no specific world of its own, only the residual, paramount reality of the daily routine at home. Many informants, especially women who were more bound to domestic duties, pointed out that there was less and less to talk about. HEATHER spent her days caring for her two small children and other children whom she baby-sat. In the evenings, she did the books for her husband's small business. Financial troubles had forced them to sell their trailer. She felt encapsulated, even a bit entombed.

We find that we don't go as many places. And when we're home, we don't have as much to talk about. The last year, we watched TV more, which bores me to death. But it's just because it's something there. To do together. Because there's nothing to talk about.... *He doesn't want to hear all day long about kids. He doesn't want to talk about his work all the time. The conversations get smaller and smaller. You get kind of in a tunnel.*

In this case, unemployment not only widened a pre-existing gulf in the couple's experience, but frayed the lines of communication that could be thrown over it.

Some of the younger informants shared the same threadbare joblessness as their partners, and the feeling of being closeted was strong. PAUL and his partner were trying to find work in the glutted restaurant sector. He described the constant imposition of the partner's presence: *"We get on each other's nerves a lot more, just sit there staring at each other or at the four walls. Up until a couple of weeks ago, we didn't even have a television or a telephone.... We couldn't afford it. So we were fighting a lot more, because there was nothing else to do. We didn't even have the money to go out and have a beer. We would just sit there, practically 24 hours a day."*

The impinging of not just his partner, but his parents as well, put a crushing burden on KARL's marriage. He was 38 and had been un-employed for nine months, after being laid off from various warehouses and garden centres. His East Indian wife was pregnant with their second child and could not work. All KARL brought home was an Unemployment Insurance cheque of $488 a month. Fortunately, in a material sense, he and his family were able to live with his parents. But being home with his wife, he claimed, exposed him to the gamut of her frustrations and rages. Her family, Hindus and Indian Catholics, included professional and business people whose successes were regularly chronicled by his wife, thrown like salt into KARL's wounds. *"She cries a lot and yells a lot and gets really upset...Mostly I just say nothing and wait till she yells herself out."* Every morning before he looked for work, she commented critically about his appearance, as though he were her child. KARL's parents were slightly resistant to Indian food, making it difficult for his wife to cook. The parents also took issue with the way they handled their child. Their domestic situation, needless to say, discouraged them from entertaining friends. Whatever the objective reason for KARL's exclusion from the labour market, it was construed as personal failure in his relations at home.

The mutual impingement of informant and partner in an environment that provided little to talk about led to constant arguing, especially about money problems. One spouse played the immoveable object against the irresistible need of the other for funds. Whatever the arguments' themes, they strained the informants' relationships, even (in four reported cases) leading to marital break-ups. It seemed that unemployment created con-ditions that struck at the heart of intimate ties. While all relationships have constraints, at their centre is a voluntary choice that conceived the rela-tion and must sustain it. Part of this voluntariness is the freedom to *withdraw* from interaction time, to take up other pursuits within self- or societal time. Just as conversation alternates speech and silence, a relation-ship mixes presence and withdrawal (assuming there is a world to withdraw *to*). For the informants whose unemployment made them de-pendent on their partner, the respect for the boundaries between self and other began to deteriorate. The couple became increasingly inbred and localized in their concerns.

When the partner took steps to withdraw from interaction time at home and go to an outside life, the informant "left behind" felt envy, regret, or sadness. STAN, a househusband, spoke of his partner's career as an ex-perienced teacher: *"The biggest thrills she gets in life are out of her work. I'm sorry to say that but that's true. I'm sorry to say it because I think she should be getting more strokes from her personal life, but basically she worked hard for what she has and I can see the benefit."* MATTHEW clearly sensed his wife's impulse to flee the home. *"She'd much rather be out working because we don't have to see each other. If we constantly see each other 24 hours a day, it bothers her as much as it bothers me. She likes to get away from the house: she's got things to go to, she can talk to people, she's out working as well, and she brings home a paycheque."*

Dividing Domestic Labour

Domestic labour became an important issue in relationships, particularly for women. We will look first at the women in couples (most of whom were wives), and then the men (househusbands).

The Women (Wives)

The unemployed wives were virtually unanimous that massive amounts of housework were imposed on them.

> *When I was working, it was more of a joint effort between my husband and I to get it done.... But when I was off then—I don't know if it was me or just the way things went—it became more my responsibility, which I really hated. There was no escape from.... There would always be something to do.... I hate it.*
>
> SUSAN

> *I feel he takes advantage of me a little bit more now that I'm not working. He didn't always expect dinner. He didn't always expect me to make his lunches.... And now he feels I should be doing all that. And I hate it.... You know, I went to university for four years, and worked really hard to get a degree, and I did that so I wouldn't have to make lunches and do breakfasts.*
>
> MYRA

> *He expects me to do it all...I really get mad at him for not helping out as much. I feel he should be helping me more.... But I go back to the old thinking that, well, he is working everyday, and he should have hot meals.... Then I switch back and think, "No, I'm here with the kids all day, and he should be able to help." I get to the point where I have to be very pushy about it.*
>
> HEATHER

> *When I worked, my husband helped [laughs]. It took me 15 years to get him that way.... When I'm working, I can walk in the house, and the house is clean. When I'm not working, that stops. He doesn't put the kettle on for tea; I serve the tea. I've become the lackey. He just does nothing.... He comes home and showers and just sits, watches TV. I make the meals, bring his tea, I do everything. That happens automatically as I'm home.... When I'm not working, she's [i.e. her daughter] like him. I really am aware—where I wasn't five years ago—that my husband is supporting me. I don't know what I'd do now if I were separated.... I really try to show [gratitude]. I do special baking when I'm home. I do all nice little things for*

them. I want to show them that I appreciate them.... I've become a char lady. And it's something I don't like to do. I resent it. But I don't now that I'm unemployed. I feel that I have to do it.

ERICA

I do everything now. The only thing that he does is take out the garbage.... He was always good [when she worked]. *He would do the dishes as quickly as I would.... He gets off at three. When I got home, dinner was almost on the table.... He never even thinks to do anything like that now.... His mother never worked. And now, it's just like it was his parent's family. It really is. Even leaves his socks lying around downstairs. He likes coming home—he's mentioned this many times—with the house nice and clean. He likes me doing the cooking.*

JOANNE

For the wives the onset of unemployment brought a structural shift in their relation to the domestic scene. The whole of housework devolved to them virtually by default, as though some older role were springing back into place. They did not so much *decide* to contribute to the family in this way; rather, they found themselves slipping back into the domestic role they had assumed in the early part of their marriage. However established the wife's rights had become over the years, there was now a reversion to a mute, pre-conscious state, as though her domestic role were being re-woven back into the order of things.

This time, however, she was not starting a marriage but stepping down from a position of maturity and attainment. Having cut a figure in the world of work, been recognized by other adults, rewarded, deferred to, the return to a solitary role as "domestic"—which even in its own domain was losing its definition as worker—was a double loss for the woman. She lost her public role *and* her standing in the family. Indeed, as JOANNE's quote indicated, she had become a kind of unpaid employee of her husband, who was almost glad to have her back servicing his daily needs.

What kept the re-alignment of the unemployed wife's situation in check was partly the unspoken acquiescence of the husband and family. Also implicated, however, was the wife herself, especially her guilt and her reinforced sense of being dependent on her husband. In the previous comments of HEATHER and ERICA, there was a marked ambivalence that swung from the conviction, "I should be treated equally at home," to the resigned acceptance of the reality that "He *is* supporting me and is therefore entitled to meals and a clean house," and back again. The social support for the egalitarian self-understanding of the wife seemed to wither under the force of economic pressure. Whereas, in contrast, the social support for her subordinate role in the home hardened, underscored by older cultural assumptions which came automatically into play.

The effect on the *personal identity* of the wife was two-fold: a slow erosion of her perceived role as a worker (both in public and at home), and a loss of her sense of being an independent person. That both role "exits" could be devastating blows was attested to by the emotional intensity of their expressions.

> *I'm more depressed...I just kind of feel that everything is slipping away in its own slow way.... I feel rather trapped, I guess. I have to rely on other people for things, and I'm not too impressed with having to do that. I'm much more independent. I guess I put other people first ahead of myself.... I feel at times that I wish I didn't have any children.*
>
> HEATHER
>
> *I've missed out somewhere.... I'm nothing.... I feel like a has-been, I'm ready for the pasture.... I don't have the confidence I would have had, say, 15 years ago.... I feel like I'm 65, that life is over.*
>
> ERICA

Within a market economy where jobs were scarce and selectively distributed, within a patriarchal culture and social system, the losses of these precious contents of the self may be irrecoverable. Societally engendered, socially supported in the family, and finally lodged in personal identity—the process of marginalization, this time keyed to gender, continued apace.

Househusbands

The househusbands, for the most part, claimed to do more housework now that they were unemployed and their wives were working. A very few said that they did most of the housework. For some of the men, their intensified domestic labour was seen simply as a practical solution to an imposed requirement. Someone had to be with the children in the evening when the wife was working; the meal had to be prepared if she got home at 6 p.m. *"Work has to be done, who's got the time?"* asked BOB matter-of-factly. This from a man who believed that the Biblical order of things required the wife to stay home with the family and the husband to earn its bread. This was how he described his typical day:

> *I make a pot of coffee and watch Donahue. Clean up the house. The baby—whatever that entails in the given day. Feeding. Mondays and Thursdays, the diaper service. The laundry to be taken care of. General maintenance of the house.... I do the kitchen and Betty does the bathroom.*

Invoking the norm of fairness, he added: *"If I don't get the housework done, she has every right to get upset with me. Because, what have I done all day?"*

It is difficult to generalize from only 10 cases, but the househusband role tended to be more acceptable to the man if he was:

- Middle class;
- Familiar with the ethos of feminism, which provided an ideology for the sharing of housework;
- Confident that he would find work, that the househusband role would be temporary;
- Not straining the family's finances by staying home.

A few informants, such as TONY, positively embraced the role. Stretching the housework to fill his time, he worked with perfectionism and style. He took a cupboard apart and organized it, or cleaned rooms that were rarely used. There was even a tone of domestic snobbishness in some of his remarks:

> *Do you know one thing? This is really weird. The way your kitchen looks.... The rings around the stove. You can make them shine or you can just wipe them, right? For the first time, I thought, well, I can really make these shine.... Even when I walk into someone's kitchen, I notice these things. I can sort of understand my mother-in-law coming in and criticizing my wife because there's dust here and dust there.*

He had taken on the habit of drawing out mundane tasks to make time go faster. When on occasion his elaborated housework betrayed itself for the make-work it really was, TONY suddenly stopped himself in the middle of a task: *"What am I doing? What do I care? I never cared about this before but now I care about it."* It was though his self had snapped out of the "automatic pilot" of filling time and assumed conscious control.

Even for those who accepted housework, the thought that it would be a full-time career was discarded out of hand. In a cash economy the role was inescapably a dependent one. *"Now I can't see living off somebody else— that really bothers me. And she is the same way. I could never see myself in the situation of the husband supporting the wife or vice versa"* (STAN). SIMON found that it was *"just not socially acceptable.... Not only in my own family, not even with my own wife."* For those with wives in low-income jobs, the houseworker role was a chafing one, traced with a guilt that they was not adding to the family income.

The working-class househusbands tended to find the role unsuited to them. One of the pre-test interviewees, REGGIE, was a laid-off electrician with two children. While he loved his children, their needs had always been in the background, attended to by his wife. Now their daily needs were *his* business. He knew this was fair but felt estranged from the role. *"It's not that I mind. I just don't want to be here. She'd rather be here, because she gets more involved 'n stuff with education...I'm a little lax about these things.*

As long as it's above board. She'd be better here than me." In BOB's case, he sadly pointed out that his baby was not bonding to the proper parent:

> *She* [his wife] *comes home some days and she picks up the baby…and then I smile at the baby from across the room, and the baby wants to come to me.… Betty is now the "father" in the house, second place to "Mommy." I'm "Mommy" all of a sudden—in sociological terms. And it hurts Betty; sometimes she just sits there and cries, because the baby does not respond to her the way the baby used to.*

The househusbands, in sum, differed from the wives in that they did much but not all the housework. Their domestic labour was not as taken-for-granted as that of the wives. It was made to appear weightier by its voluntary nature and its role in the working of justice in the family. That being said, the househusbands did contribute significantly and did feel some of the frustrations (if not the anguish) of the housewife. They felt the long passage of time and wondered at what they had accomplished all week.

Children

Caring for Children

Given that unemployment reduced contact with the outside world and compressed activity into the home, how did it affect caring for children? This is far from an easy question. Rearing children plainly differed from other kinds of interaction time. Unlike friends who could be turned to voluntarily, children compelled attention, often summoning parents to attend to their needs. Furthermore, informants' relationships with them were so complex and ambivalent, and fed from so many sources, that it was hard to tell what independent impact unemployment had at all.

For some informants, caring for children was an inescapable mandate which the self had not so much chosen as found itself attached to. RUTH, a 51-year-old single parent, was living in government housing with the last three of her seven children. Her husband had deserted her when she was home with all seven. Not having worked for pay for 20 years (now on Mother's Allowance), RUTH and her family lived in considerable social isolation. In the interview her manner was depressed and timid. In her years at home, she had done what she was supposed to do: raise her family. Of course, it was not in the cultural script that her husband would abandon her. Now, with her last children in their teens, she worried about the future. She *wanted* a role in the adult world, but what? *"When my children would be grown up, what would I do? Right now the only thing that keeps me going is with them. I'd have nothing to keep me going, just sit at home and be bored."* Her increased self-time at home kept casting her back. *"When you're home, it gives you time to think. Mother's home with seven children and the husband deserted them. I don't get anything out of it—I'd rather be out."*

The extravagant investment by some mothers of their personal *identities* in their children seemed to rob the self of its autonomous powers. This was the case with MARTHA, a 44-year-old divorcée with two teenagers at home. Like her own mother who had stayed home all her life, MARTHA assumed that *her* life would be cut to the same pattern. With her husband in a good job, she took up her place in the home and loved it. She was a Brownie leader and deeply involved with children. *"I raised two beautiful kids."* Like RUTH, she was unprepared for the separation.

> *I never even dreamed I would be separated. Now I find I'm struggling. I'm not prepared. I don't have the education, and it's hard out there.... I feel the clamps are put on me. I didn't take care of myself, and I should have, and kept working....* I had kind of cast off myself. *I had not even thought about what was going to happen to me.* [emphasis added]

The one continuity in her radically changed situation was her children: *"I tend to centre my life around my kids, because that's all I've got."* But though her children might offer her security later, *she* had to face the adult working world in the present. Armed with an opinion of herself she described as *"zilch,"* she admitted to being *"scared, really scared."* MARTHA's close relatives were worried about her being unemployed. *"They know I'm not destitute for money, but they can see what it's doing to my...self."*

What was the *quality* of time spent with children, according to these unemployed mothers? For a few former workers, the added time with children made possible by unemployment was an unalloyed pleasure. The personal relationship with children seemed to take on a new depth and richness. Here was how JOANNE, just released from an oppressive job situation, described it: *"I've had more time just to sit and listen. Rather than have to say: 'Well, I'm busy right now; we'll talk about it later.' There isn't anything I can't stop."* She has taken her son to the library to show him how to operate the computer and the microfiche. *"If I were working, I wouldn't have had the time to do that."* If she and her husband had not needed a second income, she would have stayed home longer.

There were mothers who, deprived of productive opportunities elsewhere, thought they could at least perfect the artifact that was their child. ERICA, struggling with long-term unemployment and its legacy of uselessness, made sure that her daughter was *"well turned out."* Having fallen from a middle-class lifestyle, she could not *buy* much for her daughter, but she could wash certain clothes by hand, sew, and make things. As with the mothers discussed earlier, who sacrificed their own needs to their children's, there was a refocussing in which the unemployed self shrank behind an enlarged other. The child—the hope and prestige of the family in the public realm, its claim on the future—was readied to walk the stage of the world. The mother and the family home had become the backstage for this endeavour.

Caring for children could shift from active to passive voice, when the unemployed mother ceded the personal structuring of her day to the child, almost by default. BRENDA, a 21-year-old single parent who had worked at a donut shop part time, had a three-year-old Down's Syndrome child. She was so bored in the mornings when her daughter was at Day Care, that she found herself going there just to watch her child. In the afternoons, the two of them watched TV, or visited friends or parents. *"We seem quite dependent on each other,"* she remarked uncomfortably, adding that, before, at least she had been employed. Once again, unemployment seemed to contribute to undermining the will of the self to control its time. Within the field of that depleted energy, objects, pursuits, and relationships began to overmatch the self, consigning it to passive voice.

There was a clear case of a child being deliberately conceived by a young single woman to fill an emptiness. TRACEY, a 22-year-old with a four-year-old daughter, had some high school classes and a secretarial course behind her. Regarding little Julie, she admitted: *"I had her on purpose. Because I needed something to fill an empty spot in me. Which she did."* Whatever void the child filled—low self-esteem, boredom, poor occupational or school prospects—she had set up an agenda for TRACEY's life. The mother's day was completely structured around the daughter: bathing, feeding, taking her out. When she was in school, her mother planned things to do with her. The highlight of the day was from late afternoon when Julie came home until her bedtime. While the child was home, TRACEY stretched out activities to keep the little one interested.

All her other relationships now pivoted around this immense "we-feeling" with her daughter, who had become an extension of herself. She had to defend her full-time child-rearing to her own mother, who had been urging her to look for work instead of collecting Mother's Allowance. She recounted their painful discussions: *"So I said, 'You know, Mom, sure it was OK when we were little, you went to work, but we didn't get you. Sure there was a little bit of money hanging around, but that doesn't compare to having a parent around.... I just want to be around her for a while.'"* Her relations with friends were affected: she broke off with her old single crowd, because they showed no understanding of her responsibilities with the child, and she was tired of their pointless pursuits. As for meeting men and making new contacts, she was holding back. She wanted to avoid involvements because *"it's going to affect me and it's going to affect Julie."*

The vantage point of TRACEY's life was now "we," not "I." Having a child extended the self, made it feel loved and needed, structured its time whereas before there had been an empty slate. Of course, it is reasonable to conclude that for many such women, the slate had been wiped clean by a society with little to offer young people. The choice of having a child was partly conditioned by the lack of alternatives.

The devotion of so much interaction and self-time to children exacted a price from these mothers: it made them less confident in dealings with adults, especially strangers. SUSAN found that, between courses, when she was back at home with the children: *"I really felt myself falling back into not feeling sure with myself. So I think a lot of it has to do with not being around adults all the time."*

If the interaction time with children was too engulfing—a situation which unemployment helped bring about—the quality of the relationship deteriorated. Children may have offered an outlet for loving and proud feelings, but also they impinged relentlessly, making it easy to displace anger upon them. Providing for them was a hardship, minding them a restriction of freedom. Parents reported turning off attention, not wanting to be bothered, or getting short-tempered—which was normal. A few, however, talked of taking it out on the kids, suggesting a situation that was more explosive. A woman explained: *"you take out stuff on the people that are closest to you."* When MONICA, became tense she asked her sister-in-law to mind her son. This happened a few times a year *"when things would get out of hand. I'm not saying I would hit him, but…"* JANINE and her husband had their first child taken from them by Children's Aid, on grounds of mistreatment. She disagreed with their decision, but felt they would be better parents if they both had work.

The clearest expression of the dark side of the mothers' ambivalence towards children was HEATHER's. She had been laid off from a factory post, then had some bad jobs, and was now home tending to her small children. She and her husband were struggling economically. A few years ago, a crisis had occurred in her life. During a medical at the factory, she found out that she was pregnant. At the time, her husband was unemployed and in an addiction unit for alcoholism, so the family depended on her wages.

> So after seeing a marriage counsellor…and deciding I had to be more independent and do things on my own, I decided to have the pregnancy terminated. Which was really hard, because it was really a wanted baby. But I felt that I couldn't be at home with two small children in an apartment. I felt that I would never get out of that rut.… I didn't want to live that way, I didn't want to be on assistance, I didn't know if things would work out between he and I.

In what was a powerful bid of the self for freedom, she concluded: *"I have to work. I have to get out of here."*

Parents and Kin

Re-Intensifying Bonds with Parents and Kin

Many informants, especially the single ones, socialized much more with members of family than before: spending weekends with them, visiting, taking trips. *"I don't see my friends as often,"* commented FRANCES; *"I have that real social life now within my family."* This helped to take up the slack created by the diminishing social contacts with friends. Increased interaction with the extended family helped to overcome the isolation of joblessness.

The wider family was sometimes immensely synergistic, connecting the informants with people, services, and perspectives. Here is a sampling from the vast number of helpful practices parents and kin engaged in:

- Lending or giving money;
- Offering free land to build a cottage;
- Providing odd jobs for pay around the house;
- Driving the informants around or lending the car;
- Letting informants do laundry at home;
- Suggesting job ideas, turning up contacts, arranging job interviews;
- Taking over car payments;
- Paying for child care;
- Sewing clothes;
- Listening, trying to understand, encouraging.

The availability of these supports was a prime factor in keeping people close to their kin (and therefore reducing their mobility). DIANE had moved back to London to where her family lived: *"I knew I was going to have a tough time so I needed some supports."* DONALD, the unemployed cook, had moved to Edmonton for work but was now back in London where his family lived. They gave him odd jobs, some money, a place to stay for a few months.

The informants appreciated the low-keyed support offered by parents and relatives. For CONNIE, it was important that her parents were *"just there. They don't bug me, they try to do what they can to help. Which is largely by not bugging me* [laughs]." People appreciated it when relatives showed no elaborate concern or did not fuss about their unemployment; calm reactions seemed to normalize things and offer perspective. One young man found gratefully that his relatives were not surprised about his unemployment, putting it down to a *"sign of the times."* Young KIM's parents were used to her being out of school, but insisted that she not lie around at home, but look for work or do volunteer work. Her father was a trucker who, though not at home much and occasionally ill-tempered, was very understanding with her.

> *If I have a problem, I'll go and talk to my Mom, like I'll tell her I want to be myself, I don't want to be nobody else, and she won't understand what I'm talking about. And I'll wait until my Dad...and he'll say, you know, "You are who you are, we're not making you be another person."*

The parents who were similarly attentive and empathetic, listening to the outpourings of confusion and self-doubt, were the most cherished.

LAURIE's mother was supportive in this way during a period of struggle. "*The pain of certain emotions, certain adjustments I had to make to finally leave adolescence behind, and finally grow up. She knew what it was about, because she had been there in her twenties as well. She had been separated and then divorced, she'd had to work on her own, she had to raise children, she knew the trouble I was having in my mind. She was supportive for me and...I'm grateful for that.*" VINCENT was also fortunate in his mother. "*I guess my Mom and I have the same philosophy about things. She understands my situation. [She doesn't pressure you to conform?] No, no. Well, she does say, 'If you leave your hair like that, it will be easier for you.'*" He suspected that she worried about him, but overall she accepted and supported him, always pointing out the consequences of his choices rather than forcing his hand. For a young man who was being denied the means to adult self-determination by the job market, being treated like an adult by his mother was most important.

Parental support was often crucial for informants, as in the case of KEN-NETH. A graduate of the co-op engineering program at the University of Waterloo, he was overweight, sensitive, living with his parents. His father went through the Depression, "*so understands exactly.*" Were his parents emotionally supportive? "*Yes. That's the one reason I've been able to cope with it so well—because my parents are willing to listen, they are supportive.... That's the only reason I've been able to withstand it this long.*" For MYRA, whose "ethnic" husband and in-laws wanted her at home to be his traditional wife and support his career, her parents' understanding of her need to work outside the home was vital. That support helped keep her sane in an uncomprehending atmosphere.

What complicated this increased time with the family was that much of it involved the passive receiving of help, services, and support. People felt reluctant to borrow or take money from the family. DICK needed money, but his father still had four mouths to feed, and his relatives had bills to pay—so he held back from asking. Certain informants refrained from unburdening themselves to their parents, some of whom were too anxiety-ridden to be of much help. Some of the working-class informants deprived themselves of emotional support by not talking about their problems, not wanting to *"put everyone down."* This contrasted with middle-class individuals who wanted to talk freely about their problems.

Relationships with the extended family often became strained when the unemployed person approached them. Reduced in dignity and circumstances, the person faced the family again—opening the self to whatever prejudices or power urges existed in the family. Some relatives almost examined the informant like a defective machine, assuming there was something which they could fix or reform in the person. EVELYN had been the youngest of 13 children. Her older brothers and sisters did not understand her condition, partly because, as the youngest, she had identified with a more rebellious generation than theirs. She had travelled a great deal, made a living as a singer, and was a political activist. Now separated from her partner and supporting a child, she was back in the orbit of the family again. Her parents put her up, but the old antagonisms soon resurfaced.

> One of my sisters-in-law called me up one morning and said, "How come you're not strawberry-picking?" She said, "They can pick you up at six in the morning, and drive you out and you can pick all day, and earn lots of money." I said, "What am I going to do with Becky? Dad can't take care of her, he's too old. What am I going to do, yank her out of bed at five, and either take her with me all day, or drag her over to a neighbour if a neighbour would take her?"

Her sister-in-law insisted she could find somebody to take the child, and finally EVELYN said, *"If I can possibly do it, I'll do it; if I can't find a solution, I won't."* If EVELYN were employed, she would not be subjected to this kind of indignity; lack of money and independence meant she had to suffer the family fools, if not gladly.

Family members sometimes became critical and patronizing, reverting to older authority relations. EVA's mother had a way of helping her that made her feel inadequate. *"She keeps forgetting that I'm 23, that I've been through university, that I've got my degree. And I know what's going on in the world. She treats me like I'm 16."* MONICA's brothers and sisters were extremely mean-spirited. *"My older brother, when I lost my job, he was ashamed. I remember him saying, 'There's a lot of jobs out there, there are tons....' I said, 'You find me something.' And he couldn't—he was lying through his teeth."* She was forced to ask him for a loan, and offered to pay him back with a higher rate of interest than the bank offered. Her brother not only refused, but complained to the social worker. *"And he gave her a speech about, 'Look, I work hard for my money. I pay my taxes, my taxes are paying to support her, and that's not right. She should be able to work.'"* In addition to his harsh behaviour, her sisters also refused to help her. One terrible week she did not have enough money for food. She asked both of her sisters if they could buy her groceries for that week: *"Their attitude was, 'Look, it's too bad, tough luck.'"*

Parents sometimes tried to mould their adult, unemployed children after the pattern of their own early years. JANE's father, something of a self-made man, interpreted her joblessness according to truths from his own past, which he mythologized as the model of ideal human action:

> My father's attitude—he worked his way across Canada—he sort of put into me that work gets you there. There's a job out there, go get it. Say you can do something. [How does he define work?] *Labour, for a wage. He doesn't consider art work. You know, a little dab here and you walk away.*
>
> *He said he knew how to drive a tractor trailer...and he didn't have the license.... Then he got a* [farming] *job and he had to practice before work every day between seven and eight. My dad worked his way through plowing and...he was an uneducated man. He is in a position now that nobody would suspect he only had a grade four education, because he's self-taught. So you can't tell my dad you can't get a job. My dad won't believe that sort of thing.*

Her father turned dubious generalizations into moral absolutes: that work only meant something practical (not Art); that work was synonymous with paid employment; that the unemployed were shirking work; that people were better off taking whatever job they can get. This kind of talk, received while under the parents' thumb in dependent conditions, was particularly stinging to the ears.

Other troubles were mentioned in relations with parents and extended families. Some families could only communicate at a shallow level. They recited old platitudes: "You can do it, you'll get a job," as though ritualistically keeping the trouble away. One woman had tried to take them deeper, but became convinced that they did not want to penetrate her situation. MARIANNE described the difficulty in making her daughter and husband understand; she was just starting to break through. When asked if they were now supporting her? *"Oh, yes. Mainly because I have told them, I've stuck up for my rights. Before, I used to be apologetic all the time, and now I say, 'It's not my fault!'"*

Some families did not know how to cope with failure and difficulty. ERICA's mother, for instance, only involved herself in her daughter's life when ERICA was doing well. For example, she had received vicarious pleasure when ERICA had been secretary to some eminent men. Now the daughter was one of the long-term unemployed and out of money, *"true to form, she's not involved at all."* SALLY felt a change in relationship with both mother and sister. Now that her sister was *"becoming the glorious R.N. my mother wanted me to be,"* the mother's interest was drifting away from her over to the successful sister. The ways in which unemployment shuffled the fortunes of family members fueled the resentment and rivalry that often lay below the surface of family ties. The unemployed felt diminished next to their successful fathers or the in-laws who had worked all their lives.

So keen were the sensitivities of unemployed family members that they did a good deal of "second-guessing" as to the real feelings of the family. As with friends, their parents and relatives' feelings were hard to read. Some were convinced that others judged them a failure. MATTHEW felt a negative judgement from his father-in-law.

> He's probably saying, "That bum, he married my daughter and can't even support the family." [Has he actually made that statement?] Yes, he has.

Informants, even without concrete evidence, projected their self-disparaging feelings onto others. Withdrawn from others, self-regarding, the informants (not surprisingly) found it difficult to distinguish between their own projected feelings and the real feelings of others. So STEVE's mention of his working-class family's antagonism towards his art was tempered by his awareness that it might be *his own* definition of the situation. Speaking of the guilt he felt in doing artistic work, he tried to separate his own feelings from theirs: *"It is more something that I impose on myself than they impose on me. I feel guilty, it may not necessarily be them imposing on me."*

Parents—particularly when faced with a jobless son or daughter—would revert to older patterns of support of their children. HEATHER, 27, described her relations with parents and grandmother—who continually doted on her, asking her if she had money.

> I can't visit with them openly.... If I say, "God, I was really ticked off because I didn't have enough money to buy this," they would give me the money. I don't want that, I don't want to owe them something, to be dependent on them. I feel like a little girl all over again when I don't have money. My independence...

Once, she had received a cheque and was looking forward to buying a much-needed coat for one of her children. To her dismay, she found that *"Dad had already gone and bought Jackie a new coat. And it was, like something I wanted to do for her."* They were forever probing to see if she needed money. *"Every time they call: 'Do you have enough money? Do you have enough to pay the rent? Are you sure you're telling us the truth?'...which made our relationship more tense, because I wasn't open to saying things to them."* The family's provision of economic support, while important, could (for some) change the syntax of action firmly to passive—even more intrusively than the government agencies.

Parents nagged at the fact of joblessness, keeping it thematic in the informants' lives. ERICA's father called her every day and asked her if she was working. He could not fathom how she, with her intelligence, could not find work. Having had a stroke, he was in a wheelchair and bothered her even more. The *"major topic of conversation"* between many informants and their relatives was: *"Have you found a job yet? When are things going to change? Are you taking the right courses in school?"* As EVA pointed out, it distorted relationships. Her father

> *...calls about once a week: "Got a job yet?" Every week, every week, he asks first thing on the phone, "Got a job yet?" And I say, "No, not yet." "Any prospects?" "Well, yeah, there's always a few hanging around someplace." He's not supportive, he's not negative.... It irritates me the way he treats it, not "How are you, Eva?", but "Got a job yet?"*

> *Another thing, nobody really says, "How are you?" They're always circling around, "Do you have a job yet?"*

Consistent with this, EVA's mother thought that every time her daughter looked "down," it was due to her unemployment. In some families, it seemed, one could never escape the nagging stigma of unemployment. It became a central concern whether one wanted it to be or not.

The follow-up to the family's thematizing of unemployment was the glorifying of that *job* that would finally redeem the family member from unemployment. EVA's mother would say, according to EVA, *"Everything's going to be great"* when she gets a job. But EVA had her doubts: *"I really believe it...and yet, everything won't be that great."* Informants were skeptical about *"that mythical job"* (as LAURIE put it). It was as though unemployment had so increased the self's vulnerability that no mere job would be enough to restore it.

There were a few exceptions to the general pattern of re-intensified family ties. In some of these cases, there was an "arm's length" relation; in others, the reconstructed connections were quite negative. Some informants would not think of depending upon their families. As MATTHEW said: *"My parents always taught me to be self-reliant. Never to go to anybody unless it's dire need. I have never asked, and I hope I will never have to ask."* BETH, an educated woman with a well-to-do sister in the suburbs, went on welfare rather than having to depend on her sister: *"I didn't want her to feed me."* In the case of BOB, there was a strong antagonism. As we have seen, BOB was a fundamentalist, living in poverty on the wages of his wife. His in-laws lived in Prince Edward Island, a *"healthy distance."* If his mother-in-law ever interfered, he said, *"she knows that she'll get her face punched off."* He was quite emphatic that *"nuclear problems belong in the nuclear family. Unemployment is not a problem for the extended family."* This defensive stance was not taken out of hatred for his wife's parents—indeed they were loving and supportive—but out of a powerful familism. He thought the Bible sanctioned the ultimate integrity of the nuclear family, which must never be violated. BOB's was an extremely pure form of the more general belief that the nuclear family should be independent from others.

Conclusion

The idiom of practices within the family was decidedly two-edged. Relations with the partner could be rich and fulfilling in many ways. But if the partner was well-connected to the outside, hence having more money and mobility than the informant, the relationship could shift into one of passive dependence on the comings and goings of the other. One relied on the other for stimulation and vicarious life, watching as though on the sideline of a playing field. When the other partner's condition was also unemployment and poverty, there was neither sufficient distance nor stimulation—only an isolated dyad whose internal resources were wearing thin. Both partners contributed to domestic labour but, for the men, it was felt as a synergistic contribution to the family, while for the women, it was taken as their natural duty. This degradation of the woman's housework role, coming after a loss of employment, carried a particularly hard blow to the personal and social identities of married informants.

Children impinged on the mothers who were unemployed and poor, perhaps even more heavily than on employed mothers. While these young ones deepened the humanity and sense of community of family members, the synergy they offered was too limiting, and weakened the confidence needed in the adult world. In the absence of a (sought-after) productive role in the community, children could become the means of vicarious fulfillment for their mothers, to be made perfect and free from the deprivations of adulthood. While offering an agenda for people without a place in society, they could overwhelm and make passive the selves that were so devoted to their upbringing.

Parents and extended kin formed the most important mutual aid network for the informants, which at its best offered empowering support and a lively synergy. Relations with the older family, however, often would fall back into traditional authority patterns, stripping the family member of the dignity of independence.

Macrosocial Impacts

The macrosocial consequences of (especially) this re-intensification of extended family relations should be pointed to. Particularly for the single unemployed, even at mature ages, parents, siblings, and relatives were the most vital continuing social support in their lives. They formed the strongest cords in what might be called a "social safety net." This partial re-integration of adults into their families of orientation had quite a few general effects. Relying on the *social* safety net of the family meant much less pressing for claims and entitlements from the *governmental* safety net. Having family support as a fall-back position might have blunted the collective edge of the movement for welfare rights (which the London Union of Unemployed Workers fostered, for example). Many were able to avoid being processed by social benefits agencies; some who had family support did not even file.

Another general consequence is upon job-seeking behaviour: people hesitated to leave the area where their social and family support network was, thus were rendered less mobile and flexible. Of course, the parents—once again supporters of their "children"—were also rendered less mobile. This and other factors added to a perhaps unrecordable shift towards greater class disadvantage. After all, some of the parents of these adult dependents were pensioners or were themselves low-income—the support they extended probably cemented them even more firmly into their disadvantaged niche in the class structure.

Unemployment seemed to bring in its wake an enhanced traditionalism, with many people stepping back into the family and into their past. No social formation covered in this book could be as engaging and restorative as the family, yet also, none could take the unemployed person so low. In the final analysis, dependence on the extended family was clearly *not* the answer—especially in a culture where independent nuclear families were the norm; where families were increasingly in the labour market; where they often lacked the means to put up relatives. A vital social safety net, the family was nevertheless an imperfect vessel to take on the burdens of being rejected by the labour market.

CHAPTER TEN

The Self

Thou art a soul in bliss; but I am bound upon a wheel of fire.

Shakespeare, King Lear, iv, 7

I'm home a lot, don't converse a lot. Not in the downtown situation, the people situation. It's like a wheel. You see less people, you do less things, and you're constantly taking more wear on that wheel.

MARTHA, unemployed 10 months

Concepts

The exclusion of the unemployed from the social order is, ultimately, an injury to the *self*. It is the self which absorbs the lessons of rejection, which feels the syntax of practices shifting out of its control. Nowhere in the social order is unemployment so reflected upon, so infused with feeling, as within the unemployed self. Particularly in the personal consciousness of unemployment, the informants' accounts must be taken as privileged. They who live with it are the teachers; those of us who do not are the pupils.

Practices

The practices to be described in this chapter are subtle and often interior; in a sense they could be called "psychological." But they are so clearly the products of a *social* dislocation that they are better named as "social," or "socially conditioned," practices. The first to be considered, "Introspecting," defines the basic action context within which the self dwells on its personal and social identities. The second, "Coping with Unemployment Over Time" looks at the critical impact of the *duration* of joblessness on the self. We then deal with the cycle of social and socially conditioned practices which make up the experience of "Being Marginalized." The concluding practice encompasses positive efforts at "Transcending Unemployment."

Introspecting

The informants indicated that the self became preoccupying and thematic throughout the day. Especially on bad days, DOROTHY said:

The only thing I have on my mind on those days is me. Nothing else.

DESMOND claimed that unemployment gave you *"a conscious feeling of yourself."* Much "idle" time was taken up with these attentions to the self which we call "introspection." What were these experiences like?

Only a small number of informants said they valued introspection and in some cases sought it out. Some of them were planning creative work. Others just needed to think about their lives. *"I'm sort of an inert person by nature,"* PETER admitted. *"So I do a lot of sitting, apparently doing nothing. I enjoy it because there's always things to look at and listen to."* In a few cases, the introspection was needed, not because the object of thought was satisfying, but because it allowed informants to take stock of their lives. In some cases their jumbled internal themes simply were not communicable to others. Young GLENN, unemployed nine months, did a lot of sitting and thinking, mostly in the park and just before going to sleep at night.

You feel like you've wasted the day. But another side of you thinks that you haven't, because you've done a lot of thinking and sorted a lot of things out.

[What do you think about?]

I don't really know. Why I'm unemployed, whose fault it is, why I can't find a job, why no one will hire me, things like that?

[Come up with any answers?]

I come up with a lot of answers but none of them really work.

Another young informant was TERRENCE, 18, whose account was detailed and helpful.

I love to go down to the park and think.... I'm doing something, I'm thinking about how I can be a better person, how I could latch onto this awesome job.

He thought about what it would be like finishing high school, being a father, raising a family. Unemployment had given him the *"time to really understand myself."* When asked what he thought about at night:

It's about myself, I'm not feeling good about myself. And I'm always thinking, you know, "I can do this and I can do that, what am I going to do, and I got to have money for that, where the hell am I going to get it?"

While at times he wished his friends knew what he was thinking, he kept his worries in a locked room, to be examined only by himself.

I want them to know that everything's OK.... But, deep down, I know that everything's not.... I don't care how close they are—I don't want anyone worrying about me.

As for the structures in the social order which excluded him, or the social and political character of unemployment, these were opaque to him. As an individual in a liberal capitalist society, TERRENCE was conditioned to deal with such social contradictions as personal struggles in his own mind.

For most informants, introspection was a psychic quicksand to be avoided. *"I think and get very introspective,"* said DOROTHY, *"then I decide, this is crazy—you can only do so much of that."* During a period of personal stress, she felt *"the introspection contributed partially to my self-absorption.... There has to be a cut-off point and only the individual knows how far he or she can go."*

Beyond the cut-off point, what awaited the unemployed person? LAURIE described it as a *"funk."*

> *If you're not busy, you have time to think. And if you're bored with what you think, you have time to brood and get into a negative mindset, which prevents you from getting out of that rut you're in that's making you depressed.*

Without the anchor of a positive social identity and responsibility, the self could expand omnivorously and begin to "feed" off its own past. Informants with some experience of unemployment told of struggles to contain the hyper-conscious self by keeping busy. MARIANNE, frequently laid off as a secretary, said: *"The first time I was unemployed, I was bitter and angry and mad at everybody. But now that I've had it happen to me so many times, what's the use? I have to look after myself, my mental attitude and everything, and so I have things to do."*

One can see the attraction of TV in this context. While television brought in the images and voices of the outer world, its "competitor," introspection, gave a view of the inner world. The inner "screening" (to continue the analogy) replayed past hurts and rejections, whether by employer or ex-spouse. It unearthed suppressed longings, and images of roads not taken. The worst time for informants was lying in bed at night. As GAIL indicated:

> *I try not to spend time thinking what would have been, what could have been, thinking back is lost time and it's a bloody waste. You just put your time in the best way you know how.*

When she introspected, old sensitivities stung again: *"Pretty soon you're taking everything wrong. Someone will say something and you're immediately defensive.... Maybe my hostility does come through on certain things."* Since introspection threatened the unemployed person with a loss of emotional control, many preferred to try and keep the room locked.

Introspection could be the means of a more general enervation—thus voiding the constructive coiled tension and objectivity which purposeful human beings bring to tasks. For that reason, when asked to give advice to a newly-unemployed person, LAURIE counselled immediate job-hunting. *"If you wait too long, insecurity sets in. And you get to reasoning and you get to thinking how bad things are—and you say, well, what's the point of look-ing.... There's nothing."*

The expanding self-absorption that threatened the unemployed person ultimately falsified and subjectivized its personal history as well as its present. Martyr-like, it took the whole brunt of the structural problem of unemployment on its shoulders. What could be more convenient for the perpetrators and the system which engendered this social pathology? In the condition of unemployment, we find a new variant of "false consciousness" to add to the Marxist analysis: *"self*-consciousness." A new politics would have to find a way to fuse together all these isolated selves, which are so fragmented by capitalism.

Coping with Unemployment Over Time

Any generalizations about the temporal patterning of the self's experience throughout the jobless spell are risky because of the latter's sheer variety (Sinfield, 1981: 152–156). The literature suggests that the first stage is often shock and immobilization. Shortly thereafter, there may be some optimism and minimization of the problem, as the person defines the inactivity as a kind of holiday. Then, as the months draw on with no success finding a job, there is a second broad stage characterized by emotional turmoil, depression, and withdrawal. Here the belief that "things will be all right" is undermined and one's identity comes under strain. With prolonged unemployment, a third stage emerges, involving the scaling down or readjustment of hopes. The individual starts to accept the fact that the standards of the employed past are not going to be a reliable basis for evaluating achievements in the present. There is less active distress at this stage, with the emotional trajectory slightly rising and stabilizing (Hayes and Nutman, 1981: 19).

Our treatment here will look at the *initial reaction* to the termination of employment, and then the *later phases* of the lengthening unemployment spell. The pivotal figure is the unemployed self, and how the generally changed social identity following job loss affects *personal* identity.

Initial Reaction

Of the 41 "job losers" in my sample, 10 informants expressed *shock* when their employment was terminated. NORMA, 24, had been working for five months as a bus driver at the London Transit. Late one night, in an act of horseplay, she had climbed through the window of her parked bus into the bus driven by a friend of hers which had pulled up alongside. A passenger spotted it and reported her. After being asked for an explanation by management, she was fired three days later. She was in her fifth month of a six-month probationary period within which management could dismiss employees more easily. At a time when women L.T.C. bus drivers formed only 1% of its work-force, NORMA was thinking of challenging the dismissal on grounds of sexual discrimination. Similar horseplay by men—she knew a man who drove occasionally with his foot out of the window—had resulted in only a fine or suspension.

When asked how she felt at the time: *"I was in shock, I couldn't believe it.... He asked, 'Do you have anything to say for yourself?' and I said 'No'. Like, I couldn't believe what happened.... I went out there laughing."* She went over to some other drivers and told them and they laughed, hardly believing anything so ridiculous. *"But the day after, it hit me. And I was crying like anything."* She stayed inside away from her friends, and had little motivation to look for a job. The only thing she had ever wanted to do was drive a bus.

BERNARD, waiting for a good job which would let him fly his fiancée to Canada to begin their family, was laid off from his labourer's job at a tree farm. *"I was so set back.... I kept in bed, slept the whole day. Then watched television through the night.... I got into serious drinking, trying to drown my problems."* A similar reaction was expressed by LORNE, fired from a dishwashing job: *"I didn't want to be talked to, didn't want to be seen.... It's like I lost my best friend."* He had been called on the phone by the employer and told not to bother to come in that day, that his work had been too slow. *"I was in shock; I didn't say anything, just OK."*

Being suddenly banished from a familiar environment left the self feeling wounded and out of place. MONICA had been given a poor evaluation as a receptionist by a supervisor who allegedly did not know her work, which had been praised by others who did. The oral report of the evaluation was made to her in about four minutes:

> She told me everything on it [the three-page evaluation] *in about four seconds flat. Her mouth was going a mile a minute. She gave an evaluation. And I remember being so shaken up by it that I couldn't talk....*

> And then she said "Do you have any questions?" Well, I couldn't speak.... I was so shocked. And then she said, "OK, then, that's it." And she stood up to walk out, and I felt like saying "Don't open the door." Because I was crying, and there were all counsellors outside.... Like, we were in there a good four minutes. That was the evaluation, four minutes. Rather a rushed thing, because she had other things to do. As if my job.... It was my job that was on the line. And then, she had left.

She sat there and took some deep breaths. Others had gone into a meeting and she was supposed to answer the phones. *"I was so upset that I couldn't work anymore, I couldn't think. If the phone rang, I didn't even know it was the phone. You know, all I could think about was my child.... You know, I had done this for two years. It was my routine, and I enjoyed it. I enjoyed the students."* While the counsellors were in a meeting, she sat typing, not really knowing what she was doing. Yet she must have looked stricken, because when a couple asked where a room was, they took one look at her face, apologized and left.

The worker, as a factor in the productive process, worked. But the worker's *self* on the job wanted to do more than work. It wanted to "appropriate" the job into its identity-formation, to use it as a vehicle for communicative and craftlike purposes. So offices, machines, and work areas, while nominally owned by the company, were often felt by the workers to be their own personal possessions and territories—a kind of ownership-by-involvement. Being laid off, then, for some, was to be deported from a fellowship and a personal territory. Not surprisingly, a few of the informants compared being laid off to losing a best friend.

WARREN's last job, sponsored by the Welfare Department, had been with a demolition company. Every dollar earned was a dollar taken off benefits. Though the work was dirty, involving cleaning and wrecking, and the pay insufficient, WARREN valued it:

> *Dirty, tough, but I tell you, I felt a hell of a lot good. I came home, I could sleep good at night, the wife and I got along really great,... We had a little bit of money to go out, wasn't much, maybe she'd go to Bingo, I'd go to a movie...and we had a little bit of money to spend for the kids.*

With every expectation of continued employment, WARREN was quietly handed an envelope containing holiday and severance pay; the boss had not said a word. He described his reaction as *"nauseous,"* as though someone had dropped a twenty-pound weight on his stomach.

> *I just kinda felt like, like there was a void in your stomach.... Like, wow, you had work and all of a sudden, it's not there. Like a friend, you know, like a real close friend, and he moves away and you feel, wow man, that's gone.*

Back in the home, he was fighting with his wife again. While employed, his marriage had been *"great"*; now, *"we just live, that's it."*

The initial phase of shock experienced in a sudden layoff was not undergone by all the job losers in the sample. Some experienced anger, some saw the layoff coming and were resigned to it. Another reaction, reported by about seven informants, was a feeling of *relief* at having been set free from the previous job. In a few cases, the job had involved working nights, which disrupted normal family routines. SIMON, fired from his job, felt that the night work was dead-end and poorly paid anyway. BRENDA, a waitress at a donut shop, quit, partly because she was required to work at night and partly because of the refusal of the boss to put her on full-time and rotation. For a time she briefly experienced that sense of being on a holiday (*"I was having a ball"*) which was sometimes associated with the early phase of unemployment. But now, jobless and on Mother's Allowance for a year, she was bored and restless and wanted full-time employment.

Some people reported being glad to be free of the constraining aspects of the job. FRAN quit her job as office manager and secretary-receptionist at an office rental agency. She had become dissatisfied: the original owners were not involved anymore, there was too much pressure, and she wanted to do less typing and more headwork. While upset at quitting, she quickly felt much better at the widening of options. She did some job searching, then went back to school, and was using her intelligence more actively. Knowing that she did not have to stay where she was, excited her. She was not as tired as when working and had a more energetic and pleasant social life. She was on Unemployment benefits, and had the whole-hearted support of her extended family. (*"I'm very lucky."*)

If the job was hated, unemployment could come as a relief. Some of the younger men, supported by parents and their peer group, were glad they were not doing kitchen work. As HERB remarked:

> *Why should I have a job doing something I don't want to do? Because that would definitely lower self-esteem, as far as I'm concerned.... There's too many people working and all they do is complain about, "I hate my job." So why don't you quit, do something else?*

In some cases, however, the relief could be short-lived. GAIL had stood up to an emotionally abusive boss who screamed at the top of his lungs for her to sit down as he prepared to tongue-lash her, unjustly in her view. She simply turned heel and left his office. That act gave her *"one half second of satisfaction and a lot of woe after."* She was relieved to be out from under his authority, but, as a 50-year-old divorcée living alone, with few prospects after five months of unemployment, she wondered about the wisdom of her act. Chain-smoking, anxious, she bitterly contemplated the high price she had paid for the exercise of her autonomy.

The comparisons between the "shocked" and the "relieved" were instructive. The "relieved" more often had quit their jobs, hence had controlled the timing and prepared emotionally for the event. Except for GAIL (above), the other "relieved" persons had some financial and social support, such as an employed spouse or a parental home and income to draw on. These people had options and resources.

By contrast, the "shocked" and immobilized were more likely to have been involuntarily deprived of paid employment, and thus lacked emotional preparedness or control over timing. Their job loss shattered their time frames rather than being integrated into them. More of them were unattached individuals, or single parents, possessing fewer resources of financial or social support. Four of the ten were from out of town, having extended kin in Exeter (60 miles away), other parts of Canada, the United States, and Kenya.

To sum up, those with financial and social (especially familial) support could choose a living situation which enabled them to pursue personal goals. People without such resources also lacked the accompanying freedoms—for them the job's enabling characteristics were desperately clung to. The job was more pivotal in their search for community, for self-esteem, and for an income. Being deprived of that job involuntarily, suddenly, was a profoundly threatening experience.

Later Phases

The cross-sectional rather than longitudinal design of the study makes generalizations about temporal effects on job search rather tentative. It may still be possible, however, to determine effects over time by grouping the sample into segments according to *duration of unemployment*. Were there significant differences in attitude and behaviour regarding job search among the various groupings?

My findings, as in the case of the initial impact of unemployment, partly corroborated and partly complicated the pattern sketched in the literature. For the long-term unemployed, there was considerable flattening of affect and morale, with resigned hopelessness replacing more active distress. In addition, new assumptions about one's relation to the environment and to the future appeared in seminal and developed form in the long-term unemployed. What was unexpected were the similarities which appeared across the board.

For those *unemployed three months or less*, there was some buoyancy expressed about the job search. BRENDA, with her small retarded child, was energized, even possessed, by the job search. It served as a welcome contrast to being in the home. For married TONY, the job search was, for now, a relaxed and self-fulfilling adventure. His wife supported him financially and emotionally in his desire to find exactly what he wanted, and he had not yet been rejected that often. But in some of the accounts by those unemployed three months or less, there appeared a pessimism, a defeatedness, an attitude of coasting—which were usually associated with more prolonged unemployed spells. What explained it? This "premature" sense of defeatism seemed to possess those who had experienced unemployment and the frustrations of the job search in the past, often more than once. Their past employment had been sporadic; as they began their latest job search their attitude was part dread and part resignation—"Here we go again."

In those *unemployed four to six months*, the theme of *"being dragged down,"* of experiencing a loss of enthusiasm and confidence, was more pronounced. There was still an alternation of emotional "highs" and "lows." But the "lows" were starting to have a cumulative, qualitative impact on the job search. This was expressed by SIMON, unemployed five months:

> Every letter of rejection hurts in a sense, you know, it's one more disappointment, and feel kind of, almost used to it,...like you kind of expect it, and so the next time I do a letter of application, I kind of feel, well, I'm just going through the process, I'm really not going to get the job.

> The longer I'm without work, the more letters of rejection I get, the less likely I am to apply for the next job and the less confident I feel about it. And I'm sure that that colours the interview that I have, if I'm lucky enough to get an interview.

Over time the job search was becoming an empty ritual, devoid of meaning and personal implication. The self recoiled from it, partly out of protection, partly because, *as work*, repeated job-hunting offered no consummation, no result.

In the group *unemployed seven to twelve months*, we notice a number of patterns, some of which will appear in mature form in the long-term unemployed. One of them was *dread and anxiety* about the future, with an accompanying desperate sense that one must hold on. This was particularly evident among those in a disadvantaged market position, especially older women. The end of work seemed to bring home thoughts of one's mortality. GAIL talked of clinging to life: you simply could not allow yourself to die, or crawl into a shell. JOANNE had an almost paralyzing vision of her own contingency:

> There are times when I am so scared that I'm not going to find a job, I think, "What the hell is wrong with me?" Even if I can't find a job in the field that I want, I can always work as a temp, and stay busy. My head knows this, OK?—but my guts go like that, and they just start wringing and I can get scared to death.... I'll have periods of insomnia. I'll get very short-tempered with my husband and with the children.

As she continued, notice how JOANNE's realistic anxiety about her market position veered into self-disparagement and a fear that her life would unravel: "*Sometimes I think there is something wrong with me. I ask myself, 'Why are you permitting this anxiety to come into your life?' And yet I seem powerless to stop it.*"

As the job search lengthened, the sense of oneself as a *worker*—which is central to our social identity—tended to weaken. FRAN, unemployed for 10 months, remarked:

> I don't think I've ever been unemployed as long before. So it's getting used to seeing yourself as unemployed too. Like you always looked at yourself as a worker.

One woman said that one looked over the jobs on offer and began thinking, "*I can't do that, I can't do that.*" People started settling for less, hence their talents came to be under-used even if they did find work. DEBBIE put it clearly:

> *I think you tend to have a defeatist attitude about yourself and about the kind of jobs you can do so you start looking for things that aren't as demanding. And also if you haven't been working, employers are less likely to hire you, if you haven't been involved with some kind of job.*

"*At the beginning,*" commented BETH, "*I was feeling so good about myself that that was a lot easier.... Towards the end I was feeling like such a loser.... You portray this, it's written all over your face: 'Nobody wants me, please take me,' so that makes the communication and everything else.... You're almost begging for a job. That's humiliating.*"

In those *unemployed more than one year*, we see a kind of entrenched adjustment to unemployed conditions, both tender- and tough-minded. The "tender-minded" spoke in a resigned, muted tone when talking about the prospects of finding employment. Several could no longer believe that their unemployment would end. CONNIE, single, laid off from an advertising firm, had the attitude of "*Why bother, I'm not going to get it anyway.*" Her job-hunting had fallen off in frequency. She had also considered suicide. There was a suicidal hint in the words of AGNES, unemployed 27 months:

> *I'm terribly depressed. I wonder if there is anything ahead, or should I just depart? [Laughs] Really, you do get to that point. I mean there's absolutely nothing ahead for me. Remarriage—that would be the only thing that would do something for me right now. And there's not too many men my age that I could live with.... I think our whole system is in very big trouble. And I am just one of the victims.*

All five informants who had hinted at suicidal intentions at one time or another were longer-term unemployed. MONICA talked of a phase when she did "*self-destructive things.*"

> *I'd be driving and I'd drive real fast and hope to hit a bridge or something. Then I'd say, "Come on! Your son's in the back seat."*

The long-term unemployed were represented in all the categories of pathological behaviour. Of those informants who had explicitly mentioned depression as a problem, who had complained of anxiety, who had mentioned blaming self, who had admitted to excessive sleeping, who had had problems with drinking or desiring to drink as an escape—in all these distressed categories, those unemployed six months or more predominated.

Having so little leverage on their future, some long-term unemployed assumed religious postures. The question of whether they would find employment shifted to "Is there a role for me in the social order?" The responses to the question ranged from faith to agnosticism to plain existentialist waiting. MARTHA, when asked what advice she would give to a newly-employed person, replied: *"I guess in some cases religion. You've got to believe. A lot of people get strength from religion. I just think that better things are to come. There's got to be something out there for me."* A few were skeptical that they will ever find decent work, adopting a certain resignation.

The *tough-minded* response was not to look to the future, but to live existentially. Faced with a future that seemed indeterminate and fateful, people relaxed their attempts to influence or anticipate it—in effect, lowering their expectations of life. Young PETER stated that he did not plan, but just looked *"forward to what might happen. I don't have specifics, but I just look forward to continued life."* GORD, unemployed for over two years, had given up the idea of a family. He had abandoned planning, figuring it would be a long haul which would not get any better, so he had best find a calm way of coping with it. The various expressions had a similar ring:

> *I take the day as it comes. No use planning because you don't got the money to plan with. (DICK)*

> *What's the sense in setting a time-table, because I'm not going anywhere. (MATTHEW)*

> *I don't make plans. I just sit at home, waiting for a letter to arrive or a phone call that will have some good news, but it never seems to come. (ANDREW)*

COLLEEN, though not long-termed unemployed, has waited a long time for even the chance at a good job. She offered a sort of parody of planning. *"I sit down, have a cup of tea and my cigarette, and think about what I'm not going to do today."* The woman suggested, more seriously, that her life was lived within each day, not the longer time spans. *"You try to do something. Either go to the bank, make some kind of outing. Go to the store."* As the unemployment dragged out, people who used to plan veered to the opposite of the planned state and lived intuitively—as if spurning the future that had been taken from them: *"It comes and goes.... Whatever my mind swings to, I'll do that. No, I don't have any fixed periods of time."* (MATTHEW)

Some adjustments were more focused than others. NANCY, 28 and single, laid off as a sales representative, and unemployed for 18 months, was looking forward to a course for women in trades. She talked of the effect of her long-term unemployment as involving a *"a total change of attitude... Go with the flow."* She and one other long-term unemployed woman drew *radical* not quietist conclusions from this, however. Having tried so hard, taken the right courses, "paid her dues" and still not found work, she concluded that the fault was not hers and she must not blame herself. On the strength of this, she worked with the local Union of Unemployed Workers to help the unemployed to make their just claims on society. *"Go with the flow"* meant that the self should cease its lone struggle against a society which overburdened selves with undeserved blame, and join itself with forces that sought to change society.

Most were not so fortified, however. A few spoke of adjusting themselves to a new order, wherein high technology provides little full-time work. GORD felt that his underemployment was a harbinger of tough times to come. He continually made a virtue of his necessity. He compared

> *sitting and reading for four hours, and doing some job that's useless, that there's no need for, that's not helping anyone, or not helping yourself either. Just the idea of keeping your hands busy, to me it's senseless. I'd rather sit down and read. You're not screwing up the environment, making a mess.*

His defense of his odd-jobs way of life seemed partly genuine, but also fueled by resentment. GORD resented the fact that his unemployment and poverty made him unattractive to women—so he criticized the women of today as shallow (as though *he* were rejecting *them*). Having been rejected by his family during some drinking years, he posited the view that one should never get close to one's family.

His ambivalence at being on the margin was caught in this passage:

> *Well, I've resigned myself to the fact that I'll never meet anyone and have a family.... And I have a kind of resentment against that.... Maybe my feeling of self-worth has gone down.... I probably wouldn't meet anyone and have one or two children. I've resigned myself that will never happen.*
>
> *To be honest, I don't really give a shit.... It doesn't really matter.*

Plainly it did matter, but he had to find some way to live with his unsheltered position in the marginal work world, as well as social rejection. GORD's "coming to terms" with those probabilities which hedged him in was chiefly the consequence of his marginalization but also partial contributor to his predicament. The self's "co-authorship" of its own marginality is our next topic.

Being Marginalized

Of the many metaphors or similes used by the informants the *"tunnel,"* the *"jungle,"* *"killing time,"* a *"piece of trash,"* *"just a number,"*—perhaps the most apt was the figure of the "wheel." *"Spinning my wheels on ice"* was how FRANCES described her unemployment, but the classic expression was MARTHA's in the epigraph to the chapter. Like a good writer, she expressed the general—i.e. the unstimulating situation at home—by means of the concrete. *"It's like a wheel. You see less people, you do less things, and you're constantly taking more wear on that wheel."*

I wish to use the wheel as more than a figure of speech; for the wheel or cycle suggests the process of social reproduction wherein people absorb and enact their social structures each day. One of the insidious impacts of unemployment is that the labour market rejection or discrimination so conditions human selves that they *reproduce* the circumstances of their marginality. This is by no means inevitable or completely deterministic—that there is a "jagged edge" to the wheel is attested to in the next section, "transcending unemployment." By and large, however, the condition of unemployment acts to marginalize people in the way MARTHA alludes to.

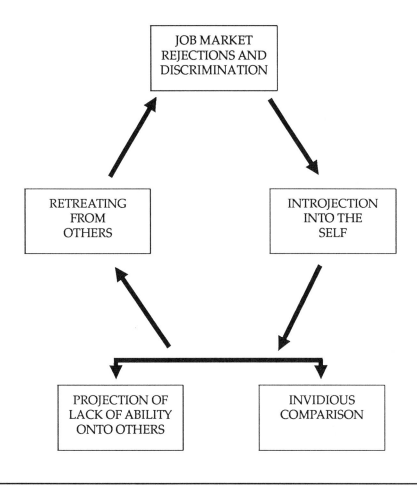

FIGURE 10.1: *The Cycle of Marginalization*

Figure 10.1 suggests the shape of the wheel or cycle of marginalization. An exposition of the stages of this model, though by no means exhaustive, will pull together many diverse observations that have been made in this book. The processes to be described are dynamic and might be visualized as moving through the time spans of the unemployment spell and the life cycle—suggesting the action of a wheel.

Job Market Rejections and Discrimination

People were sometimes socially rejected before they appeared on the job market—for a disability or some other ascribed trait—and the employers might only have replicated that rejection. For some women unemployment was partly generated, not by the labour market, but by the expectation that they take the principal responsibility in the home and family. In most cases, however, the initiating factor in economic marginality was labour market rejection.

Those who were surplus to the shrinking labour requirements in the early 1980s simply were not employed—this in a society that placed one's occupation at the core of social identity and where it was often necessary to have two incomes to maintain a family's standard of living. There was no role offered by the government agencies that could replace the "self-reliant" worker's role.

Introjection into the Self

Irrespective of whose fault the high unemployment rate was, people were often drawn to consider their own personal responsibility for their misfortune. People claimed ownership of their difficulties. As BOB remarked:

> *Being unemployed…it's taken me down a peg or two…. Right now I would consider being unemployed as being my problem. If I am unemployed a year from now, that is my fault. And we will see.*

Especially within the introspective mode, self seemed to have the capacity to scapegoat itself and to blame itself for its constricted functioning in the social order. Given the individualistic terms of the culture, the self was the only agent it understood. *"On a bad day,"* said DOROTHY, *"I'll take it personally. Those are the days I feel incompetent, very unsure of myself. Fortunately those have been the minority. On better days, I am taking a more objective view; the realities of the situation are beyond my control. And on those days, I feel that I am very competent."*

The scapegoat which the self set up was a sort of double or *Doppelgänger*, which was a version of the social self filled or emptied by the choices of others, which then took on total responsibility when it was screened out. ROSS hinted at this unreliable social self and how it distorted the reading he had hoped to get from his deeper self.

[How has your unemployment affected you personally?]

I feel—although I know it's not correct—I feel it has lowered my self-esteem, although I know the reality is not the case. So what I have to do is cope with that and keep telling myself, "Look, it's not me." [emphasis added]

When people simultaneously blamed themselves and the market, then, they were not contradicting themselves—only continuing to accept responsibility for all the commotion unemployment had thrown up at them. ERICA commented:

It's a lot my fault, because of poor planning and where I am now. But I also happen to feel...it's the market.

Elsewhere she stated: *"There's really no reason why I should not be working, other than the market."* She also said that, because the issue of unemployment was so complex, then (almost by default): *"You blame yourself. You blame yourself."* Few informants (except young social isolates) spontaneously blamed themselves; rather they *arrived* at self-blame through other routes (e.g. lack of knowledge).

What finally made the job search so inextricably linked to the self-system was that the successful applicant was *chosen*, and the unsuccessful one was not. DONALD could not find work in 1981 because the restaurant field in London was glutted. *"Why can't I find work? What's the matter with me?"* Then he went to Edmonton and, within two weeks, he was employed. His response: *"So I said, 'Well, I can't be that bad.'"* Again the personal reaction to fluctuating market conditions. Though GAIL was qualified to do office work, the fact that she was, predictably, having difficulties finding employment led her to lose her self-confidence: *"Am I qualified to do anything or am I over the hill?"*

Invidious Comparisons

Corresponding to the diagram in Figure 10.1, there seemed to be a number of inter-subjective processes flowing from the introjection of societal discrimination. One was the widespread tendency to compare oneself and one's condition with others. The use of the adjective "invidious" follows its dictionary definition which refers to comparisons or distinctions which are "unfairly or offensively discriminating" (Collins English Dictionary). These comparisons tended to take two forms: comparisons with those less well off ("internal differentiation"), and (by far the more common) comparisons with those who were better off.

One way in which groups with negative social identities handled the resulting stigma was to distance themselves psychologically from those among them who were worse off (Marshall and Rosenthal, 1986, 150).

Informants sometimes took pains to express their differences from such people. People—especially those contemplating welfare—shudderingly distinguished themselves from "bums" or "loafers." Single parents in London Housing objected to women who did harbour male providers. There was resentment of those whose behaviour tainted the general view of the unemployed. As ANDREA indicated,

> *I am sure there are people out there that have no intention of working, but every kind of society has those kind of people. There's a very small number of people that abuse the welfare system and the unemployment system.*

In her case, the distinction was not a snobbish one; she simply resented the way the negative view of this noticed minority spread to stigmatize *all* the unemployed. When people asked if she was working, and she said, "No," their attitude changed. *"Like my word doesn't have the value it does...or I'm not of much value."* While partly condemning the general societal tendency to stereotype, she still blamed those who really did not want to work. *"Everybody pays for those few people, which I think is very unfair."*

The far more common comparison was with those who were better off. ERICA compared herself to those women who had raised their children and were just beginning a career. *"And I, who have worked all my life, am a has-been. There just doesn't seem to be any common sense to it."* She compared herself to those women who had played it safe by entering a large corporation at a young age and worked their way up—as opposed to her pattern of working for doctors and professors and in agencies. MATTHEW often sat and cried at night, thinking of people his age who had reached the top of their professions. *"Here I am, after all these years, and nothing to show for it."*

Informants expressed envious resentment about immigrants who were thought to be taking jobs away, and who had special government attention. Those younger, slimmer, more affluent, or employed, were singled out for envy. Married women who were working when their husbands could support them were thought to be *"selfish. Make way for those who need the jobs."* There was some negative feeling among older women about the social wages offered young mothers on their own, wages not available before.

These comparisons should not be dismissed as the inevitable rumblings of the envious in a competitive society. For the unemployed of this time and place—an affluent society undergoing high unemployment—were *immersed* in injustice. Both job search and community movement inevitably mixed the unemployed with the employed. What separated the two were *not* differences in talent or ability, or in quality or worth as human beings—but luck, attractiveness, economic advantages which permitted the gaining of credentials, connectedness, and so on. The formulation of these advantages into a *class system*, buttressed by the internal differentiation of the unemployed by the state welfare system, made the divide between themselves and the prosperous, both wider and more entrenched.

The accumulated advantages and disadvantages which pulled the two groups farther apart in sympathy and equality of life chances, in freedoms and dignity—and the sheer arbitrary injustice of being on the wrong side of this divide—struck some of the unemployed with the suddenness of being wakened from a dream. In the dream state the injustice was taken for granted, as though it were a natural state for the self. With a start, people woke up to the *unnaturalness* of social inequality.

> *I walked down the street one day—. God, how do people buy their clothes, where are they getting their money, how come they have a job?... Like, I just thought, SHIT!* [emphasis in original]
>
> JANE

> *I often find myself walking down the street, looking into people's houses and feeling jealous of people. I've never done that before.... I go downtown and see people eating in nice restaurants and shopping in those clothing stores....I really get mad at people.... What's that? Some kind of state where you grab, where you start revolutions? Where you start to take what you think you should have? That worries me.... It's so unfair.* [emphasis in original]
>
> ERICA

ERICA went on to say, "*I never wanted to be on top of the heap. I just wanted to hold my own.*"

The inequality of power and wealth and purpose—accepted by some as the environment within which one moved—became clear in these moments. The meritocratic mystifications, the false consciousness of self-blame, no longer obscured the structure of inequality—which could be seen in all its perversity. Those moments for most of the informants were few, however. The uneven development that resulted from capitalism was, for them, virtually a theme of daily life. Any synergy or solidarity among the victims of such a disunifying system was difficult to sustain.

Projection; Retreating from Others

Another common process by which the labour market's discrimination affected relations with others, after being introjected into the self, was "projection." It in turn contributed strongly to a "retreat" from others. Projection was the growing assumption that others—prospective employers, friends, members of family—shared the view of the unemployed person as a loser. Another word for it is "altercasting," i.e. casting others in rejecting roles. We dealt with this in Chapter Three in connection with the self-discrimination of older workers who withdrew from labour markets.

The possession of a stigmatized status, which so blighted social identity, tended to make some informants think (or imagine) that they were surrounded by a community of rejecters. HEATHER wondered about her employed friends: *"They're always chatting about people they're working with…and I wonder if they're mentioning us to their friends. How she's only staying at home, how she's not working."* KARL, who had worked in the past to improve worker's rights, felt that he was being punished by present employers. In the silences after applying, he imagined that they were discovering his record. Given the social distance from those who hire, and the insufficient reasons for their non-response, this was not paranoia but a rational speculative hypothesis.

One's self became so defended and preoccupied in serious unemployment, that the capacity to accurately read the feedback from others became dulled. One could not be sure whether their felt negativity was real or imagined. *"It bothers me when I think of other people…how they view me,"* HEATHER admitted. WARREN depicted his friends as thinking, *"You're a welfare bum, I'm supporting you, what the hell are you doing here?"* Then he reflected, *"Maybe it's a paranoia I have."*

HEATHER, at home all day with the children, felt that her situation was boring and limited. Notice how this spread to the view of her friends:

> I find that I don't have as much to say to them…They're not going to be interested in hearing about my kids all the time. They are more interested in what other adults are doing…. They're not going to be as stimulated by what I have to say…. They're going to think I'm boring so I don't talk to them.

Closely linked to the projection—virtually its complement—was the *retreat* from others: in HEATHER's words, *"I withdraw from them. I don't say as much."*

LORNE reported avoiding his friends because, *"it's me feeling bad and thinking they're thinking that."* How could one disentangle one's own negative view of self from the view of others towards self, when the former tended to taint and distort the latter? The confusion was well expressed by DICK, who was asked how his employed friends have reacted to his unemployment:

> If I could read their mind, right, so that I know what they're saying, "Well he's unemployed, he's getting nowhere," right? Because that's what I'm doing right now, getting nowhere.

The wounded self-perception usurped the role-taking process, contributing to a withdrawal (*"I stay home more often"*) which further obscured the feedback from social relationships.

There developed, especially in the long-term unemployed, a general mistrust of people in employed society. *"When you come right down to it, nobody cares,"* commented WARREN. *"As long as they can put their finger in the pie and pull out some money, they don't care."* The public realm—where people made their living, and made politics—was depicted as a *"jungle," "dog-eat-dog," "every man for himself."*

Returning to the diagram (Figure 10.1), the wheel had come full circle; the self had been conditioned to reproduce its own marginalization. The introjection of unemployment into the self led to invidious comparisons with those worse and better off, decreasing the synergy and solidarity with them. One projected one's damaged self-esteem onto others, both employers and friends. This brought about a withdrawal from these others. This of course increased the probability of withdrawal from potential contacts or employers and decreased the prospects of employment. And the cycle of marginalization—the depleting wheel that MARTHA referred to—continued.

The informants most caught up in this cycle were those who were unemployed for a long time, those who were poor, those without social support (especially older workers), and some housewives who found themselves back in the home after being in the workforce. Those with more than one of these elements were much more likely to be marginalized. But who were those who managed to *transcend* unemployment, who were on the still-jagged edges of the wheel?

Transcending Unemployment

Those who seemed to weather the atomizing, a-socializing effect of unemployment—and even occasionally to rise above it—were those insulated by one or more of the following factors: non-stigmatizing financial backing, social support, education, and collectivist ideology. We will review each in turn.

Non-stigmatizing financial backing could come from a number of sources. It might have been a disability allowance, an adequate Unemployment benefit, room and board in the parent's home, savings, or a sharing of the spouse's income. If it was a social wage, what made it non-stigmatizing was the clear understanding of the informant that it was his or hers by *right*, and that, far from resulting in a reduced, dependent existence, it was a "ramp" to a fuller life in the community. Whether disabled or on Unemployment insurance benefits, such people were freed from some of the constraints of poverty to take courses, to move about in the job search, to explore contacts and opportunities in a community that was still theirs. If the support was from a spouse or parent, what made it non-stigmatizing in some cases was the trust invested in it. There seemed to be an understanding, sometimes unstated, that human life was worth more than its productivity or marketability, that there were times in life when a proper orientation to the public realm required a period of reflection and relief from its demands.

Social support came from many quarters—from spouses or partners, from friends, relatives, parents, fellow volunteers, other unemployed people in the intermediate organizations. The acceptance by these people of the unemployed person helped to reconnect the ligatures that were broken by the jobless condition. By continually treating the informant as a *person*—not atomized or abstracted, but as a concrete being capable of a life extending beyond the present—these supportive others reminded the person of the humanity which the public realm could not apprehend. By interacting with supportive others, and seeing that others were in a similar situation, one's social identity was preserved from collapse into self-blame. LAURIE came out of her "ruts" by reminding herself that this was a *social* experience she was undergoing:

> There's more to life than this, and this is not the end of my life. A lot of other people are hoeing the same row and I don't need to feel so inferior, and…degenerate and lazy and no good—because it's a worldwide condition anyway. And we just need to cope with it together.

Though *education* did not conclusively deter the negative impacts of unemployment, it did provide the analytical tools to generalize about the condition. Those without these tools felt personally distressed and powerless, as did ERICA:

> The man on the street can't do anything because he can't understand it. I can't understand it. There's got to be an answer. Who is going to provide the answer?… I don't think people are going to ask why, I don't think they know where to start. Why? Why aren't I working? Are there less jobs now than there were 20 years ago? Are there more people?

The response to this complexity, ERICA thought, was the blaming of self.

The educated, by contrast, had a better chance to address the problem intellectually. COLLEEN, with a psychology degree, matter-of-factly distilled the problem of unemployment in a few sentences. She thought governments were holding the reins on social spending, and employers were taking advantage of the oversupply of labour by demanding high experience and qualifications for low pay. Another university graduate, TONY, looked at the situation as a personal problem but a structural issue:

> I'm the only one who's going to get myself out of this…but I also see it as a structural problem which society has to deal with. There are 150 people looking for work and 100 jobs. It doesn't matter if the 50 people are working like mad to get a job. If it's not there, it's not there. No one's going to give it to you.

He felt that a post-industrial revolution would decrease the number of jobs, taking jobs from the blue-collar area and adding them to the white-collar area but in smaller numbers. *"We have to look in radically new directions,"* he concluded.

Finally, those holding a *collectivist ideology*—the main variants being participatory socialism and Marxist analysis—were intellectually fortified against the misplaced egoism of self-blame. The holders of this perspective believed that the major responsibility for the high unemployment lay with business and government. According to the most articulate spokesman of this view, JIM, the roots of the present crisis lay in the objective contradictions between capitalism's world-wide search to maintain its rate of profit and the interests of communities and the working class. Subjectively, business and government were using the unemployed as a tool to *"reduce the price of labour payout, of forcing those who are working to work for less."*

> To the extent to which they can demoralize the unemployed, they have a potential scab...and a capacity to intimidate workers.... [There are] large numbers of people who are scared, looking for work, not ever knowing what is expected of them.

It was in the interests of big business and government to have *"broken-down individuals as opposed to collective forces."* Not only in their analysis, but in their organizing and egalitarian practice, the leftist informants tried to counter this atomization, refusing (in JIM's words) to be *"pushed around and carried by blind forces."*

The leftists seemed determined to stand united against the assault on the working class represented by unemployment. JIM's advice to the unemployed was also aimed at the unemployed *person*, who had to be armoured against the marginalizing currents of capitalism:

> The essential thing I come back to is a sense of your person. Don't let them grind you down. Don't let them give you the impression you are all alone, don't let them atomize you.... You didn't make the situation, but you can have a hand in changing it.

These analytical tools were not just theories, but were an indispensible part of radical practice. Only such an analysis of the whole situation, it was thought, would prevent the unemployed from being crushed by their sufferings. And only in the collective struggle which followed from the analysis would the self come into its own—not in the private absorption or psychologism of liberal-capitalist society.

Conclusion

In the socially-conditioned practices of the unemployed self there were two idioms—that of the wheel or cycle of marginalization, and that of the "jagged edges." We will take each in turn.

The marginalization of the unemployed self meant that the personal identity had lost its mooring to the social identity. Cut off from significant personal agency in the social world, the practices left to the self to "write" became ever more circumscribed. Introspecting, disconnected from active social roles or contents upon which it could reflect, it became increasingly self-referencing and subjectivized. Communal ties, even thoughts of the outside world, became fewer. Social injuries were transmuted into personal hurts. The mind cast back to past events which become exaggerated in their present influence.

Over time the self lost its sense of entitlement to the future. No longer acting in the future perfect, one prepared for a long accommodation in the present. The goal now was self-maintenance. The view of society became more cynical, and one kept a well-rationalized distance from others. The extreme situation to which entrenched unemployment drove the self left it the author of its own practices, but those practices did not enter the collective making of the society outside one's door. Marginalization had finally reached into the self and become reproduced in the self's own processes.

The idiom of those who were able to *transcend* unemployment, on the other hand, was determinedly active or at least self-protective—whether it was based on the confidence of a sense of entitlement, of intellectual comprehension, of active collective opposition, or of income. The key here was support, willingly offered and received, which was the lifeline that sustained a sense of agency in a community. Whether the others were family, friends, contacts or fellow unemployed, with them one was able to turn modest resources into rich returns in the community. By fighting for a place in the social order—as well as in the future—one not only improved the prospects of finally being employed, but also resisted the hypothesis of self-blame. The personal identity was turned outward, to its social identity, and to how it might connect with the collective life of its time and place.

CHAPTER ELEVEN

Conclusions and Initiatives

Though fortune's malice overthrow my state,
  my mind exceeds the compass of her wheel.

  Shakespeare, 3 Henry VI, iv, 3

The social practices covered in this book occurred in (1) a *microsocial sphere* of individuals, families, and groups of friends; (2) an *intermediate community sphere* of unemployment organizations, union locals, church groups, small enterprises, and social networks; and (3) a *macrosocial sphere* of state bureaucracies, corporations, and large unions. Within these societal frames the thesis and findings of the book will be briefly recapitulated, and certain *initiatives* pertaining to the problem of unemployment will be advanced.

Recapitulation

Macrosocial processes and institutions combined in recent years, in a partly deliberate, partly unintended manner, to sustain a punishing level of unemployment among Canadian workers. Unemployment rates were especially high in the early 1980s, and, for some groups and regions, have continued well into the late 80s. It was working people and the poor who suffered the economic crisis in the very marrow of their bones. Whenever the political and economic elites talked of "belt-tightening," ordinary people felt the pangs. The government's decision to target inflation, not unemployment, while eroding its spending and services to economic victims, deferred to the business class and the vagaries of the marketplace while putting people's human needs in second place.

After all, inflation is much more injurious to the wielders of capital than is unemployment. Since industry requires predictability for investment plans, restraints on the inflation rate are demanded of government. Employers also require the flexibility to lay off workers at will, to increase the number of part-time and temporary workers, to restrain their wage demands, to replace labour input with technology, and so on. So in the recession years of the early 1980s, not only was unemployment tolerated by political and business leaders, it was a (partly welcome) *discipline* for a work force whose growing wage demands and sense of entitlement were seen as threats to competitiveness and profitability.

This subordination of the interests and needs of people to the demands of the marketplace is mirrored in the way informants were handled on the job market. They were treated as if they did not matter, as if they were articles at a lawn sale in late afternoon. The inaccessible employers and their front line—even when they would communicate—seemed themselves to be mere instruments of some more profound process that was writing their own practices.

Government officials seemed similarly tied to an extrinsic, systemic logic, in this case one of legislation and bureaucratic rules and policies originating from centres of power. Both employers and government officials seemed unable to permit or imagine people's co-authorship of their practices in macrosocial domains. Individuals could not therefore express themselves in an active, collaborative idiom.

To express any personal agency at all the informants had to look to the intermediate and microsocial spheres of local community and family and friends. On intermediate ground, a substantial minority became involved in the unemployment organizations which were set up to serve their needs. These offered a social life of sorts; a place to drop off children for "parent relief" and job-hunting; assistance with typing and copying and résumé-writing. Most importantly, they made it possible to see one's situation as a collective problem and to identify with the unemployed as a source of learning and strength, instead of failure. As did "free zones"—like libraries and parks—unemployment organizations sheltered the unemployed from the discriminating materialism of the urban scene. Individuals could drink coffee, read a paper, take a fitness course without feeling second-class.

There was an exciting synergy among some of the younger informants who worked together in International Youth Year projects, which promised to lead on to careers and future collaborations. The friendships that emerged from active involvement with unemployment organizations and the working-class movement were also important—and were all the stronger for being formed in a common struggle.

The *microsocial* sphere of family and friends, especially if not relieved by civic involvement in the intermediate sphere by social support, could become a de-socialized place of suffering—where the force of societal rejection was felt directly. In private life the self had so much leeway and so few resources that its practices became ingrown. Being unemployed meant that one's negative or ill-defined social identity penetrated the personal identity and even influenced reading the intentions of others. At home other people, routines, even objects could become distractions or obsessions, concentrating alienated energy within themselves.

Yet this home sphere could be a constructive place for the autonomous self. Freed from the "straitjacket" of the full-time job, one could pursue art, enjoy children, prepare for future directions or projects. One could find useful, unpaid work which needed doing and which structured the day.

It is with this potentially autonomous and ego-involved microsocial sphere that we begin the discussion of initiatives.

Initiatives

Microsocial Sphere

When we look at the various projects of unemployed individuals, and their families and small groups, we are driven to make a distinction between *work* and *employment*. Though not "employed," the informants "worked" at many tasks (some of which earn wages in the service sector): housework, child care, volunteering, playing music, collecting food coupons, job-hunting, sewing, making repairs, and so on. While some of these unpaid work-tasks were imposed, and could come to seem meaningless during an unstructured day, many were performed with energy and a grateful sense of purposefulness. *These* were more likely to rescue the individual from idle time than leisure pursuits, which the informants either could not afford or feel entitled to.[1]

The Lottery Question

In order to gauge how the informants felt about leisure, work, and employment, they were asked whether they would still work if they won a great deal of money in a lottery. Freed from a compulsion to earn their living, how would they live? The response was overwhelming: *all but ten informants said they would want to work*—though sometimes in some combination with leisure. The pattern of responses is worth exploring.

Of the 10 who said *no*, six were youthful and lacking in skills or definite occupational direction. Some indicated that they would sit around and do nothing. There seemed to be a defiant, if unfocussed, rejection of the work ethic which had punished them. As well, their future work seemed not to have taken shape even in their imaginations. One woman, SILVIA, admitted she worked from necessity; she would like to spend her time travelling to see distant relatives. Two were self-directed artists, who only wanted the conditions for autonomous work and personal integrity and therefore were "workers" by our definition. STEVE would be glad not to

---

[1] Certain definitions are needed at this point. I define "leisure" as activity enjoyed more for its own sake than for any purpose it is assigned. "Work," on the other hand, is complex, purposeful activity more clearly focussed on its objective. One form of work is the social institution of "employment," where people are paid to carry out work (Fryer and Payne, 1984: 285).

have to sell his art: *"I would prefer just to do my art, just to be left alone and not have to sell it. I don't enjoy that, because it's not a part of me—it's like prostitution."* CHRIS saw work-tasks in terms of his personal needs rather than as goals in the environment: *"If you had the desire to work, you could always shovel in your garden until you were physically tired, or if you wanted mental entertainment, you could always read a book or learn a language."*

All the others wanted some form of work which would extend them beyond the self or the immediate pleasure of the task. MARIANNE shyly showed the interviewer a huge pile of typescript which contained part of her life story. *"I just kept typing and typing, seeking a position, being interviewed over the years."* If she won the lottery, she would retire from paid employment and try to write her book. In a similar vein, SALLY quoted a writer who expressed his joy that his writings were read around the world, and yet were still his own. She envied that personal identification with work and wanted the satisfaction of seeing the end product.

"If I won the lottery," DOROTHY commented, *"there are only so many times I could travel around the world."* She would want to work to reclaim the things she missed in her old job. *"I miss the stimulation. I need that, I need a sense of purpose.... I need that amount of structure in my life.... I miss the interaction with co-workers."* Informants talked about having more choices to do work that they really wanted to do, or that would develop creative ideas. They would accept stimulating and challenging work. DICK's answer was simple, *"Yeah, I love working."* Some spoke of working as being *"fun," "productive,"* and as contributing to something; they showed contempt for just sitting around like a millionaire, or being out on the golf course. As BRIAN remarked: *"You've got to be active.... You've got to rub shoulders with people all the time and the golf course isn't the place to do it.... You've got to get with the little guy."*

Many would ease into work gradually, after travelling or developing talents. Some would open their own hotels, restaurants, businesses, farms, carpentry shops. Others would be glad to pursue a career after some years in university. Some simply would be glad of employment, provided by someone else, giving them a mooring to the social world. Two long-term unemployed men, MATTHEW and GORD, spoke of a good job in tones of reverence. To the question, MATTHEW answered feelingly: *"Oh, yeah.... If it deprived another person of work, maybe not, but a created job.... I would work. I can really identify with unemployed people. I know what it's like. If I could use that money to help some other unemployed person."* GORD answered:

> Yes, I would want to work more than ever.... It's just doing something useful. You just can't sit around and do nothing. You've got to do something, even if it's interview work.

Some would do volunteer work, helping other people.

People did not discount leisure: they would want to travel, to read, to experience the pleasures of the world. But above all, they would want to *work*. LAURIE gave the most moving and perceptive account of why she would work:

> *Working would still appeal, because you have to have somewhere to go in the day, even if you don't need the money to live. It's just* something about working that clicks into something in you...*that even socializing, or even the most transcending experience outside just doesn't do. There's just something about working that keeps people together and keeps them going. And it makes them friends.*

Working gives one a moral entitlement to a place in society. And in the shifting arenas of the modern city, where one's family name or religion no longer identify a person, doing work "clicks" into the need of the personal and social identity to be a part of the social world.

Those theorists who believe the future points to the abolition of work and the expansion of leisure (e.g. Gorz, 1982) cannot be encouraged by the evidence from the lottery question or from the informants' accounts of their daily lives. Without employment, or any other *socially-grounding* work, leisure is sterile and without point. The work-oriented motivations among the unemployed, their socialization into a consuming culture, the failure of communities to offer alternatives to the dynamic of consumption, all suggest that we are far from ready to institutionalize a leisure society.

The Myth of the Self as Hercules

Psychological and individualist variables do not explain the phenomenon of unemployment. Though they are keys to understanding the experience of unemployment, these variables are "proxies for more complex social factors" (Fryer and Ullah, 1987: iii), which have been described in this book. But so powerful is the individualism of this culture that some informants could not even consider that their suffering may stem from a wider social malaise.

Some informants felt that the only role was to wait in a kind of splendid isolation for business conditions to improve. As BRIAN said, *"It's within the individual. Nobody feels sorry for you. There isn't one soul on God's earth that cares one hoot one way or the other if you go bust today, other than possibly your own immediate family."* People felt that unemployment had reminded them that, in COLLEEN's statement, *"the onus is completely on me.... I have had to come to take stock of myself. You really get to know your own attributes, when you're trying to sell yourself to people all the time."*

The self in this bleak isolation often suffered greatly from the absence of a sense of solidarity. CONNIE defined society as *"only a compilation of in-*

dividuals." When asked if *"society"* was helping her, she replied, *"A lot of individuals are helping me. My friends, my family, my doctor, etc. But society in general, no.... I don't feel society really gives a damn. I don't feel they have any obligation to me."* When asked immediately afterward what advice she had for other unemployed, she said softly, *"Jump off a bridge."* Another immense sufferer, BOB, said, *"The number one responsibility for all this rests on the shoulders of the individual. This is not Russia where the state takes care of you.... The number one responsibility is on the individual to get his own work."*

While important in its own right, initiatives for change lie beyond the microsocial sphere. Most of the unemployed's psychological sufferings and sense of emasculation stem from being cut adrift from the main productive work of their society. We now turn to a wider spheré.

The Intermediate Community Sphere

The civic space of the community must come alive to provide present work and to prepare for the new forms it will take. This intermediate ground, however, is no longer held firm by the roots of religious or other organic communities. Left to the developers and the buyers and sellers of the consumer marketplace, the social fabric of this spheré is constantly being weakened. Yet this community ground is the most promising for fusing together individual projects into common collective purposes. To hold it together, government revenues must *underwrite, but not control* initiatives in the intermediate sphere.

Form Small Enterprises

People should be helped to form small enterprises, according to LAURIE. Society can help the present situation *"by fostering or kindling the spirit of entrepreneurship. Like small businesses. Like, somebody has a great idea; give them government grants, make them more accessible."* LAURIE recommends a supporting, not controlling role for government.

> I think the things we can do for each other are very personal. They don't have to be legislated. Self-help groups, community centres, the churches, the libraries for meetings. It's stuff like that, that doesn't cost a lot, that doesn't make a lot of paperwork, that's person-to-person. And the government doesn't have to worry about them. You just get the feeling that the government's there to do what it can and we do what we can. You see, I've never really identified with the government, it's more the community.

I would not agree that the government role should *generally* be a minimalist one (especially in the macrosocial sphere), but in the community enterprise it should be a low-profile role.

Individuals who were helped to set up enterprises, whether capitalist or non-profit, were very grateful for the confidence shown in them. There was a moving account of MONICA receiving financial backing from a stranger, with apparently selfless motives, to set herself up in self-employment in sewing. His decision to trust her with his capital inspired her to do good work and to want to do the same thing for others: *"I know the first thing I would do: I would be helping the next one, like another mother or something, because I was helped."*

Some of these community enterprises which spring up around a need or a good idea should be worker co-operatives, which are synergistic and involving. Workers learn the laws, the techniques, the economic environment, the financial restraints and capacities, in far more detail than in conventional businesses. They are participants in a collective effort and share in its struggles and rewards. Whether their activities involve homebuilding, glass recycling, or the provision of neighbourhood services for the elderly, worker co-operatives deserve extensive public support.

It is possible to weave non-monetary relations even more boldly into the social fabric of communities. In a later work of Gorz (1985: 62), he cites a Swedish account (Akerman, 1979) of an interesting exchange between producer co-ops and community members, which originated in Quebec:

> a union of local co-ops, bringing together an ever-widening range of products and services, and entitling all its members to the equivalent of all the hours they have given to the community in the form of goods and services. The union will provide, for example, a voucher for holiday accommodation, the services of painters or plasterers, consumer goods or materials, in exchange for a given number of hours worked for the co-op or community. These hours can be worked by individuals, groups or families intermittently or occasionally according to respective needs and opportunities.... Exchange assumes a non-market form (Gorz, 1985: 62).

There was some support expressed for the skills-exchange idea among informants, because it led to a knowledge of people and work methods in the community. DEBBIE commented: *"If it's extended, it does create more of a sense of community, because people have to work together.... You have a better sense of the people around you, of what facilities are available. It's getting away from the idea of people getting something for nothing."* It gave people opportunities to contribute, instead of just receive (or purchase).

Towards People and Services

There was considerable support among the informants for the move away from producing *goods*. *"We're such a consumer-oriented society,"* commented FRANCES. *"Make something so we can buy it and play with it. I would like to see more effort and money put into fine arts and theatres."* EVA phrased it differently:

> *Any country's greatest natural resource is people. I mean, people don't have to be measured in how many sweaters they can produce in an hour, right? They are also*

measured in art, culture, everything. They [i.e. government] *have to start think-ing about how they can utilize people more than* [giving them] *jobs where they're making something.*

DOROTHY felt that the current climate was favouring a particular social type. *"You're always hearing government say that the answer lies in the busi-ness community. Well, unfortunately, not all of us are interested in, and/or skilled at working in business. There are a lot of other things to work at besides busi-ness."* She went on to suggest that when the business ethos dominated the society, there was a new class of losers. *"It almost seems…if you don't have the interest or inclination to work in business, then you deserve to be unemployed. That it's your fault, because you chose something like social services or whatever."* She recommended that when government gives handouts to business, it should then pressure companies to provide employment. She could have added that it would then be justified in supporting non-capitalistic forms of enterprise.

Many informants did not respect the imperatives shaped by a market-driven economy. When STAN was queried about a possible upturn in the economy, he replied sharply, *"That's garbage.… Who says that we want to go back in the same direction that brought us here anyway?"* He favoured the turn to services and thought they should be developed to a higher level. In-stead of cutting university staff and limiting access to facilities, he wanted higher education and training to be free. Education, culture, and the com-municative and therapeutic services possessed and needed by people were infinitely better, in his view, than the consumerist society's crass am-bitions.

Education and the New Synergy

Public space, the schools, libraries, community centres, places of work, must link human beings in conceiving and learning new forms of work. If corporations have renounced social responsibility, people must dis-cover what needs to be done to foster human purpose in their lives. People must debate and experiment with new forms of providing for themselves when the conventional link between work and income is changed.

Some informants suggested keeping the schools open after regular school hours and making them centres of community learning. Schools should be places which provide vocational screening and individualized counselling. There should be courses in practical trades and other fields of employment for those who would likely drop out of academic school-ing. Putting more teachers and workers who want to teach into jobs in these expanded schools "would provide more individually designed school programs. Work programs for academic credit should exist in all high schools and job training and placement programs should also be instituted. And, existing vocational programs have to be upgraded—not treated as a dumping ground for second-class citizens" (Levine, 1979: 9).

There was support for *co-operative* curricula that combined school work and on-the-job experience. This would lead to a better sense of what the world of work was like, away from the sheltered classroom. As KENNETH put it, *"Increase the university student's hands-on work experience with the employer's technology. That experience will prevent the university education from being irrelevant. Learn skills right at the workplace, even in high schools. More co-op programs that would increase that kind of learning."* These synergistic links from school to shop floor should be strengthened by creating apprenticeship programs. As Levine suggests, "artisans, craftsmen and skilled workers could have young people assigned to them—after careful screening—for lengthy periods of time. The youth would learn needed skills and receive vocational and other guidance from them" (Levine, 1979: 9). Such a program should be government-supported.

The best way to prepare people for a future which may not have a vast array of conventional full-time jobs for them is to give them a role in making rules and changes in their own community settings. If, in school, they can participate in designing curricula for the emerging needs of their country and community, they will be more fit as adults to do the necessary work around them.

> Job creation programs, and new business formations involving young people in the planning, learning and working, are vital, especially if these are joint ventures among public and private, non-profit and educational sectors. Innovative, cost-effective, labour-intensive cottage industries can be established that do not compete with traditional industries, yet do provide jobs and training for unemployed young people. Alternative technologies, waste recovery and recycling, urban farming…are all feasible possibilities (Levine, 1979: 9).

The vision that is emerging breaks down the distinction between the realm of schooling and the realm of society. Schooling will contain firmer links with society, especially for students who want experience in the work world. And work will continue to educate and inform the workers to keep them abreast of new social developments and technologies, as well as the history and humanities that they may have passed by in their teens.

This second level is in a way the most exciting. According to Gorz, it links macrosocially necessary work with the "autonomous activity…determined by individual choice."

> [T]his second level thus constitutes the social fabric of civil society. It is the level of debates and trade-offs; the level where decisions are reached as to what is necessary and what is desirable; the level of conflicts and plans for the future, of the "production of society"…. (Gorz, 1985: 63)

For it to occupy this pivotal role, the macrosocial sphere must be reformed.

The Macrosocial Institutional Sphere

The large-scale institutional sphere must increase the amount and the quality of its communication with individuals and small social formations. To make encounters with applicants and clients less defeating and dis-identifying, there must be increased staff to communicate with the unemployed. Personnel departments must gain higher status in companies; their people must have the skills and time to deal with applicants as if they mattered. This interaction, whatever the outcome, will at least give the applicant a vocabulary with which to assess and present his or her skills. To some degree the applicant will be kept in the conversation of public life. The job search experience will seem somewhat less atomizing and depriving.

This increased communicative content and synergy is even more necessary for government agencies. With more counsellors who are not moved to other positions as frequently, claimants and clients could present their situation and need more carefully.

One thing that would make *Manpower* more effective would be to improve its liaison with employers. Employers—who benefit from state support in ways ranging from training courses to infrastructure-building to tax breaks—should be compelled to enter a job vacancy into a computerized Manpower system as soon as it appears. Unreported vacancies should bring fines, which could go into a fund to help workers travel to where there are jobs. Employers and government should share the cost of travel grants for workers as companies would benefit from the greater variety of applicants.

There is an immense emphasis in the informants' accounts of how immobilizing unemployment is, how it fixes them in space. Not only should travel grants be more freely available to bring applicants to other cities, but *local* travel must be facilitated. Bus passes—either free or discounted—should be issued to the unemployed and to welfare recipients who have job search requirements. Given their small incomes, it makes no sense for them to be paying out of pocket for their trips to employers.

Single parents and others with children would have *their* mobility enhanced if there were short-term child care facilities where they take courses, visit government agencies, and drop in on employers. These facilities should become far more widespread, like architectural adaptations for the handicapped. There should also be more neighbourhood facilities for these children. Universal subsidized child care, well-funded and staffed, is necessary for those with children who need to participate in the work force.

Groups who have difficulty finding jobs, partly due to inadequate skills—such as younger and older unemployed persons— must be given the opportunity and means to upgrade their skills. There should be many courses on new, marketable skills, offered in churches, schools, recreation centres, and libraries. The unemployed should be encouraged to take courses at colleges and universities, and their tuition should be free or reduced. At the very least such experiences bring the unemployed into contact with other people, as well as impart the language and skills of new work processes.

The foregoing—provision of communication channels, transmission of knowledge and skills, child care, subsidizing travel throughout the city— would require the government to build and underwrite an *infrastructure for people* and their present needs. As the monetarist economist, Milton Friedman, has said, corporations have no social responsibilities—only responsibilities to their shareholders to be profitable. Corporate actions have been paralleled by the irresponsible policies and programs of neoconservative political and economic elites during the recession.

In more general terms, the government must take a more active role in job-creation. It is uniquely positioned to employ people itself—as well as underwrite community enterprises—in tasks of national importance. In countries such as Germany, environmental protection is proving to be an important source of new jobs. There should be many more workers recycling materials such as glass, paper, and automobile tires. The glass-recycling industry in West Germany "has created 3000 jobs to date and is recycling 27 percent of all glass used in the country, compared with 17 percent in 1970" (Schohl, 1985: 26). There could be more jobs in waste-heat recovery, in the insulation of buildings, in the construction of barriers between dumps and the surrounding ground water, in the repair of buildings damaged by acid rain, in reforestation. Unemployed scientists and technicians could be put to work analyzing the thousands of chemical compounds that have effects on the environment and human health which are unknown (Schohl, 1985: 27).

There are many more provisions that could be implemented. With crown corporations and companies that do business with the government leading the way, there should be a phasing out of overtime, a balanced and equitable reduction of working hours if necessary, and an encouragement of job sharing. Part-time workers must have an equitable share of benefits and wages. There should be paid educational sabbaticals, to which workers contribute by setting aside portions of their salaries.

The government should formulate plant shutdown legislation so that corporations are forced to "open their books" to prove that their disinvestment or shutdown was necessary—and face stiff fines if they cannot. These decisions must be discussed with labour unions and government representatives who will have to be convinced before they pay the price of the corporation's rationalization. Alternatives should be explored—such as worker buy-outs. Workers must be given sufficient notice of layoffs, and should be helped to secure new employment, and to retrain. Workers should be consulted on all technological changes to ensure that both the benefits and the effects of dislocation are fairly distributed (this is required by law in Sweden; see Gill, 1985: 182). An independent body should monitor technological change with an eye to its employment effects and its impact on workplace practices.

Corporations understand contracts. By virtue of the tax breaks, grants, infrastructure-building, and training assistance which they receive from governments, major business corporations have signed a *social contract* with the community. They must be made to fulfill their obligations to that community.

If the injury that is unemployment has its origins in the macrosocial sphere, then it is in this sphere that the major remedies must be sought. The "therapy" is this: people need good jobs. If the private sector cannot provide them, then the public sector must. If conventional employment will be systematically reduced, then the public sector must help people fulfill their natural desire to work at tasks that need doing. And the private sector must be made to support these goals to fulfill its part of the social contract.

Only in the company of active, co-operating men and women who are learning and working together can human beings hope to write themselves into the public script of their times.

Tables of Sample Characteristics

PERSONAL, FAMILY STATUS

Sex

Male	41 %	(31)
Female	59 %	(44)

Age

15 to 24	39 %	(29)
25 to 44	44 %	(33)
45 and over	17 %	(13)

Marital Status

Single	49 %	(37)
Married, Common Law	31 %	(23)
Divorced, Separated	21 %	(16)
Widowed	1 %	(1)

(Note: Some are divorced and common law)

Home Situation

Having Children at Home	28 %	(21)
Sole Support Parents	13 %	(10)
Housewives	8 %	(6)
Househusbands	13 %	(10)
Living with Parents	27 %	(20)
Living with Relatives	3 %	(2)

UNEMPLOYMENT STATUS

Duration of Unemployment

3 months or less	25 %	(19)
4 to 6 months	19 %	(14)
7 to 12 months	27 %	(20)
More than a year	29 %	(22)

Flows into Unemployment

Job Loser	55 %	(41)
Job Leaver	24 %	(18)
Entrant	24 %	(18)
Re-entrant	15 %	(11)

(Note: Some entrants were also classed as job losers or leavers)

SOCIO-ECONOMIC STATUS

Father's (or Mother's) Occupation

Managerial	19 %	(14)
Professional	8 %	(6)
Clerical/Sales/Service	16 %	(12)
Manual	41 %	(31)
Other (No response, welfare, housewife)	16 %	(12)

Education

University Degree	19 %	(14)
Post-secondary certificate	5 %	(4)
Some Post-secondary	24 %	(18)
High School	20 %	(15)
Some High School	31 %	(23)
Grade School	1 %	(1)

Principal Income Source

Unemployment Insurance	29 %	(22)
Social Assistance	19 %	(14)
Mother's Allowance	9 %	(7)
Disability Allowance	7 %	(5)
Parents	21 %	(16)
Partner	11 %	(8)
Savings, Alimony, Odd Jobs	4 %	(3)

Social Class Background [1]

CLASS I	28 %	(21)
CLASS II	39 %	(29)
CLASS III	33 %	(25)

---

[1] "Social Class Background" is a relative scale of the background of advantage/disadvantage. Its components are:

Education University degree = 12
   Post-secondary certificate = 9
   Some Post-secondary = 6
   High School degree = 3
   Some High School = 0

Father's Occupation (Mother's)
   Managerial/Professional = 12
   Clerical/Sales/Service = 8
   Manual = 4
   Social-waged (welfare) = 0

"Last Important Job" (self-reported)
   Managerial/Professional = 12
   Clerical/Sales/Service = 8
   Manual = 4
   Social-waged (welfare)= 0

Income of Last Important Job (Informants' Incomes Ranged in Quartiles)
   1st = 12   2nd = 8   3rd = 4   4th = 0

Out of a possible 48, those scoring
   30 to 48 are in CLASS I
   20 to 29 are in CLASS II
   0 to 19 are in CLASS III

The Sample: Important Variables

EXPLANATIONS AND ABBREVIATIONS

DURAT	Duration of Unemployment (in months)
AGE CAT.	Age Category
MAR.STAT.	Marital Status

	Com Law	= Common Law
	Div	= Divorced
	Sep	= Separated
	+C	= With children at home
	SSP	= Sole Support Parent
	HH	= Househusband
	HW	= Housewife

EDUC	Education

	%HS	= Some High School
	HS	= High School
	%PS	= Some Post-secondary
	PS.D.	= Post-secondary Degree
	U.D.	= University Degree

CLASS	(See Appendix A for details)
FAM	Overall Assessment of Contribution of FAMILY (of orientation or procreation, whichever most relevant)

	POS	= Positive
	NEUT	= Neutral, Mixed
	NEG	= Negative

MOB	Readiness to be MOBILE

	VM	= Very Mobile
	SM	= Somewhat Mobile
	IM	= Immobile

UNEM. STAT.	Unemployment Status
FIN. SUPPT	Chief Source of FINANCIAL SUPPORT

	SOC. ASST.	= Social Assistance
	MOTH. ALL.	= Mother's Allowance (Family Benefits)
	U.I.	= Unemployment Insurance Benefits

MARKET	Chief Job MARKET Being Searched
SOC'ZE	SOCIALIZES More While Unemployed, Less than, or the Same as before
DISTRESS	"Y" indicates that active distress was verbalized (talk of anxiety, suicide, etc.)

NAME	SEX	AGE	CAT.	DURAT.	MAR.STAT	EDUC	CLASS	FAM.	MOB	UNEM.STAT.	FIN.SUPPT	MARKET	SOC'ZE	DISTRESS
AGNES	F	54	45+	YEAR+	DIV+C	HS	II	POS	IM	JOB LOSER	RELATIVES	OPEN	LESS	Y
ALICE	F	21	15-24	7-12	SINGLE	%HS	III	NEG	VM	JOB LEAVER	SOC.ASST.	OPEN,REST.	SAME	Y
ALLEN	M	22	15-24	7-12	MARRIED HH	%HS	II	POS	SM	JOB LEAVER	PARTNER	CONSTRUCT.	SAME	
ANDREA	F	33	25-44	YEAR+	DIV+C SSP	%HS	III	POS	IM	JOB LOSER	DISABILITY	SOC.SCIENCE	SAME	Y
ANDREW	M	35	25-44	YEAR+	SINGLE	%HS	II	NEUT	VM	JOB LOSER	SOC.ASST.	JOURNALISM	LESS	Y
ANNE	F	18	15-24	3LESS	SINGLE	%HS	III	POS	IM	ENTRANT	PARENTS	OPEN	MORE	
BERNARD	M	27	25-44	7-12	SINGLE	%PS	II		SM	JOB LOSER	U.I.	AGRICULT.	LESS	Y
BETH	F	30	25-44	7-12	DIV	U.D.	I	NEG	VM	JOB LOSER	U.I.	PSYCHOLOGY	MORE	
BOB	M	30	25-44	3LESS	MARR+C HH	%PS	I	NEUT	SM	JOB LOSER	PARTNER	OPEN	LESS	Y
BRENDA	F	21	15-24	7-12	SING+C SSP	%HS	III	NEUT	IM	RE-ENTRANT	MOTH.ALL.	OPEN	MORE	
BRIAN	M	60	45+	4-6	MARRIED HH	%PS	I	NEUT	IM	JOB LEAVER	U.I.	OPEN	LESS	Y
CHRIS	M	28	25-44	3LESS	SINGLE	PS.D.	I	POS	IM	JOB LOSER	PARENTS	TECH.TRADES	SAME	
COLLEEN	F	28	25-44	3LESS	COM LAW	U.D.	I	NEG	SM	RE-ENTRANT	PARTNER	PSYCHOLOGY	LESS	
CONNIE	F	49	45+	YEAR+	SINGLE	%PS	II	POS	VM	JOB LOSER	SAVINGS	OPEN	LESS	Y
CRAIG	M	35	25-44	YEAR+	SINGLE	U.D.	I	NEUT	VM	JOB LOSER	PARENTS	ENGR.ACC'T	LESS	Y
DEBBIE	F	34	25-44	3LESS	SINGLE	%PS	I	NEUT	VM	JOB LOSER	U.I.	TECH.,OPEN	SAME	
DESMOND	M	28	25-44	4-6	MARR+C HH	PS.D.	I	POS	VM	JOB LEAVER	U.I.	OPEN	LESS	Y
DIANE	F	25	25-44	4-6	SINGLE	U.D.	I	POS	IM	JOB LOSER	U.I.	HUM.SERV.	MORE	Y
DICK	M	22	15-24	3LESS	COM LAW	%HS	III	POS	SM	JOB LOSER	SOC.ASST.	OPEN	LESS	Y
DONALD	M	33	25-44	YEAR+	SINGLE	%PS	II	POS	IM	JOB LOSER	SOC.ASST.	REST.CHEF	LESS	
DOROTHY	F	33	25-44	4-6	SINGLE	U.D.	I	NEUT	IM	JOB LOSER	DISABILITY	TEACHING	MORE	
EMMA	F	52	45+	YEAR+	DIV+C SSP	%HS	III	NEUT	VM	JOB LOSER	SOC.ASST.	SERVICES	LESS	Y
ERICA	F	45	45+	YEAR+	MARR+C HW	HS	II	NEG	IM	JOB LEAVER	PARTNER	OFFICE WK	LESS	Y
EVA	F	23	15-24	7-12	SINGLE	U.D.	II	NEUT	VM	ENTRANT	PARENTS	PERSONNEL	SAME	
EVELYN	F	38	25-44	4-6	DIV+C SSP	%HS	II	NEG	SM	RE-ENTRANT	MOTH.ALL.	HUM.SERV.	SAME	
FRAN	F	32	25-44	7-12	SINGLE	%PS	II	POS	SM	JOB LOSER	U.I.	TECH.TRADES	MORE	
FRANCES	F	26	25-44	YEAR+	SINGLE	U.D.	I	POS	VM	ENTRANT	PARENTS	SOC.SCIENCE	LESS	
GAIL	F	50	45+	4-6	DIV	HS	II	NEUT	SM	JOB LOSER	U.I.	OFFICE WK	SAME	Y
GLENN	M	18	15-24	7-12	SINGLE	%HS	III	NEUT	VM	ENTRANT	PARENTS	OPEN	LESS	Y
GORD	M	47	45+	YEAR+	DIV	%HS	III	NEG	SM	JOB LOSER	ODD JOBS	OPEN	LESS	
HAROLD	M	34	25-44	4-6	COM LAW	%HS	III	NEUT	VM	JOB LOSER	SOC.ASST.	OPEN	LESS	
HEATHER	F	27	25-44	4-6	MARR+C HW	HS	II	NEG	SM	JOB LOSER	U.I.	SOC.WORK	LESS	Y

NAME	SEX	AGE	CAT.	DURAT	MAR.STAT	EDUC	CLASS	FAM.	MOB	UNEM.STAT.	FIN.SUPPT	MARKET	SOC'ZE	DISTRESS
HERB	M	21	15-24	7-12	SINGLE	HS	II	POS	VM	ENTRANT	PARENTS	OPEN	MORE	
JANE	F	25	25-44	3LESS	C LAW +C	%PS	II	NEG	IM	JOB LOSER	PARTNER	HUM.SERV.		
JANINE	F	18	15-24	4-6	MARRIED HW	%HS	II	POS	VM	JOB LOSER	SOC.ASST.	OPEN	LESS	
JIM	M	29	25-44	7-12	COM LAW	%PS	I	NEUT		JOB LOSER	U.I.	FACTORY	SAME	
JOANNE	F	47	45+	7-12	MARR +C HW	%PS	I	NEUT	IM	JOB LEAVER	U.I.	OFFICE WK	LESS	Y
JUDY	F	15	15-24	3LESS	SINGLE	Gr7	III	NEUT	IM	ENTRANT	PARENTS	BABYSIT	LESS	
JUNE	F	16	15-24	4-6	MARR +C HH	%HS	III	NEUT	IM	ENTRANT	PARENTS	OPEN	SAME	
KARL	M	38	25-44	7-12	C LAW +C	U.D.	I	NEUT	VM	JOB LOSER	U.I.	OPEN,SALES	LESS	
KATHY	F	32	25-44	4-6	SINGLE	HS	III	POS	IM	JOB LOSER	PARTNER	OPEN	SAME	Y
KENNETH	M	31	25-44	3LESS	SINGLE	U.D.	I	POS	VM	JOB LOSER	PARENTS	ENGN'R,OPEN		
KIM	F	16	15-24	3LESS	SINGLE	%HS	III	POS	IM	ENTRANT	PARENTS	OPEN		
LAURIE	F	24	15-24	3LESS	SINGLE	%PS	II	POS	IM	ENTRANT	PARENTS	OPEN	SAME	
LORNE	M	19	15-24	YEAR+	DIV	%HS	II	NEG	VM	ENTRANT	SOC.ASST.	OFFICE WK	LESS	Y
MAR'NNE	F	60	45+	3LESS	SINGLE	%HS	II	POS	IM	JOB LOSER	U.I.	OFFICE WK	LESS	Y
MARJ'IE	F	18	15-24	4-6	SINGLE	HS	II	NEG	IM	ENTRANT	SOC.ASST.	OPEN	MORE	
MARK	M	56	45+	4-6	SEP	%HS	III	NEG	IM	JOB LOSER	SOC.ASST.	ODD JOBS	LESS	Y
MARTHA	F	44	25-44	7-12	DIV +C SSP	%PS	II	POS	IM	JOB LEAVER	ALIMONY	OPEN	LESS	Y
MARY	F	41	25-44	YEAR+	DIV +C SSP	HS	III	NEUT	IM	JOB LEAVER	MOTH.ALL.	OPEN	LESS	Y
MATTHEW	M	39	25-44	YEAR+	MARR +C HH	%PS	II	NEUT	IM	JOB LOSER	PARTNER	OPEN,LAB.	LESS	Y
MAUREEN	F	22	15-24	YEAR+	SINGLE	%PS	III	NEUT	IM	ENTRANT	DISABILITY	OPEN, SERV.		
MELISSA	F	20	15-24	3LESS	SINGLE	%HS	I	POS	IM	ENTRANT	PARENTS	BABYSIT	SAME	
MICH'LE	F	16	15-24	3LESS	SINGLE	HS	III	NEUT	IM	ENTRANT	PARENT	OFFICE WK.	LESS	
MONICA	F	28	25-44	YEAR+	SING +C SSP	HS	II	NEUT	IM	JOB LOSER	MOTH.ALL.	OFFICE WK.	MORE	Y
MYRA	F	27	25-44	YEAR+	MARRIED HW	U.D.	I	POS	VM	RE-ENTRANT	DISABILITY	PHYSIOTHER.	LESS	Y
NANCY	F	28	25-44	YEAR+	SINGLE	U.D.	II	POS	IM	JOB LOSER	SOC.ASST.	TECH.TRADES	SAME	
NORMA	F	24	15-24	3LESS	SINGLE	%HS	II	NEUT	VM	JOB LOSER	U.I.	TRANSPORT.	LESS	Y
PAUL	M	20	15-24	7-12	COM LAW	HS	III	POS	VM	JOB LEAVER	U.I.	RESTAURANT	LESS	Y
PAULA	F	22	15-24	7-12	DIV +C	HS	III	NEUT	IM	RE-ENTRANT	MOTH.ALL.	OPEN, SALES	MORE	Y
PETER	M	21	15-24	4-6	SINGLE	HS	III	NEUT	VM	ENTRANT	U.I.	OPEN, SALES	LESS	
ROSS	M	24	15-24	7-12	SINGLE	U.D.	I	POS	VM	JOB LOSER	SOC.ASST.	ENG'R,OPEN		
RUTH	F	51	45+	YEAR+	DIV +C SSP	HS	III	POS	IM	RE-ENTRANT	MOTH.ALL.	OPEN		Y

NAME	SEX	AGE	CAT.	DURAT	MAR.STAT	EDUC	CLASS	FAM.	MOB	UNEM.STAT.	FIN.SUPPT	MARKET	SOC'ZE	DISTRESS
SALLY	F	30	25-44	YEAR+	SINGLE	PS.D	I	NEG	IM	RE-ENTRANT	DISABILITY	TECHNICAL	SAME	Y
SILVIA	F	57	45+	7-12	WIDOW +C	%PS	II	POS	VM	JOB LOSER	U.I.	OFFICE WK	LESS	Y
SIMON	M	32	25-44	4-6	MARR +C HH	U.D.	I	NEUT	SM	JOB LOSER	U.I.	HUM.SERV.	LESS	
STAN	M	30	25-44	3LESS	C.LAW +C HH	PS.D	II	NEUT	IM	JOB LOSER	U.I.	LIBRARY		
STEVE	M	21	15-24	7-12	SINGLE	%PS	III	NEUT	VM	ENTRANT	PARENTS	ART.PHOTOG	MORE	
SUSAN	F	28	25-44	YEAR+	MARR +C HW	HS	III	NEUT	VM	RE-ENTRANT	PARTNER	ELECTRON.	SAME	
TER'NCE	M	18	15-24	3LESS	SINGLE	%HS	II	NEUT	IM	ENTRANT	U.I.	OPEN		
TONY	M	23	15-24	3LESS	MARRIED HH	U.D.	II	NEG	SM	JOB LOSER	U.I.	OPEN		
TRACEY	F	22	15-24	3LESS	SING +C SSP	HS	III	NEUT	VM	JOB LOSER	MOTH.ALL.	OFFICE WK		
VINCENT	M	23	15-24	7-12	SINGLE	%PS	III	POS	VM	ENTRANT	SOC.ASST.	OPEN	MORE	
WARREN	M	42	25-44	YEAR+	MARR +C HH	%HS	III	NEUT	VM	JOB LOSER	SOC.ASST.	OPEN	LESS	Y
WAYNE	M	33	25-44	3LESS	SEP	%HS	II	POS	SM	JOB LOSER	U.I.	UPHOLST.		Y

Descriptions of Informants

These snapshots of the informants are in the form of rough field notes that give a brief, but useful, overview of each person. Here, as throughout the book, names and specific places are fictitious.

AGNES

A 54-year-old divorced woman, who was left to raise five children by herself. She was on the editorial staff of a city newspaper for five years and was laid off with a week's notice. Due to auto industry cutbacks, advertising revenue of the paper was declining, and it was forced to lay off workers. She is now living with her son's family in the suburbs. She is supported by him and receives a little alimony; this is a difficult situation because she wants and values independence. She has taken "joe-jobs" that have negatively affected her self-esteem. Articulate and extremely bitter, she faces the world with an angry glare, which occasionally softens when she talks about happier times. Unemployed 27 months.

ALICE

A 21-year-old single woman, unemployed for seven months. After leaving Grade 10, she usually worked in restaurants (washing dishes). She quit her last job because she felt that the manager was too critical. On social assistance, she sleeps a lot during the day and watches TV until it goes off. Quiet and shy.

ALLEN

A married man of 22, he has been unemployed for 12 months. He quit a construction job in Toronto due to the intolerable working conditions. He left school at Grade 9. His working wife's low wages can only support the two of them at a poverty level. A reluctant househusband, he spends his days job-hunting and volunteering at the London Union of Unemployed Workers.

ANDREA

A 33-year-old woman, divorced, with a 14-year-old son. She injured her wrist while working at an auto parts assembly plant and receives Workman's Compensation. A feminist, she now has a more positive sense of herself which has led her to reject manual labour. She wants work in which she can relate to people; work that will make her want to get up in the morning. She is struggling to educate herself in order to improve her prospects. She is close to her support group in the city. Unemployed 24 months.

ANDREW

A 35-year-old, living with his parents, on social assistance, he has been without work for 16 months. For his last five years of employment, he worked as a journalist, but was dismissed, allegedly for his political positions. He felt rejected when he was not offered an editor's job on the last paper for which he worked. A loner, he lives an unhappy existence with his parents, who are pensioners. He talks of suicide and feels that his life is over. Espouses violent revolution.

ANNE

Unemployed for two weeks, this 18-year-old girl lives with her parents. She has done odd jobs, mostly in the summer (e.g. corn detassling). She wants to work with children. Her family and friends are supportive. She is weary of seeing jobs that require experience.

BERNARD

A 27-year-old immigrant from Kenya, he was first trained and skilled in electronics. He was employed as a farm labourer, then was laid off, and has been jobless for eight months, while drawing benefits. His poverty and the racial discrimination he encounters anger him and his feelings run high. His unemployment has affected his morale and personal functioning to a marked degree, leading to drinking and depression. He is too poor to bring his fiancé over from Kenya.

BETH

A 30-year-old former clerk, she is divorced and has been unemployed for seven months. She receives Unemployment Insurance benefits. Her last job was on a project working in the vault of the city hall basement—which was the most depressing experience of her life. That experience and the fruitless job search had demoralized her, but she is pulling out of it. She has been exercising and has decided to go on to graduate school in psychology. Having just been accepted for school, she was feeling buoyant.

BOB

A 30-year-old married man, with an infant child at home, he has been out of work for two months. Because of the ripple effect of Conservative government cutbacks, he lost his job as a computer operator in Ottawa. He and his wife are fundamentalists, and he derives some support from his church friends. He feels the househusband role is contrary to the Bible. He and his wife are in dire poverty, forced to charge medicines on their credit card. Partly because of his belief in the work ethic and individualism, his unemployment is a desperate torment. Enormous suffering.

BRENDA

A 21-year-old single person with a three-year-old daughter who is mentally retarded. She only has Grade 10, and receives Mother's Allowance. She quit a part-time job as a waitress at a donut shop in frustration with the boss who would not give her full-time work. She has been out of work for a year and is very bored. Wants full-time work.

BRIAN

A 60-year-old married man, who was once an interior designer. He left that career, partly because of disenchantment, partly because of financial problems with his company. He has some chest problems of an undefined nature. To qualify for Unemployment Insurance benefits, he took a gas station job. His benefits now are low, and he is bitter about age discrimination. However, he does enjoy the added time with his wife. Unemployed about six months.

CHRIS

He is 28, trained as a technologist in chemical and electronic fields. He worked in California and Alberta for short periods of time, and now seeks work in the glutted technologists' market in his home town of London. He is single, living with his parents, and has been jobless for three months. Since he began a course in upholstery at a community college, he has been taken off Unemployment Insurance benefits and is upset.

COLLEEN

She moved from Alberta in July 1982. As she and her man had no money, they went to the tobacco belt to live and work for six weeks, until frost ended the season. Before that, she had worked at low-paying jobs in the grocery business. Since finishing her university degree in psychology, she wants a good full-time job that will enable her to use her knowledge. Her partner is supportive as she turns down poor job offers. Her partner works part-time and is starting university. 28 years old.

CONNIE

A 49-year-old woman, she has been unemployed for two years. She had worked in customer relations in an advertising firm and was declared redundant when the firm lost two contracts. She has suffered from severe depression, for which she has seen a therapist. She made suicidal hints during the interview. Her days are less empty now that she has discovered Womanpower and does some English tutoring with a Vietnamese person. Much support from her parents.

CRAIG

An unemployed civil engineer, he is 35 and single. He is living with, and is supported by his mother in her home. He has been out of work for 18 months, since the loss of federal contracts in Windsor resulted in a large lay-off. Having few contacts or friends, he works hard sending out applications.

DEBBIE

A single woman of 34, unemployed two months, she was a lab technician and library assistant in the recent past. She has 17 years of schooling but has been unable to get secure work. She is bracing herself for another bout of poverty. On Unemployment Insurance benefits.

DESMOND

A 28-year-old black man, originally from Angola, he is married with two children and has been unemployed four months. After obtaining community college training in administration related to insurance, he could not find a job in that field and had to work at a gas station. After being subjected to harassment and threats there, he finally quit in disgust. He would like to work in business. His last important job was manager in his father's grocery store. He feels passionately that dependence on one's wife is emasculating, and resents the indignity of the job search. Is extremely bored.

DIANE

An attractive, tense, 25-year-old, single woman who has worked in the social service field on a project basis. She has had anorexia and some family difficulties in her past. With a Bachelor of Arts degree, she is aiming for a career in social work and has worked hard to keep up her morale during her six months of unemployment. As she has been unemployed before, she desperately wants to avoid being demoralized. She receives Unemployment Insurance benefits.

DICK

He is 22 and lives with his girlfriend. He has been unemployed for two months, and has never had a job for a long period of time. He has done mostly seasonal and unskilled work (e.g. tobacco work). He has Grade 9 education. Receiving social assistance, he is really adrift and not coping at all well with unemployment.

DONALD

A single man of 33, a cook by trade, he has been unemployed for two years. He was laid off from a restaurant in Edmonton, and is now on welfare. He is unhappy that Manpower has discounted some of his training and work experience. At the moment he has to settle for pizza-driving work. He relies on his family, who put him up and give him money.

DOROTHY

A 33-year-old single woman, she has been unemployed for six months. She taught at Robarts School for the Deaf in the 1970s and, after becoming blind from diabetes, went to university to get a bachelor's degree in English. She then went on to re-train as a social worker by earning her Bachelor of Social Work degree. In this post-university period, she is experiencing difficulties finding work as a teacher and is supported by long-term disability and Canada Pension payments. She is articulate and determined to find meaningful work.

EMMA

A 52-year-old woman, she has been unemployed for four years, and is divorced and living alone with her daughter. She has worked on a tobacco farm for most of her life, also as a factory worker, and recently as a laundromat attendant. She expects to begin a job soon as a housekeeper/nanny. Receiving social assistance, she feels deprived by society and criticizes age discrimination. She is alienated from the city around her, whose prosperity she and her daughter do not share.

ERICA

A 45-year-old married woman with a 16-year-old at home. She was a consumer advisor at a business association for two years, after which she resigned. Her bosses were making her job miserable by piling on work, isolating her, limiting her budget. She has been unemployed for 19 months. Feeling now like a "lackey" as a housewife, she yearns for the independence that a job would give her. She thinks age discrimination is a factor. Her solid background in business has not enabled her to compete with the young and attractive new office girls. She is depressed, feels hopeless about ever finding work, and has hinted at suicide.

EVA

A university graduate, Eva has been jobless for 11 months. At 23 and single, she is primarily supported by her mother. Her last job was a project of limited duration. She very much wants to break into the personnel field and is full of energy and fervour. Very insightful.

EVELYN

A divorced single parent of 38 with a six-year-old daughter, she is on Mother's Allowance. She tried to make a living as a musician. After an embattled relationship with her man out west, (he and his friends advised her to take therapy because she refused to accept his irresponsible behaviour), she grew emotionally stronger. Experiencing the injustice of poverty and unemployment has hardened her resolve not to blame herself. She hopes to learn the causes of social problems by embarking on political-social studies. A community activist, she plays her music at functions, and helps with the London Union of Unemployed Workers. Unemployed for 18 months.

FRAN

A 32-year-old single woman, who quit her job as secretary-receptionist at an office rental agency, she has been unemployed for eight months and is on Unemployment Insurance benefits. She is enthusiastic about her involvement in a Women in Technical Trades re-training course and never wants to go back to office work. Her family offers strong support and wants her to find work that will make her happy.

FRANCES

A 26-year-old single woman with a master's degree in sociology. Despite some odd jobs in telephone sales and real estate, she regards her work as a teaching assistant as the last real job she had. When that contract ran out, she became unemployed. This jobless stretch has lasted 18 months and, to her frustration, she has been forced to live with her parents back in her small home town. It is hard to maintain contact with her social network of academics and fellow graduate students but she tries to cultivate those relationships. Her funds are dwindling and her student loans are coming due. She has become something of a domestic at home, baking and doing housework. But she keeps a sense of humour and appreciates the family support.

GAIL

A 50-year-old divorced woman, she quit her job as secretary. She walked away from what she describes as an undeserved tongue-lashing from a tyrannical boss. She has done secretarial work at the executive level for years and is somewhat rueful about the price she is paying for her few minutes of defiance. Chain-smoking, honest, she is fighting back desperation about her prospects as an older woman in a young woman's market. Unemployed five months.

GLENN

An 18-year-old single male, unemployed nine months. He quit his position as cook after being denied a promised promotion. He lives with and is supported by his parents. Discouraged, lacking in hope, and confused, he is planning reluctantly to go back to school. He blames himself.

GORD

While basically chronically unemployed, Gord, 47, has worked at odd jobs for the last 15 years. He is divorced and has been a loner for some time. His nonconformity is derived partly from a need to rationalize his marginality. He has harboured suicidal intentions. Having the friendship of a woman, but experiencing only rejection from his family, Gord lives day to day. A reformed alcoholic, he finds some fellowship at Alcoholics Anonymous.

HAROLD

An 18-year-old, unemployed for five months, he is on welfare. He worked for a photo shop for a while, and did some phone selling. Was fired from his last job. He quit high school after Grade 11. He is single and has a gay lover. His friends are in a similar situation and are supportive. All his family, except for his antagonistic father, are emotionally and financially behind him. Still, his poverty is a daily affliction.

HEATHER

A 27-year-old married woman with two small children, she has been unemployed for six months. She was laid off as a production worker at a local factory. Although she appreciates the time with the children, she is eager to re-train and advance herself. Confinement to the home and children has left her feeling isolated and uninteresting. Her husband has had a drinking problem. She had an abortion which she says was linked to her joblessness as she simply could not handle another child in her present situation.

HERB

A 21-year-old single man, he has been unemployed for 10 months. He is living with and supported by his family. He was last employed as a kitchen worker. Discrimination is a problem for him, not because of his gayness, but because of his "new wave" appearance. A youth on hold, not yet bothered by his unemployment.

JANE

A 25-year-old woman, unemployed for three months, she is living in a common-law relationship with a man and with a daughter from a previous marriage. Her last important job was as a visual arts monitor, from which she was laid off. She attends university to study visual arts, but really wants to work in human services and do her art in her spare time.

JANINE

An 18-year-old married woman, unemployed for five months, she left school at Grade 11, and worked at "candy-striping" (i.e., as a hospital volunteer) and as a labourer in her father's home repair business. When she became pregnant, she left her job and married. Her child was taken away from her and put into a foster home due to suspected child abuse. According to Janine, her unemployed husband wants to block her plans to go to hairstyling school because he is worried that she might meet another man. Lives in straitened circumstances.

JIM

A 29-year-old man, living in a common-law relationship, unemployed for eight months after a layoff from his factory. Extremely active in the London Union of Unemployed Workers, of which he is a founding member. He believes that, in this crisis of capitalism, the unemployed must not allow themselves to be passive, individual victims but must organize to demand jobs and, failing that, to assert their entitlement to social wages.

JOANNE

A married, 47-year-old woman, unemployed 10 months, she had worked in Property Management as an administrative secretary. The job was traumatic, the employer abusive, and when the stress became intolerable, she quit. In the past, she had suffered some abuse from her husband, but with therapy she (and he) have resolved this. He still controls the money and does not help with the housework. She likes the extra time with the children and is almost reluctant to go back to work, but they need the money.

JUDY

A 15-year-old girl, unemployed less than a month, living with her mother (who is on welfare). She wants baby-sitting jobs, but the neighbourhood children are growing up. She wants more income to keep up with the consumption standards of her peer group. Feels rather immobile and bored when jobless.

JUNE

A 16-year-old single girl, unemployed six months, having lost her job due to a move here from Edmonton (where she did telephone sales). She left school because (she claims) she had been badly treated by teachers here (accused of stealing, belligerency). She lives with her family, in poor and disorganized conditions. Has done some baby-sitting.

KARL

A 38-year-old married man, with a young child and one on the way. Although he has a bachelor's degree in history he has usually worked at unskilled jobs in industry, business, and farming, for low pay. He was fired from his last job at a garden centre. His East Indian wife nags and complains about his unemployment, and how far behind they are compared with her relatives. They are living with his parents, who support his family but do not get along with the wife. He is unhappy and believes that age discrimination is hurting him, as well as his past stands for workers' rights. His family has moved around somewhat. Unemployed nine months.

KATHY

A 32-year-old divorced woman with two children no longer at home, she is presently living in a common-law relationship. She has been unemployed for 12 months after the business in which she worked as a sales clerk closed down. She is involved in the London Union of Unemployed Workers and finds unemployment frustrating and immobilizing.

KENNETH

A 31-year-old single man, unemployed for six months, he was in the Co-operative Engineering Programme at the University of Waterloo. While taking a government program which would have led to employment, he was asked to leave by his instructors who felt he was not up to the demands of the course. He is very overweight and sensitive. He is living with his parents.

KIM

A 16-year-old girl, unemployed three weeks, living with her family, she dropped out of Grade 10 and is doing volunteer work at Crouch Resource Centre. A bit overweight, she is not very academic. She does baby-sitting and loves to help out at home, where her mother is ill with cancer.

LAURIE

A 24-year-old single woman, who lives with her parents, and has found that the loss of independence has deflated her ego. She lives on the edge, with poor housing and poor food. She had displayed some emotional instability, which is still evident in her mannerisms. She has studied design and fine arts, and done odd jobs. She values her connections with others of her generation, and her community. Thinks deeply and is spirited and articulate.

LORNE

A 19-year-old man, unemployed for 18 months, he left school at Grade 9 and has deeply disappointed his parents who are both professionals. He has few friends. The only work he has done is dishwashing, but was he fired for not keeping up with the fast pace. He is gentle and can find no place in society. He faces poverty and growing hopelessness. On social assistance.

MARIANNE

A 60-year-old divorced woman, laid off three weeks prior to the interview, she has done secretarial work for about 23 years, though never for long at any one place. Her aging parents treat her poorly. Her daughter and son-in-law have not always appreciated her situation but she has finally won their understanding. She is extremely insightful and angry at the system for depriving her of the right to make a living. She does have a supportive "gentleman friend," who has stood by her for five years.

MARJORIE

An 18-year-old, unemployed six months, living on social assistance, the only work she has done has been baby-sitting. Living in poverty with a few young men, she does not see her immediate family. A quiet, reluctant informant.

MARK

A 56-year-old man on welfare, living on the underside of society, he takes whatever casual labour comes his way, generally from the Public Utilities Commission. He has a drinking problem and has been separated from his wife and family for many years. He suffers from ulcers and stress, and has had a nervous breakdown. He is eager to hold onto his room as he does not want to end up at the Salvation Army dormitory.

MARTHA

A 44-year-old divorced woman, with two teenagers at home. She is a sole-support parent, who has been without work for 10 months. Before that, she worked as a stenographer, sales representative, etc. Her re-training as a travel agent had given her some confidence, but that was soon destroyed. She was duped into working for six months for a travel agent, who did not pay her. She was devastated by this, but finally managed to get some money out of the bogus employer. The job search wears down her self-esteem, and she experiences some age discrimination. She receives some alimony. Leads a middle-class lifestyle.

MARY

A 41-year-old divorced woman on Mother's Allowance, with children 9 and 15 years old at home, she lives in government housing, having been unemployed for four years. Her last job was as a part-time counsellor at a group home for the mentally retarded. She quit this job, partly because she could not turn it into full-time employment, and partly because of welfare hassles and separation troubles. She is overweight. She wants work and wants to get out of government housing.

MATTHEW

A 39-year-old, he was laid off from a factory and has been unemployed for three years. Married, with four children, he began his career in computers, working on and off for 15 years, though he was without formal training. He and his family are often desperate and occasionally are given food relief from a local church (he is too embarrassed to be home for the drop-off). His wife works temporarily, and he looks after the children on those days. From time to time, he gets a short-term job (e.g. driving a rental truck to Toronto). Family life holds him together, despite the strains between him and his wife. Rejected by many employed friends, he is alienated and deeply anguished. Does not see his unemployment ending.

MAUREEN

This 22-year-old single woman lives with her foster father. She was enrolled in a community college child care program, but was forced to leave due to illness. She is now able to work and her volunteer work at a library was much appreciated. Much of her time is spent baby-sitting. On disability allowance, she has known grinding poverty and has received a food basket from a local church.

MELISSA

A 20-year-old single woman, unemployed two months, she has completed one year of university. She wants work for the summer, as she plans to return to school. Her unemployment is not upsetting her and she lives comfortably in the suburbs with her parents.

MICHELLE

A 16-year-old girl (just finished Grade 9), unemployed a week, living with her mother who is on welfare. Like her sister Judy, she wants baby-sitting but the local children are no longer the right age. Her life alternates between boredom and wrangling with her mother when she is jobless, to eager socializing with her peers when she has a job.

MONICA

A 28-year-old single mother of a seven-year-old child, she has been unemployed for four years, apart from occasional baby-sitting jobs. Her last important job was as a receptionist at a local college. She was fired from this position due to a poor evaluation from a supervisor who did not know her work—a shocking injustice from which she has never recovered. She is on Mother's Allowance and receives $576 a month. She feels hopeless at times, angry, even suicidal, but her child keeps her going. A person of deep feelings.

MYRA

A 27-year-old married woman, who worked as a nutritionist for over four years after university, but was unable to continue due to a disability known as systemic lupis. Unemployed for 14 months, she has been supported by her husband (who is training to be a doctor), long-term disability, and private insurance. Though her traditional husband and in-laws feel her proper place is in the home, she is discontented with the domestic role and wants to work. Her own parents support her aspirations and therefore understand her frustration. She expects to have her old job back in the future.

NANCY

A 28-year-old single woman, unemployed for 18 months, who is currently on social assistance. She has a bachelor's degree in fine arts. She was laid off with two weeks notice from her job as sales manager for a tourist-oriented display-village. Though her unemployment has been hard, she is extremely excited about her retraining for technical trades as part of the Women In Trades and Technology program and lives for the course.

NORMA

Single, 24, this woman was employed as a busdriver with London Transit on a trial basis—the only job she had ever wanted. After five months on the job, she was reported for a prank in which she climbed through the window of another driver's bus, and was immediately fired. She intended to complain on the grounds of sexual discrimination, since a fine or suspension was the usual consequence of this sort of prank. At the interview, however, she was still in shock and ashamed, and was not able to see anyone. She was afraid to tell her family, who lived out of town.

PAUL

A 20-year-old man, living with a gay partner, he has worked sporadically as a waiter, which is the kind of job that interests him now. He was fired from his last job, after being accused of stealing and other offenses. He believes that his gayness has lead to discrimination during his job search. A high school graduate. Unemployed for eight months.

PAULA

Divorced, with a four-year-old son, this black woman of Jamaican background is 22 and lives in her mother's house. She receives Mother's Allowance, and is ashamed to be doing so. She is bored, and highly vocal about such subjects as racial discrimination. She has worked at a wig shop. She claims it is hard for a black woman to get a job in London. She feels guilty and restless in her current dependent status.

PETER

A 21-year-old single male, with a high school education, unemployed for five months, and on Unemployment Insurance benefits. For a three-month project (Ontario Career Action Program), he worked in a woodworking shop. Since age 18, short bouts of work (e.g. as a janitor) have alternated with long stretches of unemployment. He lives with his brother on a limited income. He displayed an elaborate philosophical detachment that seemed partially self-protective.

ROSS

A 24-year-old single male, unemployed eight months, who previously worked as a research assistant, after completing the Waterloo Co-operative Programme in mechanical engineering. After the bankruptcy of the firm at which he was working, he did volunteer artistic work with International Youth Year. Living with parents, his interest in engineering is waning, as he has felt the attraction of artistic, or self-chosen endeavour. He is not sure what he will end up doing.

RUTH

A 51-year-old divorced woman, living in government housing with three (of seven) teenage children. She receives Mother's Allowance and has not worked in 20 years. Her last regular work was as a secretary. She has a high school education and has always accepted the traditional wife/mother role expectations. She is fearful of the outside world—not really knowing anything but children. She feels she has cast herself off all these years, and tries not to dwell on her husband's desertion of the family years ago. She would now like to work outside the home (even without pay), just to meet people.

SALLY

She is 30, was trained as an RNA and found work in this area. She lost this job when she had a nervous breakdown. She found work as library clerk at a local college, but was fired due to personality conflicts and office politics. She was blamed for an error in the distribution of a film. She is taking a re-training course to prepare her to enter a technical field. She has received therapy and been hospitalized several times. She suffers from a lack of self-esteem and an inability to handle unstructured time. Single. Unemployed three years.

SILVIA

A 57-year-old widow, unemployed for seven months, she receives Unemployment Insurance benefits. She has worked on a temporary and short-term basis in offices. Her last job (at Bell Canada) ended in a layoff, due to a surplus in office staff. She is bitter about age discrimination and the invasion of privacy by employers. She lives with her adult son who is also unemployed.

SIMON

A married man of 32 with a small child at home, his last important job was as a child care worker—a job from which he was fired. He is university-educated and is now on Unemployment Insurance benefits. He is a househusband, having been unemployed for five months. He feels his confidence sagging as his joblessness lengthens.

STAN

A 30-year-old divorced man, with a five-year-old child (non-custody), he is living in a common-law relationship. He gets work for 10-month periods at the university library, but wants full-time work, with better pay, benefits, and security. He has taken a library technician course for two years at community college. He enjoys being a househusband and contributing to his partner's domestic life.

STEVE

A 21-year-old and single, Steve has been unemployed for nine months and lives with his parents. He worked for about six weeks as a silk screen printer, a job from which he was fired. He identifies the reasons for his dismissal as making too many mistakes (but points out that he was only trained for a week) and for being too outspoken in his progressive opinions. He is artistic and works in a studio. He found his volunteer participation in International Youth Year to be most helpful, and believes it may produce leads for work in artistic photography.

SUSAN

A former bank teller of 28, she is married and the mother of two children. She left the banking field to be with her children. Now she wants to work again but in a different area as she hates clerical occupations. She is enjoying learning technical trades with the Women in Trades and Technology program. When she is trained and not so economically vulnerable, she hints that she will leave her husband.

TERRENCE

An 18-year-old, he has worked on a tobacco farm and in an auto body shop. He was fired from the farm, run by his parents, for drinking at lunch time and subsequent poor performance. He socializes with his friends a lot and has no routine. While he receives Unemployment Insurance benefits, he also always has his parents to fall back on financially. He criticizes the unemployed and states that "there's always a job out there."

TONY

A 23-year-old man, married, and recently out of university, he worked for three months on a government contract job, which recently ran out. He refuses to take just any job and is confident something will come up. His last important job was recreation supervisor for the elderly. He is a househusband on Unemployment Insurance benefits. His wife is very supportive, both financially and in other ways.

TRACEY

A 22-year-old single parent of a four-year-old, she has been unemployed for three months. She has some high school education and a one-year secretarial course. She has worked on an Ontario Career Action Program, three-month project, where she felt exploited. She has felt aimless for some years, but now feels that she is starting to find herself. She is very devoted to her child, whose rearing has helped her to grow up.

VINCENT

A 23-year-old single man, unemployed for seven months. A soft-spoken "new waver," he lives in a warehouse room. He has been poor, has done some squatting in the inner city, and has had psychiatric assessments. Dyslexia undermined his school progress and achievement. Through all of this, he has maintained a positive philosophy and is committed to his art and contemplation. He is helped financially by his mother. His last job was as a dishwasher. He now lives on social assistance. An insightful non-conformist.

WARREN

Married, with children, he is 42. He has been unemployed for three years and is currently on social assistance. Even before that, his jobs were sporadic. Formerly a bus driver in the US, he has been unable to become licensed in Canada. He is adjusting unhappily to his unemployment. He is poor and bored, has few friends and does not know what to do with himself. His marriage is strained and uncommunicative. He talked about an affair, which he started in order to escape the tedium.

WAYNE

He is 33, separated from his wife, and the father of two young boys. After being fired from a tire shop, he has been looking for work in London for three months. He is enjoying an upholstery course and is thinking of setting up his own business. He has had stressful hassles with Unemployment Insurance. He lives alone in a poor part of town, where he is unable to talk to his Portuguese neighbours. He just waits for his course to begin each day while missing his family back home.

References

Akyeampong, Ernest
1986 "Involuntary" part-time employment in Canada: 1975–1985. *The Labour Force* (Dec.) 143–170. Ottawa: Statistics Canada.

Alberta. Department of Health and Social Development
1973 *Public Attitudes Towards Public Assistance in Alberta.* Edmonton: Queen's Printer.

Ashton, D. N.
1986 *Unemployment Under Capitalism.* Brighton: Wheatsheaf.

Berger, John and Jean Mohr
1975 *The Seventh Man: The Story of a Migrant Worker in Europe.* Harmondsworth: Penguin.

Berger, Peter
1977 In praise of particularity: The concept of mediating structures. In *Facing Up to Modernity: Excursions in Society, Politics, and Religion,* 130–141. New York: Basic Books.

Bostyn, A.M. and D. Wight
1987 Inside a community: values associated with money and time. In *Unemployment: Personal and Social Consequences,* ed. S. Fineman, 138–154. London: Tavistock.

Bourdieu, Pierre
1977 *Outline of a Theory of Practice.* Cambridge: Cambridge University Press.

Brown, Roger
1986 *Social Psychology.* 2d ed. New York: Free Press.

Butler, Peter M.
1980 Establishments and the work-welfare mix. *Canadian Review of Sociology and Anthropology* 17: 138–153.

Canadian Council on Social Development
1985 Tinkering with U.I. *Social Development Overview* 3, No. 1 (Spring): 1–2.

Deaton, Richard
1983 Unemployment: Canada's malignant social pathology. *Perception* 6, No. 5: 14–19.

Dickinson, James
1986   From Poor Law to social insurance: the periodization of State intervention in the reproductive process. In *Family, Economy and State: The Social Reproduction Process Under Capitalism*, eds. James Dickinson and Bob Russell, 113–149. Toronto: Garamond.

Dumont, J.-P.
1987   The evolution of social security during the recession. *International Labour Review* 126, No. 1 (January-February): 1–19.

Fagan, L. and M. Little
1984   *The Foresaken Families*. Harmondsworth: Penguin.

Fineman, Stephen
1983   *White Collar Unemployment: Impact and Stress*. Toronto: John Wiley.

Fineman, Stephen (ed.)
1987   *Unemployment: Personal and Social Consequences*. London: Tavistock.

Foucault, Michel
1979   *Discipline and Punish*. Harmondsworth: Penguin.

Fryer, D. and S. McKenna
1987   The laying off of hands: unemployment and the experience of time. In *Unemployment: Personal and Social Consequences*, ed. S. Fineman, 47–73. London: Tavistock.

Fryer, David and Roy Payne
1984   Proactive behaviour in unemployment: findings and implications. *Leisure Studies*. 3: 273–295.

Fryer, David and Philip Ullah
1982   Editors' Introduction. In *Unemployed People: Social and Psychological Perspectives*, ed. David Fryer and Philip Ullah. Milton Keynes, U.K.: Open University Press.

Geertz, Clifford
1968   Religion as a cultural system. In *The Religious Situation: 1968*, ed. Donald Cutler. Boston: Beacon Press.

Giddens, Anthony
1984   *The Constitution of Society*. Berkeley and Los Angeles: University of California Press.

Gill, Colin
1985   *Work, Unemployment and the New Technology*. Cambridge: Polity Press.

Goffman, Erving
1963   *Stigma: Notes on the Management of Spoiled Identity*. Englewood Cliffs: Prentice-Hall.

Gonick, Cy
1987   *The Great Economic Debate*. Toronto: James Lorimer.

Gorz, André
1982   *Farewell to the Working Class*. London: Pluto Press, 1982.

Habermas, Jurgen
1970   *Toward a Rational Society.* Boston: Beacon Press.

Hasan, Abrar and Patrice de Broucker
1985   *Unemployment, Employment and Non-Participation in Canadian Labour Markets.* Economic Council of Canada. Ottawa: Supply and Services Canada.

Heidenheim, A. Paul
1984   The Political Economy of Canadian Public Assistance. Master's thesis, Department of Sociology, University of Western Ontario.

Hughes, Everett C.
1971   *The Sociological Eye: Selected Papers.* Chicago: Aldine Atherton.

Inglis, Fred
1982   *Radical Earnestness: English Social Theory: 1880–1983.* Oxford: Martin Robertson.

Jackson, George
1987   Alternative concepts and measures of unemployment. *The Labour Force* (January) 85–120. Ottawa: Statistics Canada.

Jahoda, M., P. Lazarsfeld and H. Zeisel
1971   *Marienthal: The Sociography of an Unemployed Community.* Chicago: Aldine-Atherton. Originally published as *Die Arbeitslosen von Marienthal,* 1933.

Kaliski, S.F.
1987   Accounting for unemployment: a labour market perspective. *Canadian Journal of Economics* 20, No. 4 (November): 665–693.

Kelvin, Peter and J.E. Jarrett
1985   *Unemployment: Its Social-Psychological Context.* Cambridge: Cambridge University Press.

Lemaître, Georges
1985   Flows into unemployment: the job loser component. *The Labour Force* (June) 149–159. Ottawa: Statistics Canada.

Levine, Saul V.
1979   The psychological and social effects of youth unemployment. *Children Today* (November-December): 6–9, 40.

London Union of Unemployed Workers
1985   Letter to Membership. April 17.

Lowe, Graham
1986   Job line for youth. *Policy Options* 7, No. 5: 3–6.

Marsden, Dennis
1975   *Workless.* London: Croon Helm.

Marshall, Victor W. and Carolyn J. Rosenthal
1986   Aging and later life. In *Sociology.* 3d ed., ed. Robert Hagedorn, 133–162. Toronto: Holt, Rinehart and Winston.

Marx, Karl
[1844]   *Karl Marx: Early Writings,* Translated and edited by T.B. Bottomore. New York: McGraw-Hill, 1964.

Mead, George Herbert
[1934]   *George Herbert Mead on Social Psychology,* ed. A. Strauss. Chicago: University of Chicago Press, 1964. Originally published as *Mind, Self and Society,* ed. C. Morris. Chicago: University of Chicago Press.

Mills, C. Wright
1959   *The Sociological Imagination.* New York: Oxford University Press.

Moloney, Joanne
1986   Recent industry trends in employment: Canada and the provinces. *The Labour Force* (November) 85–108. Ottawa: Statistics Canada.

Moscovitch, Allan
1986   The welfare state since 1975. *Journal of Canadian Studies* 21, No. 2 (Summer): 77–94.

National Council of Welfare
1985   Fighting poverty: the effect of government policy. In *The Other Macdonald Report,* ed. Daniel Drache and Duncan Cameron, 63–79. Toronto: James Lorimer.
1985   *Poverty Profile 1985.* Ottawa: Minister of Supply and Services.

Neugarten, Bernice L. and G.O. Hagestad
1976   Age and the life course. In *Handbook of Aging and the Social Sciences,* eds. Robert Binstock and Ethel Shanas, 35–55. New York: Van Nostrand Reinhold.

Offe, Claus
1985   *Disorganized Capitalism.* Cambridge, U.K.: Polity.

Ontario New Democratic Party Caucus
1984   *The Other Ontario.* Toronto: Ontario N.D.P.

Picot, Garnett and Ted Wannell
1987   Job loss and labour market adjustment in the Canadian economy. *The Labour Force* (March) 85–135. Ottawa: Statistics Canada.

Piven, Frances Fox and Richard A. Cloward
1972   *Regulating the Poor: The Functions of Social Welfare.* London: Tavistock.

Reisman, D. A.
1977   *Richard Titmuss: Welfare and Society.* London: Heinemann.

Schohl, Wolfgang
1985   Recovery through ecology. *World Press Review* (July) 25–27. (From *Wirtschafts Woche,* April 12–19, 1985.)

Shaw, R. P.
1985   The burden of unemployment in Canada. *Canadian Public Policy* 11, No. 2: 143–160.

Social Planning Council of Metropolitan Toronto and Ontario Social Development Council (SPC/OSDC)
1983   *And the Poor Get Poorer.* Toronto: Social Planning Council of Metropolitan Toronto and Ontario Social Development Council.

Social Planning Council of Metropolitan Toronto
1985   The rise and fall of the welfare state. In *The Other Macdonald Report*, ed. Daniel Drache and Duncan Cameron, 51–62. Toronto: James Lorimer.

Struthers, James
1983   *No Fault of Their Own: Unemployment and the Canadian Welfare State 1914–1941.* Toronto: University of Toronto Press.

Tajfel, H.
1981   *Human Groups and Social Categories.* Cambridge: Cambridge University Press.

Therborn, Goren
1986   *Why Some Peoples Are More Unemployed Than Others.* London: Verso.

Thompson, E. P.
1967   Time, work-discipline and industrial capitalism. *Past and Present* Vol. 38.

Veevers, Richard
1986   Results from the Annual Work Patterns Survey: 1984 and 1985. *The Labour Force* (March) 85–112. Ottawa: Statistics Canada.

Weigert, Andrew
1981   *Sociology of Everyday Life.* New York: Longman.

Whitehorn, K.
1987   What a month of Sundays. *Observer* (Jan. 25) 7.

Wilensky, H. L, and C.N. Lebeaux
1965   *Industrial Society and Social Welfare.* New York: Free Press.

Willis, P.
1977   *Learning to Labour.* Westmead: Saxon House.

Zaretsky, Eli
1986   Rethinking the welfare state: dependence, economic individualism, and the family. In *Family, Economy and State: The Social Reproduction Process Under Capitalism*, eds. James Dickinson and Bob Russell, 85–109. Toronto: Garamond.

Index